RED DIAPER DAUGHTER

RED DIAPER DAUGHTER

Three Generations of Rebels and Revolutionaries

Laura Bock

RED DIAPER DAUGHTER
Three Generations of Rebels and Revolutionaries

Front cover photograph: Laura's Junior High Graduation, 1960.
L to R: Mini Karasick Bock, Berta Karasick, Laura, Al Bock

Back cover photograph: A quilt made in 2012 of Laura's beloved and well-worn t-shirts. Please note her life-long love of tie-dye.

Book & cover design by Robin Brooks   www.TheBeautyofBooks.com

ISBN: 978-0-9981616-0-0
Library of Congress Control Number: 2017900690
Laura Bock, Mill Valley, CALIFORNIA

Second Wave Press: reddiaperdaughter@gmail.com

DEDICATION

To my grandparents
Lena and Morris Bock
Berta and Meyer Karasick

and
my parents
Mini Karasick Bock
Albert J. Bock

for
their legacies
and to
My Sisters of the Second Wave

CONTENTS

Acknowledgements

FIRST OF ALL, contrary to conventional form, I thank Suzanne Gary, my partner of sixteen years. Not only is she an amazing poet, gifted editor, and creative prose writer, she has been a rock, a brick, and all-around supporter of this process of writing my memoir. This included my periodic spasms of anxiety, overwhelm, and frequent distraction. Lucky, I am.

Thank you to all the members of Fat Lip Readers Theater, MotherTongue Feminist Theater Collective, and the Old Lesbian Memoir Writers Group for stimulating me to write my heart out in such supportive circles of women. It is due to you all that secrets were revealed, shame admitted, humor exploded, and a writing skill evolved.

I am beholden to all the high-tech folks who developed computer software for blind users so that I could do the very thing in the early 21st century that I was unable to do in 1972, when I left graduate school unable to complete my studies for lack of a way to absorb, process, and work research into cogent and creative papers.

The phrase "I couldn't have done it without you" is literally true when it comes to my long time helper/reader/assistant Peg Murphy.

From the early stages of scanning in piles of typed writings from hither and yon and trying to make it work with my JAWS screen reader, to typing all those pieces into the computer when JAWS would not read PDF files, to proofing endless versions of chapters, to finding the software allowing us to edit FBI files, to responding to my material with laughter (appropriately) and grimaces (also appropriate) and on and on! She gracefully tackled whatever I asked of her, putting up with my frustrations and her own, and coming back each week for more.

My dear friend Sally Goldin helped me each step of the way as I looked for an experienced editor who would make the manuscript "book ready" while retaining my voice and style. My deep gratitude goes to my editor, Paula Stahel, for her expertise and enthusiasm, and to my book designer par excellence, Robin Brooks. It was a pleasure to work with each of these professionals.

The next step was proofreading; Sally took this on. She also used her prodigious computer skills to crop and prepare all the pictures for print publication. We then researched potential online publishers. All in all, she has midwifed this book, including holding my hands through every labor pain.

As ever, errors in omission and commission are mine alone. This is my story, as subjective and idiosyncratic as I could make it. It is simply one small piece of an immense puzzle. I hope others add their pieces to the picture, for then, what a mosaic we will make!

Author's Note

IN THIS MEMOIR I have included many pieces I have written over the years. Throughout these pages I have highlighted some of them for emphasis with a thin gray line to the left of the text.

To Begin With

Why Write Memoir? Why Read Memoirs?

Exercise written for the Old Lesbian Memoir Writing Group

I like good writing, and reading a story I can identify with, describing similarities, feelings, and understandings that perhaps I have, too, but cannot adequately express myself. My reaction is an acknowledgement and confirmation, "Oh, it happened to you, too?" It's a "Yes" reaction and gratitude to that writer.

I like reading a memoir of a life entirely different from mine, of a woman growing up in Iran, Tunisia, Hanoi, Lima, or the Detroit ghetto. The settings, specific situations, and century may be foreign to me but reveal feelings I can understand and experiences that inform and enlighten. I enjoy learning about the lives of people other than white men of privilege. I like filling in the gaps in my knowledge and being swept into another's thoughtful story of her life.

I write for myself—to remember and to document the histories of my parents and grandparents.

I write to be remembered—to add to my archives, to prove I lived, to be a part of history.

I write perchance to be published in a memoir.

I write because I have no family, no younger generation to pass my stories onto, to bore with their endless repetition, and no one who will share these stories with future generations.

I write to show I mattered—I survived, I thrived, I accomplished. I was funny.

I write to share writing with other old women—to reveal our similarities as well as our delightful bounty of differences.

I write because I've never liked Swiss cheese. The holes are annoying and a waste of space—I write to fill them as best I can.

I write because I wholeheartedly believe in history "from the bottom up"—not just the histories written by the elite, the "haves," the dominant.

I write because I am sixty-seven and further procrastination is not an option.

IT ALL STARTED with an offhand comment in a meeting of our Old Lesbian Support Group in 2009. I said I wanted to write memoir with a group of women. I was sixty-four and feeling some urgency to fill in gaps in the story of my family's history. On the other hand, at this age, wasn't this a time to float, to glide effortlessly—not a time to struggle, find fresh grief, revisit losses, and even need therapy again? I wanted this to be a settled time. Yet there I was, about to organize a memoir writing group for old lesbians, jumping into the deep end, scared out of my wits.

I had already done quite a bit of writing in my day, with Fat Lip Readers Theater and MotherTongue Feminist Theater Collective, as well as letters and limericks to friends on special occasions. But there were so many missing pieces in the telling of my story so far, not to mention that of my parents and grandparents. There was no future generation to hear the stories, nor brothers or sisters with whom to share stories of our family from each of our different perspectives.

I feel the weight of being an only child to tell the world the stories of my parents, Mini and Al Bock, who led unusual and fascinating lives. I never got my dad's oral history, and only three hours of my mom on tape before her death. I waited too long. For this I carry such regret.

I fancy myself a radical feminist historian of sorts, committed to doing my part in discovering and preserving histories of the undocumented.

I want people to know about the Bock and Karasick families immigrating to this country from Eastern Europe around 1900, and about me, the daughter of one Bock and one Karasick. I want to tell of the legacy I received, the choices I've made, the amazing times in which I've lived, the paths I've chosen, and my activism in reaction to those influences.

I don't want our lives expunged when I die off, as if we had never existed.

A memoir-writing group seemed the first and crucial step. Throughout my adult life, whenever I've been faced with some new and perhaps scary change or just wanted to challenge myself to action, I've looked for other women to join with, in a support group with a shared affinity. And if there was not one already, I started one, sometimes with the help of an interested friend. This included a fat women's support group in 1975, started by the San Francisco Women's Centers; a coming-out support group in 1981, sponsored by Operation Concern; a disabled lesbian support group in the mid-1980s, also at Operation Concern; a Jewish women's study group in the late 1970s, organized with my friend Miriam Weber; a hard-of-hearing support group in 2004, which I requested when I was a client at the San Francisco Hearing and Speech Center; an old lesbian grief and loss support group, started by New Leaf Outreach to Elders; a break-up support group, which I started when I was experiencing that unbearable pain; and others. You get the idea. Friends have teased me about being such a "groupie."

So it was in 2009, in that old lesbian support group, that I mentioned my desire to start writing personal history with other women. I said I would be willing to organize it but would prefer to do it with another woman. One of the other group members, Sheila Goldmacher, tentatively responded, "That sounds very interesting, Laura, but I can't write and anyway I'm way too scared to try." She was adamant. I replied, "I understand, but let's do it anyway!"

To Sheila's everlasting credit, I talked her into it and we set off to organize such a group. I knew I did not want an outside "expert" facilitator/teacher but rather, to have our members rotate that role weekly. I knew I wanted to use an existing "how-to" book to help us get started. Sheila and I chose Natalie Goldberg's *Writing Down the Bones* and, in our ads and outreach for members, we asked that women get and bring a copy of that book to the first meeting, which Sheila and I would facilitate.

That first meeting was held at 190 Coleridge, a senior housing facility in San Francisco's Bernal Heights. Several of those who responded to our "call" lived there and arranged for the group to meet in the community room without charge. In that fall of 2009, thirteen of us met in that poorly ventilated and badly lit room. We sat on uncomfortable metal folding chairs around two long tables pushed together and covered with butcher paper. And we continued to meet there for four and a half years!

On that day something magical began. The most amazing writing has come from each of us. Yes, including Sheila, who turned out to be a natural writer and has amazed herself and wowed us with her eloquent and descriptive stories.

The women had a variety of reasons for writing memoir: some to pass their stories on to their children and grandchildren, some to challenge themselves to add a writing practice to their lives, a few of us thinking about a book in our futures. All of us came for the pleasure of gathering together with other old feminist lesbians to tell and hear our unique yet familiar stories.

Lynn had already written a memoir but enjoyed writing groups. Polly had felt blocked from writing for decades and didn't think she could, but proved to be an exquisite nature writer. She wrote up a storm. Toni and Carly had been in other feminist writing groups and brought their experience and evocative writing, which frequently led us to laughter and tears. Sandy was scared and reluctant but put pen to paper nonetheless and produced poignant and moving tales of her past. Sheila M. added her stories as a native San Franciscan proud of her Puerto Rican roots, writing of being a young hippie during the summer of love in the Haight Ashbury. As a child, she had lived across the street from Orlando Cepeda, the San Francisco Giants[1] star first baseman and outfielder, who taught her to salsa. My partner, Suzanne, an award-winning poet, wrote eloquently of her life in Grosse Pointe and Ann Arbor, of

---

[1] The San Francisco Giants baseball team

her marriage, and coming out as a lesbian. We looked forward to her powerful and at times hilarious punch lines. There was Tita, who wrote of being born and raised in Guatemala and later immigrating to the U.S., eventually becoming a hippie mom. We were mothers and grandmothers, as well as those of us who had chosen not to have kids.

We were in our sixties, seventies, and eighties. We needed to learn to accommodate each other's disabilities and physical challenges: hearing, vision, and memory loss for example. We were often utterly amazed at the memories that surfaced.

As each woman took her turn as facilitator, she brought thoughtful prompts for writing exercises and her own way of moving that particular session forward. There was no requirement that we all read aloud what we wrote, but those who did could ask for the kind of feedback we wanted, or none at all. For the most part our comments were supportive and appreciative, sometimes asking for clarification or making suggestions for fleshing out some aspect of the story. Often, as each woman finished reading her piece, the rest of us sat riveted by her tale and astonished by the quality of the writing.

For the first several years, we organized the group into sessions of eight meetings each. At the start of each session we went around the room voicing our personal goals, and at the last meeting we again spoke of how we met or shifted away from those expectations. At that final meeting each of us decided whether or not we wanted to continue with another eight-week session. This was not a drop-in group. Rather, we were women committed to each other and our writing for at least eight meetings at a time.

Over the years, some women left and others joined, as priorities changed. We were never more than twelve or thirteen and frequently fewer on a particular week, as we were challenged by illness or other temporary interruptions.

We became a family, taking this journey together. At times it was painful, at times joyful. As in all families, we occasionally had misunderstandings and hurt feelings. We faced losses when Tita died and when Sherrill's Alzheimer's, which was minimal when we began, advanced and prevented her full participation.

Time and again I went out on a limb, writing pieces that made me feel utterly vulnerable, telling secrets and putting my fears and horrors to paper to be shared in such a public way. I grew to trust these women completely and cherish our time together. I was continually amazed at how brave they—we, were in our writing.

Eventually I filled in the holes in my written herstory and made the hard decision to resign my membership in May 2014. I knew it was time to edit all my writing and consider how to get it out into the world.

To this end I took the first step. I learned that the GLBT Historical Society of San Francisco agreed to take my papers and create the Laura Bock Collection in 2013, which includes all my writing up to that time. It would be housed in their archive for researchers and curators to use. Those papers have now been organized, preserved, and made ready. Anyone can review the collection in the finding aid[2] at either of the following two links:

OAC Collection Guide: Laura Bock Papers
(http://bit.ly/2nUNGFR)

---

[2] A "finding aid" is a document detailing the contents of an archival collection

GLBT Historical Society: Finding Aid to the Laura J. Bock Papers, 1945–2014 (http://bit.ly/1PAtyA7)

In November of 2014, with bravado I did not feel, I thought, "Why not a book or several small books?" Perhaps one might be titled, *Looking Bock*, but that is a groaner to be sure.

The prospect of writing a book is entirely daunting, and I wonder if I have the arrogance to think anyone might be interested in reading it. I don't know, but I have gone ahead anyway. After all, was I not the person who declared to Sheila in 2009, "I understand your fears, but let's do it anyway"?

Oh, but of course, I would need a new group! This would be a group of women also editing their writing for the purpose of putting together their books.

The material in this volume is based on four and a half years of memoir writing in that wonderful old lesbian writing group. In addition, there are poems and narratives written over an eighteen-year period as a member of Fat Lip Readers Theater, for numerous scripts performed far and wide. There are pieces written for MotherTongue Feminist Theater Collective as we worked on scripts focusing on themes of aging, disability, and sisters. Some of these pieces you will find highlighted throughout the book. There are also a few letters and even part of a class paper written for a women's studies course I took at San Francisco State University with Ricki Sherover Marcuse on "Jewish Women."

So there you have it. Here's the deal: You, as reader, have stepped up to fill a crucial role for me, as receiver of the tales, and believe me, I am extremely appreciative. Feel free to pass these stories along, embellishing as you will, and be sure to add some of your own.

As for my end of the deal? I will do my best to intrigue and entertain you, to inform and perhaps amuse you. I may even anger you. I feel sure I will not put you to sleep because, after all, how many memoirs have you read by the likes of me, i.e., a fat-liberation, feminist, lesbian activist, veteran of the political movements of the 1970s, '80s, and '90s who is a Jewish San Francisco native, blind, low hearing, and a Red Diaper Baby whose four grandparents were socialist revolutionaries in Lithuania and Russia before emigrating around 1900; whose mother was hit by a Molotov cocktail while addressing a huge rally for agricultural workers in Santa Clara Valley, and whose father spent six months in prison, having been convicted of labor union organizing, prosecuted by the district attorney of Alameda County, Earl Warren? How many folks do you know whose parental advice as they went off to college was, "Now, you make sure you get arrested for something political and not just for drunkenness!" To top off this unusual picture, I was extremely shy and self-conscious about my fat body, without romantic or sexual experience until the age of thirty-six, whereupon I found myself onstage in a performance called Fat and Sexy, doing a striptease to packed audiences!

So, is it a deal?

Avanti! Let's go.

Buttons

2

Subversive Roots

A Tale of Two Sisters

Written for MotherTongue Feminist Theater Collective, 1999

Once upon a time, long, long ago, there lived two beautiful princesses, Mini and Reggie. They were both fiery of temperament and spirited of nature. They tried hard to please their parents and fulfill their destinies.

Their father, King Meyer, and their mother, Queen Berta, had fled their native land, running for their lives, hated by the evil czar and hunted by his marauding bands of thugs called Cossacks. They had been branded as revolutionaries (admittedly, they were rather unusual royals) and once arrested they were to be sent east, banished to a cold and remote kingdom called Siberia. Eluding capture, the couple traveled for days and months over vast lands and churning oceans, until they reached an island called Ellis—the gate to the land called The Lower East Side.

Now, upon the births of each of the two baby princesses, there was much rejoicing. These doting royal parents, Meyer and Berta, lovingly clothed them in red diapers as was the fashion among their people and, as the little ones matured, provided them with soapboxes and colorful banners as befitting their station.

The sisters were tutored in flaming oratory, elocution, Marxist theory, and civil disobedience, as well as the usual tenets of revisionist history and literature. Naturally, the sisters excelled in their studies.

Mini and Reggie looked to their father—a poet, a quiet visionary, for a faith in a future where all the people of the land would share in the wealth, and to their mother—a wary, pragmatic, nuts-and-bolts kind of queen, for dire warnings to beware of the dreaded *agent provocateur*, the rampaging anti-red squads, the evil giant J. Edgar Hoover, pesky Trotskyists, and men in general, for they would attempt to divert the girls' attention away from their true path and into deadly domesticity.

There came a time when Mini and Reggie, now women, left the comforts of the family castle-tenement and set forth to test their wings and spread the doctrine—Princess Mini to the infamous territory of San Francisco, accompanied by her consort Albert, an anarchist (alas), and Princess Reggie to wander the globe with her Prince Gene, the future heir to the throne of the region known as CPUSA[3].

Both the sisters led lives of purpose and principle. In time, they begat children, who also learned their lessons well and carried on the family business in their own ways. The sisters remained close always and as old women were just as fiery, strong, confident, and opinionated, and much loved and respected.

Sadly there came a time when the princesses Mini and Reggie left this world, never to return. However, I can, with assurance,

---

[3] Communist Party of the United States, aka the C.P.

inform you they are as busy as ever organizing the hell out of heaven, and quite soon there will be the International Sisterhood of Angels, Local 1.

The Karasicks

I KNEW MY grandma Berta as old and wrinkled. But I have photos of her holding me, baby Laurie, beaming with love. As I was growing up, she and my grandpa lived on 17th Street near Castro in San Francisco, next door to her sister Chaya. I'd spend time there, with and without my mom, going back and forth between the two apartments. Aunt Chai was warm and nourishing, feeding me toast with melted peanut butter, and we would all sit out on the front steps visiting, exchanging greetings with neighbors. They were an important part of my life until they died—Grandpa Meyer in 1957, in Agnew State Hospital for people with senile dementia, and Grandma at the Jewish Old Folks Home in San Francisco in 1963.

Grandfather Meyer was born in 1894, and my grandmother, Berta, in 1892. They may have been second or third cousins or at least family friends. They lived in shtetls, little villages located in an area called "the Pale,"[4] where Russian Jews had been forced to live and survive as best they could. These shtetls were repeatedly overrun by pogroms,

---

[4] From 1798 to 1917, Jews in Czarist Russia were restricted to the Pale of Settlement, an area from the Baltic to the Black Sea. At the start of the 20th century, five million Jews, 40% of the world's Jewish population, lived there, most in impoverished shtetls.

as Cossacks and gentile neighbors rampaged, attacking the Jews as well as their homes, businesses, and synagogues.

As young adults, Meyer and Berta each left to go to the closest city, possibly Kiev or perhaps Odessa, to become literate, work, and join other young revolutionaries who were organizing and fighting against the Czar's pernicious and oppressive regime. There, Berta joined an illegal Leninist group. She and Meyer and others of their comrades were frequently hounded, beaten, arrested, and jailed for their activities.

One day a sympathetic local policeman warned them they were to be arrested once again and this time would be sent east to Siberia. Information had been leaked to the police that a printing press could be found in the basement dwelling where Berta and some of her comrades lived and wrote their political tracts.

Berta had fallen in love with a young, charismatic revolutionary but they had been forever separated when he was exiled to Siberia. When it was imperative for Berta and some of her comrades to flee Russia, Meyer offered to marry and accompany her, to make her journey safer.

A small group went underground, was smuggled out, and made their way through Germany to Amsterdam, and then to England, joining Berta's sister in London's Whitechapel district, where thousands of impoverished Jewish immigrants scraped out meager livings, saving their pence for passage to America. I never heard the story of how miserable that trip was for them and the hundreds of others crammed into steerage.

For some reason Berta and Meyer traveled on two different ships in 1904. They arrived at Ellis Island and were admitted, although Berta was detained for five days. She and Meyer then settled in Brooklyn, a

Jewish ghetto, in a tenement apartment, crowded in with relatives and borders, and worked in the garment sweatshops—Berta as a seamstress in shirtwaist factories, and Meyer as a tailor making men's suits.

They brought their political passions with them as they made a life in the sweatshops, in the meeting halls, and on the picket lines, organizing for workers' rights, for unions, for suffrage, for socialism. They helped organize the International Ladies' Garment Workers Union and campaigned for the eight-hour workday and safer working conditions. They learned English, but always spoke with an accent and preferred Yiddish, their first language. They were Socialist revolutionaries who worked tirelessly to bring about their shared dream of a workers' paradise. They must have been jubilant when the Russian Revolution of 1917 overthrew the Czar, and in 1919 when the Communist Party of the U.S.A. (CPUSA) was formed.

Grandma Was a Revolutionary
Written for MotherTongue Feminist Theater Collective May 2000

Grandma was a revolutionary—
isn't everyone's?

a rabble-rousing, card-carrying Red
run out of Russia, late in the 1890s,
the Cossacks hot on her heels
with a warrant for her arrest,
this time to be sent east.

With courage to spare
landed in the far off land known as the Lower East Side
 —tenements, sweatshops, pushcarts.
With heart on her sleeve
and body on the line,
a labor organizer, feminist,
fiercely independent.
Taught her two daughters Marxism
and speechifying, soapbox style,
and to beware of men for they will try to domesticate,
 diverting them from their paths.
Refused to teach them to knit or sew
 in fear they too would be enslaved.

She was indomitable, subject to dark moods,
 opinionated, smart as a whip, difficult, and gutsy,
 demanding, devoted to the cause.

And who was I to this woman?
Just the apple of her eye.
With love in her gaze and
gnarled fingers knitting and sewing
clothes for my dolls and me.

And do I plan to exhibit
more and more of her qualities
as I continue to age?
In spades.

> And do I have a problem with this?
> Now, what do you think?

Berta and Meyer's first daughter, my mother Mini, was born on December 19, 1905, and three years later came her younger sister, Regina, whom everyone called Reggie, born on January 1, 1909. In 1912, the family moved to Los Angeles, joining the poor but vibrant Jewish neighborhood of Boyle Heights and a community of relatives already situated there. I think Mini and Reggie had pretty good childhoods, in spite of precarious family finances. Mother remembered being doted on by her extended family as a little girl, the first girl to be born in this country. In one photo, she is all dressed up, in her daddy's arms and, she told me, ready to go to a Eugene V. Debs meeting at the age of three!

In Los Angeles there was an extended family of aunts and uncles and eighteen cousins, the latter organizing themselves into a cousins' club. Family members went camping together each summer, each family setting up their tent along a riverbank. The wives and children spent their time visiting and playing. They were joined each weekend by their husbands, who crowded into several vehicles, including a decrepit car and a wagon drawn by a trusty horse. Of course, throughout the year, the large family often gathered in each other's homes for parties.

Meyer again worked as a tailor in a dry cleaner's shop, and Berta worked when her health permitted, having asthma. My mother started working in a box factory at the age of thirteen (having told the boss she was fifteen). She was so little they had to rig up a wooden box in front of her machine to make her tall enough.

As little girls, Mini and Reggie were tutored in Marxist theory and people's history and culture, practicing oratory on soapboxes at those family gatherings starting at the age of four. Their little speeches about capitalism and working class heroes and heroines were always received with enthusiastic applause.

Both sisters joined the Young Communist League and, wearing their red neckerchiefs, attended activities organized for the children. As adolescents, they became teen YCL (Young Communist League) leaders, organizing the first Communist children's group in Southern California and cultural programs for the younger children. They made their parents proud. And when they were old enough, they "flew up," eagerly joining the Communist Party themselves.

At the age of nineteen, Reggie attended a Marxist youth camp in Woodland Washington and fell madly in love with one of its charismatic teachers. His name was Frank Waldron. They would spend a life together as partners, activists, international revolutionaries, and notorious subversives. They were completely dedicated to the Communist Party, the Soviet Union, and the international working class.

In 1930, Frank went underground to avoid arrest as a result of his labor organizing, and went to Moscow. Reggie, along with their three-year-old son, Tim, joined him later that year. They returned without Tim in 1935, and in New York en route to Milwaukee, took the names Eugene and Peggy Dennis. Many years later Eugene became the general secretary of the CPUSA.

Peggy became a brilliant writer and journalist, roaming the world covering international political movements and serving as an underground courier for the Comintern[5], supporting revolutions and revolutionaries around the world. She carried precious messages and money between people in those movements. She traveled frequently to Moscow, Europe, and several times to China with messages and funds. She wrote prolifically, becoming a journalist for the *Daily Worker* and *People's World*, the East Coast and West Coast Communist papers.

She and Gene had two sons, Tim and Gene Jr. Tim was left in the USSR when he was three, to be raised and protected from the danger his parents faced at home. Gene Jr. was born in 1942 and remained with his parents, living in New York City. He and Aunt Peg visited us in San Francisco summers. Uncle Gene was forbidden to enter California because there was a standing order for his arrest. He was eventually tried in federal courts under the Smith Act, convicted of conspiracy to overthrow the U.S. government. In 1950 he received three consecutive sentences: five years for the Smith Act, another year for contempt of Congress, plus six months for contempt of court, for a total of six and a half years to be served at the federal penitentiary in Atlanta, Georgia. Aunt Peg and Gene Jr. traveled by train from New York City to Atlanta whenever they were permitted to visit him.

It was a grueling and extremely stressful time for each of them. My aunt even lost her menstrual period while her husband was imprisoned, a not unusual consequence of extreme stress and fear. The FBI constantly hounded them and even followed my cousin to and from school.

Uncle Gene died of lung cancer on January 31, 1961, and was given a showy funeral in New York City, orchestrated by the CP,

---

[5] The USSR international department, equivalent to the U.S. State Department

which my aunt refused to attend as she was disgusted by the current party leadership.

In mid-February 1961, Aunt Peg moved to San Francisco, living with us on Willard Street for a year before she was ready to get a place on her own across the street. It was then she became the foreign correspondent for the People's World and, in that capacity, traveled abroad for extended stays, sending back her stories and in-depth analyses of conditions in various countries. She also wrote articles and pamphlets on the New Left, feminism, and other hot topics of the day, as well as book reviews for *The Nation*, *The Progressive*, and other liberal periodicals.

In her later years, Peg would write her memoirs, *Autobiography of An American Communist*, which after her death was made into a documentary shown nationally on the PBS series *The American Experience*, under the title *Love in the Cold War*.

Ultimately, she had a stroke, which prevented her from speaking or writing, and after a few very difficult years living at the Jewish Old Folks Home in San Francisco, where her mother too had resided, she died on September 25, 1993.

Berta and Meyer's first-born daughter, Mini, my mother, had a rather unusual beginning. When my grandma went into labor, my grandfather took her to the neighborhood hospital near their Lower East Side tenement. They knew little English and did not know why they were greeted there with such puzzlement and confusion. It turned out it was a home and clinic for unwed pregnant girls and thus Meyer's presence there was unprecedented. They couldn't quite figure out who he was! Nevertheless, Berta was admitted and her daughter born.

Berta and Meyer wanted so much to give their first child a good American name but were uncertain what that might be. After a few days of being pressured by hospital staff to provide a name for the birth certificate, they heard the loud speakers calling for "Nurse Mini" at the very moment hospital official had pen and paper, determined to complete the paperwork without further delay. They blurted out that name, "Mini." Mother never did have a middle name. One was hard enough for her parents to come up with as it was.

Mini, as a teenager, chained herself to the doors of the Los Angeles City Hall, along with Upton Sinclair and others, to protest the lack of free speech. She became a counselor for the YCL and wrote and directed plays and musicals on working class themes for the Young Pioneers to perform. Years later when she was the leader of my Brownie troop, she wrote a play about Harriet Tubman which we put on for our families. I was, of course a very, very pale Harriet and, needless to say, we were a rather unusual Brownie troop for the mid-1950s.

Throughout her teen years Mini led two lives, one at school and the other with family and movement comrades and activities. These worlds rarely intersected.

Mini felt lucky to go to the new Lincoln High School, which she described to me as proletarian and WASP. There she was popular and very active in the drama club (starring in a number of plays and musicals, like *Bunty Pulls the Strings*) as well as the debate club, and had plenty of dates. In her Lincoln High yearbook at graduation in June of 1922, she pasted a note from her debating coach to her parents. The note said she had excellent debating skills and predicted she would do public speaking in some fashion as an adult. Little did he know she would become a union organizer and give speeches to mass meetings and rallies around California, exhorting workers to resist and fight back. However, not all was bliss at Lincoln High. As a freshman, she dated a handsome and popular senior named Waverly. He was running for student president and was told he better stop dating "that Jew girl" if he wanted to be elected.

Mini met Al Bock when she was around seventeen and they dated, but she also was dating Will Schneiderman. She adored them both, and the three were best of friends. When the time came to make a choice, Mini chose Al, whom she described to me—her daughter, as a "hunk." Still wanting to keep Will in the family, she engineered a romance between him and her sister, Reggie. Needless to say, that didn't last long. (Will eventually became the leader of the California state CP.)

Neither Mini nor Al, nor their parents for that matter, believed in legal marriage—Mom, the communist, and Dad, the anarchist, would not give "the state" the power to legitimize their union, but they said they always felt married. Their friends gave them a "pots and pans" party and they started living together in Los Angeles. Ironically, years later, it was the CP that told Mom to marry her partner so that she would have a legitimate cover for her public activism and would not give "the law" the excuse of her living immorally with a man in order to arrest and gag her, and discredit the CP.

Somehow money was found for Mother to attend UCLA for three and a half years. She told me that she did not get to graduate because, in her senior year, she was kicked out as a result of her left wing politics and activism. But around 1973 I found out the truth.

Disclosure

Written for the Old Lesbian Memoir Writing Group

My mother, Mini Karasick Bock, aka Mini Carson (her Commie "handle"), let me know at an early age that she wanted me to go to college and get my degree. She loved books and learning, and at the age of fifty-five she attended classes simultaneously at San Francisco City College and the University of San Francisco, to become a library technician. She worked in the libraries of several primary schools, creating wildly successful and popular writing and reading poetry programs, and happily worked in the reference department of Golden Gate University. She was a natural researcher and took such pleasure in helping students, including her daughter, find the sources they needed for their papers.

When, as a child, I heard the story of my mother's tragic expulsion from UCLA in her senior year, I understood that this was evidence of and reason to boast about her values and commitment to her principles. Something to be proud of.

I went to graduate school at the University of Massachusetts for my master's. I lost my eyesight while I was there and ultimately returned to San Francisco with a high pass on my orals but with two incompletes in my seminars, having been stymied as a result of my new disability. Mother urged me to come home, where she could help me complete my research and my degree. I came home to Willard Street to do research for my classes, including a paper on Paul Robeson.

One late afternoon, Mom and I were sitting in the foyer of our Willard Street home, she in a wheelchair and I comfy in the rocking chair opposite her. No one else was around. She told me, "Laurie, I hope so much you finish your MA because I never finished my degree. I was not expelled for political reasons. I shoplifted some books from the university bookstore. I was so ashamed that I had to make up a story worthy of my family's values, rather than display my shame to everyone. I tell you now because perhaps it will help you to work through your barriers and complete what you started. I don't want you to have to live with the remorse and self-reproach the rest of your life, as I have."

My mother loved me enough to tell me her secret. She died five years later, in 1977. I never received my MA, disappointing her and myself. To this day, I wish I had completed my work for her sake and to justify the tremendous courage it took for her to reveal the truth to me on that day.

Mini and Al hitched to San Francisco around 1925 and lived communally in a series of cold water flats with other comrades, finding any jobs they could and pooling their meager wages. One of these was on Telegraph Hill, which would eventually become a very posh area of San Francisco, but at the time the hill was covered with little shacks and run-down buildings where the young radicals lived together.

During the 1920s, '30s, and early '40s, Mini worked as a presser in factories making women's clothes. She became a brilliant union and party organizer, speaking at huge meetings and rallies to organize for decent wages and working conditions, and to be in solidarity with other workers resisting oppression. She was the president of the San Francisco International Ladies Garment Workers Union, and a delegate to its national convention in New York, speaking to the 3,000 assembled.

She organized a meeting at the San Francisco Civic Auditorium where over 6,000 came to hear CP leader and candidate William Z. Foster speak. She was the circulation manager for *The Worker*, the West Coast CP newspaper. On many a Saturday Mom and a few comrades would go down to Third and Market in San Francisco, to stand on a soapbox and orate to the crowds. Within a few minutes the cops would arrest them and pack them off to jail for the night. Mom would be separated from her colleagues and thrown into the cell with all the prostitutes. Since this was a weekly "visit" they all got very friendly and each Saturday these women would cheer as she got tossed into their cell. She would be back home by Sunday evening to resume her weekly work and activism, as usual, until the next Saturday.

She survived attacks from goons, scabs, FBI agents, and plants, and, in 1931, even a Molotov cocktail that struck her in the face as she was speaking at a huge rally for farm workers in the Central Valley.

As a child, I often asked her to tell me how she got the scar under her eye. Several years ago I had a shock while reading a novel and wrote the author a letter:

November 2007
Dear Dorothy Bryant,

I have just finished reading your *Confessions of Madam Psyche* and for the first time in my life feel compelled to contact an author! On pages 254 and 255 you describe a scene at St. James Park in San Jose where 5,000 had gathered for a rally in support of striking agricultural and cannery workers. No meeting hall had been willing to open their doors for this rally. Police abounded, surrounding the throng, and there were *agent provo-cateurs* milling around, fomenting trouble. Several communist and union organizers had been brought down from San Francisco to speak to the crowd and encourage the workers. One of these, a young, slight woman, was a factory worker. She was boosted up onto the makeshift platform, threw her fist into the air and roared, "Workers!" at which point she was hit in the face with a Molotov cocktail and the police charged in, clubs swinging. She fell from the "stage" bleeding. Pandemonium broke out, police stormed, and the young woman was rushed away by her comrades.

That young woman was my mother! She was taken to a sympathetic doctor who stitched her up and treated her wounds and she got back to San Francisco. Her name was Mini Carson (born Mini Karasick, and "married" name of Mini Bock).

As I read that book and wrote that letter, I was overcome with emotion. Dorothy Bryant had discovered this story while doing research for the book and was as surprised and gratified to hear from me as I had been to suddenly read about my mother in her novel. I was thrilled and moved to know that my mom's activism had been documented and was available to future generations. This was doubly meaningful because I have lived with the regret since her death that I never took her oral history, except for a mere three hours I tape-recorded as she was dying. The prestigious Bancroft Library at the University of California at Berkeley had requested her oral history, but she turned them down, saying that her daughter was then in grad school studying to be a historian and that she would wait for me to do it. It didn't happen.

In 1934, along with Harry Bridges—the leader of the International Longshoreman's and Warehouseman's Union, Mini was on the steering committee that organized and ran the San Francisco General Strike. The strike headquarters was on Market Street above a "friendly" French restaurant and she claimed that was the only strike she was ever involved in where she actually gained weight. In a letter read at my mother's memorial Dorothy Healy—who became the head of the CP in Southern California, wrote, "I met Min when I was fourteen and she became a mentor for me in the movement. Min was a superb organizer, agitator and orator for working class justice."

As a child I, among other rapt listeners, was riveted at stories often told. One of them had to do with Mom and two of her women friends all getting pregnant. My dad was sent off to see Madam Inez, the abortion queen of San Francisco, to ask her how much she would charge for an abortion for his partner, and the abortionist gave him a price. Then he asked, "How much for two women?" She paused, looked at him, and gave him a price. Then he asked if there would be a break for three abortions. She stared at him, looking him up and down, shook her head in disbelief, and they closed the deal. I don't know where the partners of Mom's two friends were but they weren't there to own up to their roles in the matter.

According to the FBI, Mini was elected as the president of her CP group, was on the central committee of the California State CP, was education director of the CP, and spoke at the California state convention of the Communist Party in 1945.

Mother did not give birth to me until that same year, when she was forty years old because—as I was later told, her time and energy and spirit had been dedicated to her unionizing and party work. Her mother, Berta, had always warned her two daughters not to have children too young, for then the men in their lives would expect them to drop their political activities for family life while the men, of course, continued the revolution. As a mom with a small child, she cut way back on her activism, concentrating on working as a real estate agent with my dad and, when they got more financially comfortable, gave annual donations to the *People's World* holiday bazaar and to the CP, of course. Her commitment to her political principles and her intellectual and oratorical skills did not waver, however, as she was always ready with a political analysis and a dramatic or hilarious story to keep her audiences spellbound at dinner parties with friends and family.

Mini had been a good Communist, even through the Stalin revelations and the Soviet invasion of Hungary[6], until the USSR invaded Czechoslovakia in 1968. Both my parents had been excited by the rise of Alexander Dubcek and "Prague Spring" in that country, and to see it destroyed by the Soviet Union was the last straw for her. She and Dad were in Europe at that time and managed to get the last flight into Czechoslovakia along with other nationals and students returning home. My parents stayed in a Prague hotel, wandering the streets, horrified by Soviet tanks and Red Army soldiers, and were incredibly moved by all the signs of creative resistance by the people in the face of that overwhelming might. In protest, my mother officially resigned from the CP. It must have been a wrenching act for her, after a lifetime of dedicated and principled commitment.

---

[6] She did have criticisms, which she voiced within the CP family but never to "outsiders."

Mini remained an ardent Socialist, however disgusted with what had become of the communist revolution in the USSR, but was true to her beliefs, taking heart as she witnessed Salvador Allende's election as the first democratic socialist president of Chile, and other attempts at democratic socialism.

In 1950, when I was five, Mother got breast cancer. She was forty-five and underwent a total radical mastectomy and radiation treatments. As a little girl I always found her "good side" with a breast to cuddle up against. She was cancer-free for sixteen years before it first metastasized into her pelvic bones. Then came more radiation and chemotherapy. Again, she went into remission, but this time for a shorter period.

I returned from graduate school in 1973 to find her in a wheelchair and facing what was to be her last four years of life, time filled with grueling treatments, unspeakable pain, broken bones, and despair. But she was still my mom, and on one of my birthdays I walked into her hospital room to find it crowded with people. She had organized a surprise party for me. There was much jollity, which was, at the same time, fun, sweet, and rather macabre.

I found myself playing a role beyond that of her child, becoming cheerleader and caregiver. When she broke her leg due to the weakness of her cancer-ridden bones, she was put into a full-length cast and sent to the rehab floor of Mt. Zion Hospital. She became catatonic, refusing to move, speak, eat, or even open her eyes. No amount of encouraging or pleas from my dad or her friends, let alone from the medical staff, had any effect. Finally, I told everyone to leave her room and I spoke to her. I was desperate. "Mom, I want you to keep on living because I still need my mother." She opened her eyes and began to try again. I've always felt ambivalent about manipulating her in that way. While what I said was true, my words sentenced her to a few more years of minimal quality of life.

Her final year of life was spent trapped on the top floor of our home on Willard Street. She was confined to a wheelchair and could no longer travel the sixteen steps down to the main floor. Dad was magnificent, her "white knight" as she called him. He cooked for the two of them, kept her spirits up, arranged for their friends to visit, communicated with doctors and Medicare, and was all-around loving and stalwart. We helped each other with her care, agreeing that she would die at home with us. A counselor from the American Cancer Society came to teach the three of us techniques of guided meditation to help the chemo get to the right places in her body. We learned how to do catheter care and Dad, without a moment's hesitation, treated her bedsores.

Dad had always promised Mom that when the time came, he would find the drugs to help her die, even if it meant going down to Haight Street to buy street drugs from some dealer. But when that time came, he just couldn't do it. So when our old family friend Ariah Schwartz, an ophthalmologist, came to visit, he told us it was time to start giving her massive doses of morphine to help her body die. With the full co-operation of our family doctor, he arranged for a nurse to come and teach us how to give the injections. Again, my dad could not inject the woman he had loved and lived with for fifty-five years. So, using an orange, the nurse instructed me how to give the injections and I started giving Mom frequent doses of the drug. I have always been proud of the role I played in helping my mom to die. It was what she wanted.

She gave me the gift of life and I gave her the gift of death. It was the least I could do for my beloved mother, but it did take a toll.

As she died, Dad and I were on either side of the bed holding her hands and loving her. We spent five hours after death with her, saying goodbye, and our dear friend Maggie joined us. We sobbed and told stories and took our time. When we were ready, our family doctor, Sid Levin, came and pronounced her, and the mortuary came for her body.

Her memorial was held at the Friends Center on Lake Street in San Francisco. There was plenty of time for stories, including one from her friend Tillie Olsen about when she and Mini, both having young daughters, organized a Socialist mothers club. There was a long rambling reminiscence from Harry Bridges about the old days, and in particular the General Strike. There was singing and crying and much laughter. People came up to me to introduce themselves and tell me what Mother had meant to them. Will Schneiderman was there. At the memorial, Will and Dad had a tearful reunion. The conclusion was that Mini Karasick Carson Bock had lived a righteous life, a life full of principle, action, and love. I couldn't have agreed more.

The Bocks

I know so little about my father's parents, Morris and Lena Bock. I was told I have Grandma Lena's beautiful complexion. I know she died before I could meet her, in a charity hospital in Los Angeles. I know that as a young man, Grandpa Morris lived in Vilna (Vilnius), which sometimes was in Lithuania and sometimes incorporated into Poland or Russia, depending on which country had acquired it as booty.

As a boy, Morris's family lived in a shtetl called Sventana. There were seven of them in two rooms. His father was mute and worked as a tailor. At the age of ten, realizing he was needed to supplement his family's meager earnings, he went to the shop where his father toiled. He was handed a piece of material and a threaded needle. From that moment Morris began learning the trade he would ply for the rest of his working life. As a young man he moved to Vilna in search of work in the big city, to further help his family, and by that time he had grown angry at the treatment of workers. There he continued his trade as a tailor, and became an activist and anarchist in the Workman's Circle. He organized the tailors in that city to go out on strike for higher wages and better working conditions. It was a prolonged but ultimately successful action, and as a result workers in other trades began to organize themselves into unions.

Morris met Lena in Vilna and they married, immigrating to the U.S. in 1897, to Philadelphia, where my dad, one of five children, was born on March 10, 1905. The family was extremely poor, and they moved from Philadelphia to St. Louis in 1910, when my dad was five years old. By 1920 they had moved to Los Angeles, where they rented a hardscrabble farm in a rural area with other Jews trying to scratch out a living. I only met my grandfather a few times before he died. I called him "Grandpa from the skies so blue" because he came to San Francisco on an airplane to visit us.

I know Morris wrote a memoir/manuscript about his days in Vilna because there is a letter from a publisher praising him, but asking him to be more personal and a bit less polemical—a family flaw, I'm afraid. I know that many Jews wrote autobiographies and sent them to the

Daily Forward, a left wing Jewish newspaper and publisher. I know that Morris' manuscript is lost, so far.

Jews had always been deprived of land in the Old Country and, as a result, forever yearned for some land to call their own. At one point, a Jewish Farmers Association was organized to assist members in obtaining land. A large parcel was found in a desolate part of Texas, near Houston, and they cut it into sizable lots for these land-hungry Jews to buy for a pittance. Morris and Lena bought two parcels, one of which had no access by road. The family held this land for decades after their deaths. My father's generation had no interest in living on the land but hoped there would be successful exploration for oil or gas, or that even Houston might expand to incorporate the area and thereby raise land values. Leases were arranged with companies eager to dig wells but nothing ever came of it. And, as a matter of fact, Houston did expand — but in the other direction.

My father was executor of the Morris Bock Land Trust for years and once visited the land, in Liberty County. He found an arid, desolated, snake infested nothingness, as he told it. There was a family of squatters who had lived on it for several generations. He was glad to find someone actually living on the land, and assured them they could remain. He also found a local attorney to represent our interests. "Lawyer Etheridge" in Conroe, Texas would send my dad annual letters full of folksy news. When he died, he was succeeded by his son, another Lawyer Etheridge, and even a third after *his* death. For years after Dad died, my cousins and I continued to hold onto the land, I think more for nostalgia than in hope of future riches, until finally we agreed to sell the plots — my share of the windfall was $44,000. I was very grateful to my grandparents Morris and Lena for their dreams and their wonderful gift.

Growing up on the "farm," my dad had chores he hated, including taking care of the mean old goat and having to sell their meager harvest from a little produce stand along the road. My dad worked at odd jobs as well, and finally saved up enough money to buy his first suit of clothes. One day, in one of her prodigious rages, his sister, my aunt Rebecca, took a scissors and destroyed it.

My dad became bitter and angry at his brother Ed and had no contact with him for decades. He was resentful, in part, because he had to forego his own dreams to take care of his older brother. He could not go to college, having to work at any menial job to help support the family while his brother, the oldest son, went to university for a degree. Dad was smart, a thinker, a natural intellect and always wanted to be a judge. He would have relished and excelled in his college studies, but instead had to contribute his paltry earnings so that his brother might attend. And there were other issues that divided them. There also was rancor between the two surviving sisters, Bess and Rebecca, which resulted in years of distrust and no contact.

As an only child, I always yearned for siblings but, come to think of it, in my dad's case, perhaps being an only child had its advantages!

Dad worked as a door-to-door salesman. ("Never take no for an answer. Put your foot in the door and ask the *right* question!") I was told he invented the first steam iron and tried to peddle it but never patented it.

Al met Mini as a teenager when, one day, she was visiting relatives on the next farm. They got together when they were eighteen. He got the approval of her mother only when he promised to support Mini's independence by giving her their first jalopy as soon as they could afford one at all.

My dad became an activist union organizer and had the anarchist's suspicion of leaders. As a child, I loved hearing the story of when he organized the Cleaners and Dyers Union in San Francisco, and when they went out on strike he devised an ingenious plan to support the strikers. He made a deal with one plant to allow them to stay open without a picket line if they would contribute a percentage of their profits to the strike fund. The strike was successful.

My father was eventually arrested under the California Anti-Criminal Syndicalism law and jailed in Alameda County. That law was passed to attack unions and imprison their leaders. My father's trial lasted for weeks and created banner headlines in the local papers, including the *Oakland Tribune*. The prosecuting district attorney was Earl Warren, who later became chief justice of the U.S. Supreme Court. My dad spent six months in jail. His most vivid memories were of boredom and becoming expert at gin rummy. He would have been so pleased if I had looked at the microfilms of all the newspaper coverage of the trial but regretfully, I never did.

Al eventually earned his insurance and real estate broker's licenses and opened his own office. He became an advocate for clients in dispute with their insurance companies and negotiated to get them larger settlements. He was always amused at the irony of his making a living in the capitalist system while, at the same time, hoping and working for its demise!

He was never pretentious, although he had the brain and inclination of an intellectual. He could make anyone laugh with delight, groan at his puns, and was a "versifier" *par excellence*. He was never intimidated by another's class or intellectual arrogance. Once, when I was ten, the family took a vacation down to southern California for the opening of Disneyland. We had no hotel reservations and, of course, everything was booked. We arrived at the grand Disneyland Hotel to a full lobby, with lots of folks being turned away. Mom and I were distraught, but Dad simply sauntered up to the reception desk and announced that the Bock party had arrived for their reservation. The clerk searched the book and, naturally, found no such reservation. My dad said with surprise in his voice, "That's strange. Walt said he would arrange everything." The clerk blanched and asked us to please wait while he went in the back to speak with his manager. He returned and said, "We're so sorry Mr. Bock, your suite will be ready in a minute." It was all Mom and I could do not to fall down in a faint.

Another time, Dad bought a Lincoln convertible, a very high-end, snazzy car, with red leather upholstery and a square steering wheel. The car never worked right. So he got the name and phone number of the Chrysler CEO in Detroit and put in a call. With a voice filled with relaxed entitlement, he easily got to the CEO's secretary and said, "Hello. Please put me through to 'Joe Blow.' Tell him Al Bock is calling." She put him right through. After a cordial conversation, the executive was very apologetic and assured my dad he would arrange for a new car to be promptly delivered. This was long before the lemon laws protecting consumers.

As another story goes, long before I was born my dad answered the doorbell at home to find two grim FBI men looming there. They snapped, "We're looking for Mini Carson. Where is she?" Without a moment's pause, Dad donned a chauvinist mantel and retorted, "I don't know where in the hell she is. Probably at some damn meeting or other. If you find her, tell her to get home and fix her husband his dinner!" And he slammed the door on the two rather taken-aback men. He and Mom loved telling this story with dramatic flair and to peals of laughter.

Al became an ardent tennis player at some point. When I was a child, he went several times a week to the "Cal Club" on Bush Street for a game, for schmoozing, and for cocktails. He never hid who he was, his politics, or his background. Even so, many of the wealthy, conservative folks who frequented the club adored him, delighting in his company, his wit, his easygoing ways, and his poking fun at their Republican positions.

During my childhood, in the early '50s, Dad bought a gun. For some reason he was afraid for us. It was after his death, in 1979, that I found the gun and a box of bullets. I wanted nothing to do with them, putting the gun in the rear of a closet shelf and the bullets buried deep in the back of a drawer. When, in 2013, it came time to sell our family home, I needed to do something about those hidden items representing our family's fears. I called the San Francisco Police Department, notifying them of the existence of the gun and asking them to send someone to the house. Officer Mike came, made sure the gun's chamber was empty, carefully wrote out a receipt for the weapon and bullets, and took them away. I have no idea why I hadn't done this years before. Perhaps they were among those few relics of my dad's life that I hung onto, like his little tennis trophies, his high school memory book, and his letters to me, which always started off, "Hi Hon" and ended with his signing off as "Your Pappy."

In the last years of his life, after mom died in 1977, we lived together in our Willard Street home. He and I became friends and respectful peers. He was a remarkable thinker, a consummate idea person, researcher, and creative writer. He spent hours and hours in his "study," a room in our basement, surrounded by binders containing clippings and articles from the *Wall Street Journal*, *Barron's*, and other periodicals. He wrote pages and pages detailing and supporting his thesis of how democratic socialism could combine with a few of the least toxic tenets of capitalism to bring about an economic system that would work effectively for all. He remained an anarchist, his faith in Socialism intact. He believed if Socialism failed, it was due to its leaders.

After my vision loss in 1971, my dad was worried about how I would take care of myself once he and Mom were gone. We discussed my starting a bed-and-breakfast in our home. This B&B notion of his came long before they became prevalent and popular in the U.S. He also had some grandiose plans for me to rent out the house for parties. I did open Bock's Bed and Breakfast in 1980, six months after his death, and successfully ran the business for almost twenty-five years.

When, on December 2, 1979, my dad, Albert J. Bock, died at Mt. Zion hospital in the dead of night, I was waiting for news on a bench in the corridor outside of intensive care with our dear friend Maggie. They told me I could see him as soon as they got him stabilized. I know if I had realized he was dying, I would have made sure I was with him no matter what it took. When the doctors informed me of his death of a massive cardiac arrest, I told them to put him in a private room so that we could spend time alone with him. They informed me that that would not be possible. I said, "If you don't do as I ask, you will have a fat woman screaming at the top of her lungs in this hallway at this ungodly hour." It was two a.m. They hurried to move him, and Maggie and I took our time saying goodbye. I thanked him for loving me. I asked him to forgive me for disappointing him, and forgave him for his limitations, knowing that in spite of all the hard times between us, I had been very lucky in a dad.

So there you have it, my pedigree. I come from strong Socialist feminist women and men, who put their ideas and ideals to work and their lives on the line for their principles.

I've done my best to follow in their footsteps, making choices, choosing battles, taking risks, and addressing the issues relevant to my place and time. But did I do enough to justify that legacy? Did I live up to their social justice values for a "righteous" life? In other words, do I have a good, fat FBI file of my very own?

Morris and Lena Bock, Laura's grandparents. Date unknown.

Meyer and Berta Karasick, Laura's grandparents. c 1902

Meyer and Berta Karasick,
no doubt holding a precious work by Marx or Engels! c 1905

Al Bock and Mini Karasick at 18, Laura's parents. c 1923

Mini Karasick Bock, always a sharp dresser
known for her dramatic flair and posing for the camera.

Al and Mini's 50th Anniversary. 1974

3

Red Diaper Daughter

Where Did I Come From?

Written for the Old Lesbian Memoir Writing Group

I come from sturdy folk—squat, meaty, solid. My people came from The Pale, the shtetl, the land of pogroms, the streets, the resistance to the czar and his enforcers.

I come from tailors and seamstresses toiling in sweatshops and living in tenements.

I come from union organizers and strike leaders.

I come from a line of Communist feminist women and activist Socialist anarchist men.

I come from people hounded by the Red Squads, the FBI, J. Edgar Hoover, HUAC, and Senator Joe McCarthy.

I come from people who lived on the Lower East Side of New York and in the Jewish ghetto of Brooklyn around the turn of the twentieth century, and from Boyle Heights, the Jewish community of Los Angeles.

I come from a city called San Francisco, often enlightened, often accepting diversity, often boasting of its tolerance. I come from a cottage on Collingwood Street and a 1906 Edwardian on Willard Street.

I come from people un-colleged or part-colleged, the first in my immediate family to get a B.A. and almost an M.A., my work cut short by sudden vision loss.

I come from people who like to laugh. People with opinions to defend, to pronounce, to insist, to argue, everyone at the same time, in good-natured dispute and at times in anger, always doctrinaire, never timid, facing off in the bedroom, in the kitchen, the living room, the front porch, and around the dining room table stretched with leaves to accommodate whoever has come to sup and argue and thereby enjoy.

There were the crucial questions of the times: international peoples' struggles for justice, U.S. politics, the Communist Party of the U.S.A., its leadership and rank-and-file, the old days in the unions, in the streets, the General Strike, the picket line, Marxism, Leninism, liberalism, the New Left.

And there was me— quiet little shy me, sometimes fearful of the discord, the growing anger, sometimes listening and learning, but never speaking because whatever could I add to this fast-paced and informed conversation? "Well, Laurie, and what do you think?"

Yikes!

I come from people labeled "Commies," "Reds," and "subversives." And I say with pride, "You bet!!"

And I wonder in awe how people without my legacy come to a progressive politic and social justice value on their own. For me, it was as easy as strudel.

The burning question for me is, did I follow in their footsteps? Would I have made my grandparents and parents proud of me as representing yet another radical activist generation, putting body and principles on the line?

LATE IN 2014, I decided to send away for my FBI file. The psychological and emotional effort to download the request form, actually fill it out, and address and send the envelope was immense. For me, taking such a step was exceptionally difficult. After all, the FBI was an outfit detested, feared, and reviled by my people. And now I was actually and voluntarily initiating contact with them.

Then another even more horrifying thought came to me: What if I had no file at all?! How humiliating! How I let my family down! How would I admit this very embarrassing development to friends and other Red Diaper Babies? I realize this is not a reaction most would have to the prospect of not having an FBI file, but they did not have my family traditions and expectations.

I grew up in the late 1940s and '50s in San Francisco, the daughter of socialists active in the labor movement, and the granddaughter of Russian Jewish social revolutionaries. I am a Red Diaper Baby[7] who is proud that my heritage is one of resistance and defiance. I depend on this legacy as I move through the world as a fat Jewish lesbian socialist feminist. Do I have any problems with labels? Not a bit, if they are ones of my choosing.

---

[7] A Red Diaper Baby is the offspring of at least one Communist parent.

It is true I was the daughter of a mixed union. No, I do not mean that my mother was a Teamster and my father a UAW[8] member. Nor am I implying they were of two races or classes or ethnicities — they were both Jews born into Ashkenazi working-class immigrant families. No, one was not Orthodox, the other secular. Both they and their parents were atheists. So, with all these commonalities, one might ask, why were there such volatile arguments between them? Why did they set each other off over just a difference of opinion? Why were company dinners as well as family meals so frequently filled with exaggerated gestures, excited interrupting, angry voices, frequently ending with impatience and frustration? (My mother's final retort when all else failed was to toss out an exasperated, "Oh, Albert, be quiet!")

The reason is quite simple. Both were socialists but Mother was a communist and Dad was an anarchist! Oy. Both believed in the "vanguard of the working classes," but one put her faith in the Soviet Union and the CPUSA leadership, while the other was disgusted and mistrustful of leaders of any kind and thought the USSR was antithetical to democratic socialism. Ideological differences ran deep, sometimes displayed in good-natured, rollicking disputes but sometimes turning into personal and bitter attacks.

Needless to say, their only offspring had difficulties getting a word in edgewise. Once or twice during company dinners, where the talk was always fast and furious, my father took a spoon and clinked a glass for quiet — not an easy circumstance to bring about — to the astonishment of the friends assembled. The contrast between the excited noise of the moment before and the present hush was dramatic. He would

---

[8] United Auto Workers

ask, "Laurie, what would you like to add?" With all eyes upon me, awaiting some insightful comment if not a polemical discourse from Min and Al's little girl, I would mumble something and flee into the kitchen with dishes.

They were good people, my parents and my grandparents. All socialist feminists. Good stock. I am proud of them all, the choices they made, the risks they took, the sacrifices they experienced for their values and visions of a better world for poor and working people. It has been my job to follow in their footsteps, knowing I could never truly fill them.

The RDB Commandments

1. Thou shalt never get arrested for a non-political act.
2. All honor and reverence shall rest in the working class.
3. The vanguard shall lead the revolution.
4. Economic determinism is the basis upon which to analyze all social and political conditions.
5. Thou shalt not cry. Save it for something big (i.e. fascism).
6. Never be critical about "family business"—communist/socialist ideas/leaders—to non-family members. You will be feeding the fires of the right wing. (This commandment came from Mom and her comrades.)
7. Trotskyites hide under the bed at night (I was convinced of this at age five). Watch out!
8. If there are folks disrupting a meeting you can bet they are PL (Progressive Labor), Trotskyites, or government provocateurs.
9. Be alert for agent provocateurs, they are everywhere.

10. Thou shalt not join some fringe group. Thou shalt work from within. (This dictum came from Dad. As a result I was the only RDB in the Young Democratic Club at the University of Oregon.)

11. Homosexuality is a byproduct of capitalism. When capitalism is defeated, it too will just wither away. (No wonder I did not come out until I was thirty-five, after my parents had died.)

12. Never talk to strangers—they are probably with the FBI or FBI informers.

13. Never, ever cross a picket line. (Once my father and I went to a movie. When we arrived we discovered a Teamster picket line. My father, always the anarchist, said, "Come on, this union is led by a bunch of damn right wing bums." To my horror, we crossed the line, paid for our tickets, bought our popcorn, found our seats, and lasted about ten minutes. He just couldn't do it. We left.)

14. Thou shalt never watch an episode of I Led Three Lives. (A TV show in the '50s about an American spy infiltrating subversive groups.) Or, for that matter, the TV series The FBI, starring Ephraim Zimbalist Jr., whose scripts were approved by J. Edgar Hoover, director of the FBI.

15. Thou shalt cry and get goose bumps whenever you hear sung "The Legend of Joe Hill" or a recording of Paul Robeson or The Weavers singing anything. (It still never fails.)

16. Thou shalt revere the Hollywood 10 and revile the Hollywood canaries who testified for HUAC[9] as "friendly witnesses."

---

[9] House Un-American Activities Committee

17. Thou shall read all of John Steinbeck's books, venerate Upton Sinclair, and read Jack London's The Iron Heel, committing to memory if possible.

18. Thou shall not listen to any radio show or watch a TV show that is racist, like Amos and Andy.

19. Thou shall respect the Old Left. (This was our version of "Respect your elders.")

20. Thou shalt rise and stand with clenched fist whenever singing the "Internationale."

21. You get "credit" for every demonstration you attend, be it for peace, civil rights, immigrant rights, or union and workers' rights, in opposition to imperialist wars and against oppression of any kind.

22. Don't worry your parents. They have enough to worry about. (Therefore, I did not join the Venceremos Brigades going to Cuba in 1964, nor did I go to the Mississippi Summer Project to work in the Civil Rights Movement.)

23. The revolution is just around the corner. (Where, where?)

24. Thou shalt not tell anyone about your background, your family, or your beliefs. It is too dangerous.

25. Nothing today can compare with the good old days: the old struggles, the old demonstrations, the old workers' movements.

Nighttime Mantra (a prayer)

Please don't let the FBI come to take Mom or Dad away during the night. Please don't let the Trots get me. Please don't let J. Edgar arrest Aunt Peg, because then Cousin Gene will have to come to live with us and he's a big bully. Please free Tom Mooney and the Hollywood 10. Please let the Weavers survive the blacklist and Paul Robeson too. Please let my Uncle Gene get out of prison for his political beliefs. Please let the U.S. become Socialist so everyone can have enough food, shelter, healthcare, and work. Please change the motto of our country to "From each according to their ability, to each according to their needs."[10] Please don't let me have any more nightmares.

Not only were my mom and dad socialist revolutionaries and union organizers, but my uncle, Eugene Dennis, was the head of the Communist Party of the United States. I'm not kidding! I'd get birthday cards from him, with his name signed by Aunt Peg. He probably never saw them because, after all, he was a very busy man what with his big job with the CP, traveling the country and abroad, meeting with Khrushchev and other big names who, as a child, I had often heard mentioned.

I never actually met Uncle Gene. He, Aunt Peg, and Genie lived in a New York City fourth-floor walk-up. I gathered it was a shabby, run-down area within walking distance of Riverside Park, where my aunt and cousin, as a toddler, loved to walk. I never went to New York and Uncle Gene couldn't visit us in San Francisco because there was a standing warrant out for his arrest in California, and if he ever returned he would land in prison.

But he did anyway! During the McCarthy period in the late 1940s and '50s, several laws were passed to round up and prosecute communist leaders and promote widespread fear and intimidation, including

---

[10] A Marxist credo

the Smith Act and McCarran Act. Some of the CPUSA leadership went underground, some even to Mexico and other countries, but my uncle stayed put. My dad, an anarchist and always suspicious of leaders of any ilk, had to grudgingly give Uncle Gene credit for not fleeing, staying to face the persecution directed toward so many.

First there were hearings—actually we called them inquisitions—in front of the House Un-American Activities Committee and the Senate committee hearings chaired by Joseph McCarthy. Then there were the show trials in federal courts charging several leaders with attempting to overthrow the U.S. government. Uncle Gene was one of those tried. I have been told there was plenty of sensationalistic media coverage—screaming newspaper headlines, movie newsreels, and more, for weeks. Law schools still teach the "Dennis Case" in constitutional law courses.

After my uncle was sentenced and incarcerated in federal prison in Atlanta for six years, Aunt Peg and Genie took the long train ride down from New York every month to visit him. My cousin remembers sitting on the coach seat, looking out the window, feeling sick to his stomach with anticipation and fear. He and Aunt Peg were the victims of constant FBI surveillance, and harassment and bullying by neighbors and his schoolmates.

I think it also was a pretty scary time for my parents and me, but I don't remember much. I know I was scared the FBI would come to our door and take them away. After all, we were commies too. I heard my parents talking about the plan that if my Aunt Peg were also arrested, Genie would come and live with us. I wasn't sure I liked this idea, but felt guilty. After all, I still had both my parents with me. As it was, the two of them came most summers to stay with us during those years.

As a child, I would overhear quiet discussions between my parents and their friends about such-and-such a person "disappearing" (going underground) or subpoenaed to testify before the committees, or this-or-that "stool pigeon" who had been a "canary" singing out names to the committees, and always waiting for and expecting the "next shoe to drop." They were worried about their close friends, Harry Bridges and Meyer Baylin, who were fighting deportation orders because of their left wing politics and activism.

Growing up, I heard my uncle extolled for his dedicated commitment to the struggle for people's rights by my mom and family friends. I heard him vilified by the world just beyond our small circle and often by my father, as ever mistrustful of leaders.

Soon after my uncle was released from prison in 1955 to a media barrage, he was diagnosed with lung cancer. I think it was in reading the book my aunt later wrote, called *Autobiography of an American Communist*, that I learned prisons were exploiting political prisoners without their permission or knowledge, exposing them to terminal diseases and then using experimental drugs on them. Uncle Gene believed that his lung cancer came as a result of those hideous, Nazi-like experiments during his prison term.

Saints, Sinners and Martyrs
Written for the Old Lesbian Writing Group

I'm a third generation atheist. I come from people of faith, just not the worship of a heavenly father, or mother, for that matter. Some of them were communists, some were leftist anarchists. But there was a reverence toward our heroes, our saints, and stories of their lives were often repeated to me along with the usual fairy tales. There were Rosa Luxemburg and La Passionara[11]. There were Elizabeth Gurley Flynn, Emma Goldman, and of course Mother Jones and Mother Bleur.

There were our martyrs: Sacco and Vanzetti, the Rosenbergs, the Weavers, Paul Robeson, the Hollywood 10 and Tom Mooney, and so many other brave and principled people who were persecuted for their beliefs.

There was the story of our dear family friend Meyer Baylin who, as a young man, along with others, planned an "action" at the 1932 Olympics in Los Angeles. At opening ceremonies, they would suddenly unfurl a huge banner, "Free Tom Mooney,"[12] jump down onto the enormous field, and start running around the track in front of the crowds. They expected to be captured and pulled off immediately by all the cops and security people. Instead, they kept running around the entire very long track before they were arrested. They hadn't trained for a prolonged sprint! Meyer said he thought his legs would drop off and his lungs would burst before they were finally taken down.

---

[11] Dolores Ibarruri Gomez, a fiery defender of the Spanish Republic against Franco

[12] Tom Mooney was a Socialist radical activist who was arrested for a bombing at the 1916 Preparedness Day Parade in San Francisco. He was tried, convicted, and given the death penalty. International pressure, including from President Woodrow Wilson, got this changed to life imprisonment and he was eventually released in 1939.

There were villains and persecutors to be despised and resisted, like J. Edgar Hoover and his FBI, like Joe McCarthy and HUAC, like the right wing media, and the government prosecutors and judges who tried, found guilty, and even murdered our people for their beliefs. There were Trotskyites and members of Progressive Labor who disrupted our meetings and our work because of left wing doctrinal differences. There were *agent provocateurs* who infiltrated our meetings, and government plants to inform on us to the authorities.

But then again, we had our defenders, our allies, our cultural workers, our writers and poets. We had wonderful songs to sing, and admired books to read, concerts and plays to attend, and speakers to cheer. There was laughter around the dinner tables shared with dear friends and comrades, and birthday and family occasions to celebrate together.

There was fear but there was commitment and resistance. There was looking out for each other, and planning together for the "what ifs." It was the worst of times and we made the best of it.

One time there was a great deal of excited anticipation in my family. Aunt Peg was living in an apartment across the street and a dear old friend of hers was coming for a visit. I had long heard about Elizabeth Gurley Flynn—one of an honored panoply of icons we revered for her courage and commitment to a lifetime of activism for the working class and socialism, and support of the Communist parties internationally. I had been given Elizabeth's autobiography as a birthday present one year.

We entered Aunt Peg's living room and there she was—an enormous woman sitting regally in an ordinary chair that somehow transformed into a throne in my eyes. She had soft white hair and bright, interested eyes, and was happy to see Mom and Dad again. (I don't think she knew what to do with me.) I knew she was a Communist leader, a feminist, a writer, a speaker, a rabble-rouser, a saint. I was tongue-tied. What do I say to a saint?

As I have said, there was a lot of arguing in my family over political doctrine, party leadership, and tactics. It was all good-natured, arguments often repeated and issues revisited with friends over for fun dinner parties, all talking and enthusiastically gesturing at once.

But something happened when Aunt Peg came to live with us after her husband died. There were the usual disagreements, now between two communists and one anarchist—Mom, Aunt Peg, and Dad—and things could turn ugly, political and personal, between my dad and Aunt Peg.

Memory of a Sound
Written for the Old Lesbian Memoir Writing Group

I remember the sound. I was in my bed in the next room supposedly asleep, but listening, afraid the noise would become louder and angrier and would well up like big waves, unstoppable, crashing in on me, and capsizing our family once again. These exchanges started as a bantering, friendly familiar discord of ideas. Sometimes they were skirmishes that if not stopped in time would lead to the battles of words and jibes and taunts and digs and in-sults and the banishment of Aunt Peg I so feared, as I listened with dread. These were political arguments, doctrinal and situational, with my mother, father, and Aunt Peg taking their usual stances. The voices of my dad and aunt would become louder, blaming, attack-ing, enraged. I waited for my dad to shout his general indictment, "You *people*...."

There were words rolling off the voices, never to be retrieved, designed to hurt, to wound. They were words of old hurts, old mis-trusts, old envies, old betrayals. The three voices, louder and louder, racing toward the inevitable end I knew well and dreaded. I knew the outcome and, as I got older, I knew it was about being hurt and feeling misunderstood and judged and that they were alike in many ways. But as a little girl I cringed as the "discussions" progressed, fearing they would follow the familiar path. I shook with fear and sorrow. My three most important adults were tearing each other apart. Silently pleading in my little room, "Mom, Dad, Aunt Peg, please stop before it is too late to take them back and we are torn asunder again."

Twice my aunt was barred from our house for a year. Mom and I would have to see her on the sly until some rapprochement was arranged for a while, until the next breach. After my mother died in 1977, my dad informed me that he absolutely did not want my aunt or "that son of hers" invited to the memorial. He could not forgive her for staying away when Mom was dying. Aunt Peg told me she just couldn't bear to be there with us, after going through it when Uncle Gene was dying.

I found myself in an impossible position. I lived with my dad in our family home. My aunt and cousin were not included and afterwards she wrote me an angry letter, accusing me of taking sides and depriving her of this one last opportunity to say goodbye to her sister. Those family feuds can really hurt everyone for years and years.

New Left Activism

As I came of age, I found myself a member of the "New Left," not a communist, not an anarchist but a blending of some of each and critical of some of both. I was an issue-oriented activist and did not want to spend my political energies perpetuating an organization to the detriment of the cause.

Upon starting college at the University of Oregon in Eugene, in the fall of 1963, I joined the campus chapter of CORE[13], and when the Free Speech Movement started on the Berkeley campus of the University of California, I knew about it quickly because I had a subscription to the *San Francisco Chronicle*. I immediately began to organize students and faculty on my campus in support. This included a caravan of cars going down to Berkeley to add our bodies and voices to their struggles against university President Kerr and Governor Ronald Reagan. I organized pressure on our faculty senate to issue a resolution in support of free

---

[13] Congress of Racial Equality

speech and in support of UC faculty protesting the efforts to gag students in Berkeley. [14]

My new best friend, Carolyn McFadden, also a political activist, was someone with whom I could share my shock that November of our freshman year when President Kennedy was shot in Dallas.

Later that year, she decided to join the Venceremos Brigades and went to Cuba the summer of 1964 to help build the new socialist society there. I wanted so much to join her but my parents, who had taken so many risks of their own for their beliefs, pressured me not to go. In their fears for me, they sent me to talk to our family lawyer and dear friend, Frank McTernan, a radical lawyer, who told me that chances were that if I went, I would be blacklisted and never be able to become a teacher, which was my lifelong dream.

That summer of 1964 was also "Mississippi Freedom Summer," and northern college students were organizing to send young people down south to work in the Civil Rights Movement's push for voter registration. I signed up. Again, my parents freaked out. Bowing to their fears for my safety, I instead traveled by car to Chicago's South Side to live in a Freedom House, work for CORE, and establish a children's center there.

At the beginning of summer, my cousin Gene, his wife Liz, and I drove in their old sedan from San Francisco to Kansas City for a Du

---

[14] The Laura Bock collection can be found in the Special Collections Department of the Knight Library at the University of Oregon. It covers political activism in Eugene during the 1960s, from 1963 to 1968. You can access the Description and Overview at: http://bit.ly/1OWbGyA

Bois Club[15] Conference, sat in at a segregated lunch counter, drove on to Madison, Wisconsin where I camped out on the floor of Gene and Liz's apartment, and then to Chicago and dropped off at a CORE office.

Scared? Yes.

Adventurous type? No.

Pushing myself? Absolutely.

CORE assigned me to a Freedom House on the South Side, in the ghetto, in a crumbling ramshackle structure. I lived there for the summer, the only white person, and organized and ran a daycare center for neighborhood kids. I really wanted to be part of the teams going into tenements to organize the tenants into councils to confront their slumlords, but was not allowed to. These teams needed to be all-black workers approaching and talking to the renters. Some middle-class white girl would be absolutely out of place and mistrusted.

That summer was an eye-opener. My first time living in a black ghetto. My first experience living in an all-black house. The first time I went to a neighborhood joint to get some food I ordered ham hocks and beans, only to discover it was not a hunk of juicy ham as I expected but the ham bone and beans! I pretended to know it all along but realized how ignorant I was. Theory was one thing, experience was quite another. In retrospect, I think the other civil rights workers in the house weren't pleased that I had been foisted on them by the CORE office, and were, therefore, not overly friendly, with one or two exceptions. They tolerated me but I never felt part of their work or play. To be fair,

---

[15]The Du Bois Clubs was an organization for socialist communist activist youth in the 1960s.

I was very shy, inhibited, and overwhelmed, and stuck out like the middle-class white girl I was.

There were tensions in the house and in Chicago, not just because of Mayor Richard M. Daly's oppressive regime but also within activist circles. They were doctrinal, personal, and organizational and I didn't have a clue. I made it through the summer coping with all my disorientation and anxiety by being in a haze, going through the motions of my work and not feeling much of anything.

One thing I knew, I did not want to fly back to San Francisco at the end of summer. The transition would have been too abrupt. I needed time to process what had happened and time to ease back into my lily-white college life. I was not the same person who had headed to the Midwest three months before.

When I returned to Eugene for the fall semester, I could have written quite a paper on "What I Did for My Summer Vacation." Had I been in over my head? Yup. Had I learned my lessons? Sure—some hard, some lifelong. Glad I went? You bet.

Back in Eugene, the Vietnam War was heating up as President Lyndon B. Johnson sent more and more "advisors" over there and then troops. I started, with several other students, to organize a new group, the Faculty-Student Committee to End the War in Vietnam. We undertook feverish activities, petition drives, teach-ins, speakers each day at the "free speech" podium outside the student union, tabling, pressuring faculty to pass resolutions in their faculty senate, bringing speakers to campus, supporting our Oregon Senator Wayne Morse in his antiwar efforts in Washington, and doing door-to-door canvassing in Eugene to elect good people like Charlie Porter to Congress and for the reelection of Wayne Morse. Morse was one of only two senators to speak out against the war in Vietnam. The other was Senator Ernest Gruening from Alaska.

I was also in the campus chapter of the Young Democrats of America, a national organization, working from "within" as my dad would advise. There was to be an international peace conference in Helsinki the summer of 1965 that would include delegates from Vietnam. I wanted to be part of the U.S. youth delegation. After the conference, this delegation would go on to Algiers for an International Youth Festival.

The Young Dems on campus were reluctant to authorize me as their representative. They were afraid of the organization being tainted as a commie front by such an affiliation with the conference. I blew up in a meeting and got the letter of representation I wanted.

The other young folks in my delegation were from around the country and were members of Du Bois Clubs or other left youth groups. They were suspicious of my affiliation with the Young Dems, which was not known to be a radical group, of course. I was not invited to participate in their young socialist caucuses. It didn't help when I felt it was necessary to abstain from a conference resolution supporting the liberation struggles of the Viet Cong and North Vietnamese. I was wholeheartedly behind their efforts to oust the U.S. aggressors from their country, but felt honor-bound to represent the interests of the Young Dems and I assumed they would want to stay clear of such a vote. I wanted to work with them upon my return to Eugene, bringing them into coalition with more radical antiwar and civil rights groups. This further alienated me from my delegation. It was a lonely trip.

At the conclusion of the peace conference, we accepted invitations by youth organizations from several Eastern European countries, as well as the Soviet Union, to visit as their guests.

My Aunt Peg was also going to Europe at the same time, to start a year of travel abroad as a foreign journalist for the *People's World*, a West Coast Communist weekly. She and I traveled together to Helsinki, where she was to cover the conference for the paper, and then on by train through Leningrad to Moscow, where I met her son and my cousin, Tim, for the first time. Her firstborn son had been raised in the USSR from the age of three. Then I rejoined my delegation at the Ukraine Hotel and toured Moscow, amazed by the gorgeous underground subway, nearby communal farms, and an exemplary candy factory. In each place we met with the workers around a laden table, to toast each other, ask questions, and express our appreciations and solidarity. We went to the Bolshoi Ballet, attended cultural performances, and delighted in the Moscow Circus in Gorky Park.

We then had the opportunity to travel on to Uzbekistan (Samarkand and Tashkent) and then, as guests of the national student organizations, we traveled as a group to East Germany, Czechoslovakia, and Hungary. Along with sightseeing and meeting with other young folks in each country, we were taken to several concentration/death camps, like Sachsenhausen in Germany and Theresienstadt in Czechoslovakia, where our translator-guide, who was returning with us for the first time since his imprisonment in Theresienstadt, showed us where he had carved his name near his bunk. It was harrowing and very emotional. In East Berlin I roomed with our young interpreter, Heidi, who broke down and was unable to accompany us on the trip to Sachsenhausen. An older and more seasoned translator continued the tour with us in Germany to Dresden and Potsdam.

That fall of 1965, I returned to the U of O to continue in the anti-war movement, organizing campus and city actions. And yes, also attending classes as much as possible.

Write about "A Peace March You Didn't Attend, or One Which Went Awry."

Exercise written for the Old Lesbian Memoir Writing Group

We were planning civil disobedience, sitting down in the middle of the street in Eugene to protest the Vietnam War. I had been on the organizing committee, working hard to "bring it off," doing outreach, tabling, in meetings galore at the University of Oregon.

All the while, I was torn with an agony of indecision. Naturally I would be part of the sit-in and be arrested. I had been raised to demonstrate and put my body on the line by my socialist-activist parents. I admired others, past and present, who were brave and took this step with their bodies.

But I was fat. With horror I imagined a couple of cops struggling to pick me up from the asphalt and half-dragging, half-carrying me to the paddy wagon and then being unable to haul me inside. I knew I would be totally mortified, as I was self-conscious and self-hating every day, living in my body.

I couldn't face such a prospect and, ever since, I remain embarrassed and humiliated when I confess, on rare occasions, that I have never been arrested. Dad had advised me as I reached my teen years, "Don't get arrested for something stupid like drinking. Save it for a principle." Over the years, friends have been arrested in demonstrations at nuclear plants, on picket lines, on protest marches. They tell stories of jails and solidarity with fellow arrestees. I have no such stories. I have always hidden the fact of my cowardice, for how could I explain my reasons for avoiding the indignity and humiliation I feared as a fat woman?

I had wonderful friends in college, all as political and as fervent as I. There were Joanne and Janet and Case and Greg and Gene and others. Caroline never returned to school after her summer in Cuba and to this day I have no idea what happened to her. After my sophomore year, I eagerly left dorm life and Joanne and I moved into an apartment on the bottom floor of a converted old house two blocks from campus. Upstairs, in two little apartments, lived Bruce and Case. I guess our house got to be known as a center for radical organizing, and we later found out the Eugene police had us in their sights. One fellow activist, Jerry, felt certain his garbage was being examined. At the time, I thought he was paranoid, but some years later it became known that this was a tactic used by the FBI and allied "intelligence" agencies investigating the antiwar movement under an FBI program called COINTELPRO.[16]

---

[16] An FBI program conceived and implemented by J. Edgar Hoover to harass and thwart antiwar and civil rights activists and organizations, such as Martin Luther King Jr., the Black Panthers, and antiwar resisters like Daniel and Philip Berrigan, as well as many others. COINTELPRO used "dirty tricks" like burglary, illegal phone taps, planting informers, using provocateurs to foment violence, and altering documents and photographs to impugn the reputations of these individuals and organizations.

Our activities included actions at recruiting centers, and we worked as draft counselors trying to help young men decide what to do. Many were declaring themselves conscientious objectors, and some were making plans to go to Canada. Students had deferments as long as they were registered in school and maintained passing grades. In one of my classes, we had been formed into small groups for a group project. Each group would discuss and grade ourselves for the entire course. Bruce was in my little group. He did not pull his weight, figuring it would be an easy A, skipping lots of classes and not completing his part of the project. At the discussion on grades, other students wanted to give him a D. But I argued that if he didn't get at least a C, he would lose his deferment and be subject to the draft, sent to Vietnam, and very likely killed. He got a C.

I was pretty serious in my political commitments and was indignant when I found out that our numbers at demonstrations were swelled by coeds looking for dates rather than from ardent commitment to our cause. Others said it didn't matter, as long as the media noted the increased numbers. And when the hippie swell came to campus and many of my comrades dropped out and dropped acid, I was indignant with their new passivity and unavailability to our organizing efforts. I never became a hippie, needless to say.

I graduated with my BA at the end of 1967 and moved into Aunt Peg's apartment on Euclid Street in Berkeley. She was once again abroad, on an extended work assignment from the *People's World*. I worked as a Children's Centers substitute teacher for a year and then as a clerk typist at the UC Inventory Department. This office was situated in an old converted house right across the street from People's Park, a stretch of wasteland owned by UC upon which they eventually wanted to build a parking garage. People and students took over the land and planted a wonderful park. The university wanted them out and off, eventually involving the Alameda County Sheriff's Department, the "Blue Meanies," who were notoriously brutal cops, and then Governor Reagan sent in the National Guard. They killed one bystander and beat up and arrested many others. I wore a black armband to work and slipped out each lunchtime to participate in the park's defense and mass demonstrations.

Then one afternoon a memo was received at the inventory department, warning us that the next morning at six a.m. troops would attack the park to evict the protesters, and cautioning us to stay home, not come into work until the afternoon. We had already taped all the windows, to try and keep out the ever-present tear gas. After work, I immediately called a few people whom I thought could get the word out in advance of the attack, so the park defenders would be alerted and ready. Ultimately they were brutally ejected, but at least I was able to sound the alarm.

Walking through campus to and from work each day, we had to cover our faces with wet cloths to try and protect against the acrid tear gas. It was frightening to live in an occupied and armed town. At one demonstration, I could see we were being corralled by the troops and shoved down a street into a dead-end lot where we would be trapped, clubbed, and arrested. I turned off onto a side street and, taking on the persona of a Berkeleyite out for a stroll on a lovely Saturday morning, I calmly walked down toward Shattuck St. and my car. Coming at me was a phalanx of guardsmen, spread across the entire width of the street with their bayoneted rifles at the ready. Somehow I just continued walking purposefully and slipped carefully between two of them, nonchalantly continuing on my way. This was either totally stupid or I had inherited a large dose of my parents' chutzpa!

It wasn't until 1982 at the age of thirty-seven that I came out as a RDB and it was such a relief and so joyful.

These were heady and urgent times. And through it all, I never shared with anyone what my background was, who I came from. It was "skitzy." I was so proud of my legacy but so fearful of sharing it or confiding with friends and fellow activists. I had been well tutored by my parents to never mention Aunt Peg and Uncle Gene or my parents' affiliations and activities, even though by the time I was born they had "retired" from most of their political and labor organizing, as well as from the Communist Party leadership on my mom's part. However, their beliefs and ideals were as fervent as ever.

I kept secret who I really was through grammar school, junior high, and high school. I finally confided in one college friend, my best friend Joanne, one night during senior year in our darkened living room, and swore her to secrecy. It was such a relief. I didn't reveal my background to anyone else until my mid-thirties, and it took time and trust and practice not to feel frightened of the consequences.

Uncoverings

Written for MotherTongue Feminist Theater Collective

"You're a what?"

"An RDB, shush, not so loud."

"Why?"

"Walls have ears."

"So what is it?"

"Red Diaper Baby."

"What's that?"

"Parents were Communists or Socialists."

"Wow, neat! My folks were only Republicans. So what was it like to grow up?"

"Keep it down, the ghost of Hoover may be listening."

"The vacuum dude?"

"No, J. Edgar. It was way scary being a commie kid in the '50s. McCarthy, House Un-American Activities Committee, people going underground, FBI coming around, friends/family arrested, jailed. I was drilled by Mom and Dad to tell no one who we knew what we believed. They ask, don't tell."

"No kidding!"

"But I'm proud of my background and I really want you to know me."

"This is so cool. Wait 'til I tell the gang."

"Groan..."

Singing with RDBs

Written for the Old Lesbian Memoir Writing Group

It was 1982, and we were sitting around a large circle. One woman with her guitar was leading the workshop at the first Jewish Feminist Conference in San Francisco. I knew I needed to be here, with other self-defined Red Diaper Babies, and when we began to sing the old songs, "Joe Hill," "The Internationale," "Union Maid,"

"Solidarity Forever"–I cried and knew I was home. These were my people and I could finally be all of me, not hiding my "subversive" legacy. Our stories followed and I heard similar ones to my own. Our facilitator, Sally, was an RDB from the Lower East Side of New York City. She and her sister are both lesbians and to this day her mom marches in the New York Pride Parade carrying a sign, "Proud Mom of Two Lesbian Daughters." Both of Sally's parents were communist activists and her mom, at age ninety, still works for the causes she holds dear. She is, however, at times frustrated and angry when at demonstrations the cops refuse to arrest her along with the others because she is "too old!"

We all met in Sally's apartment several more times to sing, to eat, to schmooze, and share our familiar stories. We have been dear friends for over thirty years.

From that time on, I have eagerly and readily shared my background with all and sundry. My partner and I now live at The Redwoods, a senior community in Mill Valley, California. Within days of arriving and settling in, I discovered an RDB two doors away on our corridor, and within months Mary and I decided to find out if there were any others living here too. There sure were, and let the organizing and schmoozing and singing begin!

A year or so later I got a call from a new resident who had seen one of the flyers still posted on a bulletin board. She excitedly said,

"I'm a Red Diaper Baby too!" and was disappointed to learn that the RDB gatherings were long over. I invited a few of us to a little welcome "tea." It was fun to hear some of her story. Her parents named her Lenita, after Lenin![17]

This Red Diaper Daughter has been an activist until the last several years. Whenever confronted by an injustice, U.S. aggression and war, grief over the loss of an iconic figure, a celebration of a victory, and for 100 other reasons, I would "hit the streets," physically and emotionally needing to be with others who felt similarly and not wanting to be isolated in hopelessness or exhilaration. There were demonstrations for peace, free speech, civil rights, immigrant's rights, gay pride parades, against Israeli policies toward Arabs and Palestinians, lesbian/dyke marches, pro-choice, gender pay equity, "Take Back The Night" marches, for rape crisis centers and battered women's shelters, International Women's Days, memorials for Harvey Milk, Martin Luther King, and so many others.

And now, old and having an uncooperative body, I can no longer race into the streets. At this time, in the year of 2015, I want and need to be with others outraged at the consistent violence and murder perpetrated by police on black people. I want to be shouting with thousands of others, "Black Lives Matter!" and "White Silence Is Violence."

Ah, a Red Diaper Daughter is always a Red Diaper Baby even when she's blind, can't hear, and her back is killing her! *Oy!*

---

[17] Vladimir Lenin was a Bolshevik leader and father of the Russian Revolution in 1917.

And Then There Was Being Jewish

Raised in the San Francisco radical community, I barely knew I was Jewish. I remember Dad saying Hitler made him feel Jewish for the first time, and not knowing what he meant. As atheists, we did not go to temple nor did we celebrate the Jewish holidays. Instead, we observed May Day as International Workers Day, and on December 25th we had an Xmas tree with a red or white dove of peace perched on top. It was an Xmas morning complete with presents to open and a special meal of lox and bagels. Sound a bit assimilated?

A Jewish Christmas
Written for the Old Lesbian Memoir Writing Group

It was the finishing touch to the Christmas tree. It was a dove of peace, but not the color of snow. It was the color of our beliefs and what some folks called us—Reds.

We were Jews, but secular and assimilated so we celebrated Xmas. We were socialists so no Star of David or Jesus at the top of our tree. We sang the traditional carols but added in "Solidarity Forever," and "Joe Hill." I had a stocking to open early Christmas morning and many presents when parents finally awoke. In the late afternoon, we had a big open house when gobs of family friends of the same ilk came to eat and argue politics and sing and celebrate our secular Jewish Commie Christmas.

My parents spoke some Yiddish to their parents and to each other when they did not want me to understand what they were saying. I picked up only a word or two by virtue of context and repetition, like "oy," and "mashuguna" (crazy), and "mishpucha" (family) and "gepsa ha tresel" (there is a limit!).[18] I was clueless about the ceremonies and rituals of the Jewish year and, later, as an adult, felt embarrassed and self-conscious about my ignorance. What kind of Jew was I, anyway?

In the late 1970s I traveled with my friend Diana to New York City on vacation, but I also had a mission. After my mom's death, I found some scraps of letters from long-lost cousins of hers who lived in New York. It seems she had done some research in the New York phone books and found familiar names. She wanted to reconnect with relatives she remembered from the past. One of the letters I read before that trip was from one of her cousins, who wrote back to Mom. It included the info that she was working at Hadassah.[19]

Having the only-child's yearning for family, I sat on my bed in our Manhattan hotel room and asked the operator for Hadassah. To my confusion, and the operator's amusement, I learned there were many chapters in the vicinity. I started calling. I would ask if my cousin worked there and explain I was a distant relative from California. Finally, I found someone who knew her and would not, of course, give me her phone number, but promised to call her right away with mine. I waited on pins and needles.

When she called, she sounded lovely, warm, and welcoming and invited us over to her apartment in Brighton Beach, wherever that was. We were about to go upstate for five days and made a date for when we returned to the city. On that day, I called to get directions and was

---

[18] I haven't a clue how this is spelled. This is how it sounded to me!

[19] A national Jewish Women's service organization with chapters throughout the country

told that they were sitting shiva[20] for the death of one of her husband's relations, but that we should come over anyway. I knew next to nothing about the protocols of sitting shiva. It was a Saturday and the Sabbath and no places open where we could buy bagels to bring. But I wanted to take something. We got a beautiful large bouquet of flowers.

When we arrived at their skyscraper and door-manned building (what the heck do you do with a doorman?) we rang their bell and greeted each other and I gave my mother's cousin the flowers. I thought it was a bit strange that she said nothing, laid them on a chair, and thereafter ignored them. (Years later I learned you never bring flowers to someone sitting shiva.) All the mirrors in the apartment were covered with black material. Diana and I were placed in an anteroom while they and their guests finished dinner and then we were invited to join them for dessert. I knew I was in a foreign world. That was, as I discovered, just the start of it.

It turned out that the family who remained in New York was entirely different from the folks who went west to Los Angeles. The former were middle-class or higher, the women not needing to work, the men professionals or shopkeepers. The children were bar and bat mitzvahed and all attended synagogue and shul (Yiddish for Hebrew school) regularly. And what's more, they were Republicans! At the table that evening, my new cousin recalled the last time she had seen my mother. Mom was in New York City to address a big convention. She visited her cousin and was asked, "What do you do, Mini?" That evening, my "new" cousin recalled her amazement at my mother's response, "Mini said with pride and passion that she was a *worker*." At the conclusion

---

[20] Religious Jews sit shiva for eight days following a death in the family, remaining at home. Friends and family visit, bringing food and solace.

of her story about that visit with my mom, everyone at the table laughed at the outlandishness of it. I remained puzzled and dismayed.

So much for finding family and expecting instant bonding. Diana and I soon said our goodbyes. Neither my cousin nor I ever initiated contact again. We were foreign to each other on many levels.

I continued, however, to search for my Jewish identity and a community with whom to find common cause.

Rosh Hashanah
Written for the Old Lesbian Memoir Writing Group

Definitions:

Shana—pretty

Punim—face

It's Rosh Hashanah time once again. For me, not a time for prayers or temple—a time for remembering the year past, appreciating the bounty of my present, and hopes for the New Year. A time for emptying my pockets of the regrets and sorrows. A time of introspection and expectation.

It was during a Rosh Hashanah many years ago when I planned to attend an event at the San Francisco Women's Building where I knew I would see Judy Freespirit. She and I were founding members of Fat Lip Readers Theater, working hard for the cause of size acceptance and fat liberation. She was someone for whom I had tremendous respect, some awe, and was a bit intimidated by her force and spirit. I wanted to be thought well of by her—cool, savvy, smart.

Growing up in a secular Jewish family, I was new to the rituals and practices of Rosh Hashanah. A friend taught me how to say

"Happy New Year" in Hebrew (Yiddish?): "L'shanah tovah"—and I practiced and practiced in anticipation of going to the event and greeting Judy with my smooth salutation.

When I saw Judy, I cheerily went up to her and said "La Shana Nova.[21] La Shana Nova!" She smiled, twinkled and said, "And a pretty car to you too."

I was mortified. My attempt to impress left me with egg on my punim.

We were radical commies and anarchists. We were labor people, surrounded by friends of our ilk. We were thinkers and writers and speakers and arguers. We ate and drank, breaking bread and polemics with others. We expected education and good peasant food. We were atheists and non-conformists and, peripherally, we were Jewish, I supposed.

We never went to a synagogue or fasted on Yom Kippur. I didn't take a school holiday on Rosh Hashanah, but did on May Day. That day, also known as International Workers Day and commemorating the Chicago strike for the eight-hour day in 1886, was our holiday. The only time we went to a Passover Seder, our friends used a "Red" Haggadah.[22]

The only times I identified us as Jewish were the occasions when my dad and I went down to McAllister Street to the Jewish delis and butchers and bakers, and brought home our "hazarai[23] meal": lox,

---

[21] A car made by Chevrolet
[22] The ritual script used at a Passover Seder
[23] Hazarai: Jewish junk food

bagels, smoked cod, poppyseed Kaiser rolls, pastrami, pickles, schmaltz herring, cream cheese—and we set to…

We didn't identify with Israel or Zionism, and if pushed to it I would say I was a Jew from the secular radical social-justice side of Jewish tradition.

Then, in my early thirties something shifted in me. I saw other women around me, in the mid to late '70s, redefining themselves as Jews, choosing what was relevant from Jewish history and practices, and reinterpreting and redrawing others to fit their left feminist values. I met these feminist women—including lesbians, radicals, secular and differently religious, at the Jewish Feminist Conference in San Francisco in 1982.

Along with my friend Miriam Weber, I organized a Jewish Feminist Study Group to meet, nosh, and discuss. To my chagrin, instead of finding a sisterhood of like-minded Jewish women, there was anger and frustration and discord around Israel and other topics. My yearning for community was left unfulfilled, for the time being.

What to do with my budding identity as some sort of Jew? When in doubt, *research*! I went to the Jewish Library and took out books on Jewish holidays—exploring to see if any of them appealed to me and if I could incorporate and reinterpret parts of them. For example, during Rosh Hashanah, there is a practice called "tashlik." You empty your pockets of all the lint and detritus of the past year into a moving body of water. This prepares you to welcome in the New Year. I fill my pockets with breadcrumbs (in lieu of lint), go to the ocean, and think about the regrets and sorrows and losses of the past year as I toss the crumbs into the surf.

I attended my first Passover Seder at Sally's, using her wonderfully transformed lesbian feminist political Haggadah, and have joyfully anticipated this annual occasion. Each year at Sally's Seder I find my tribe once again and am renewed and so moved by her refigured Haggadah. Each of us at her big table—Jews and non-Jews, old-timers and ones new to a seder, read portions, sing, and feel such strength and affection for one another. In her Haggadah, it is not only about the liberation of the Jews from slavery in Egypt. It is about all enslaved peoples and the universal liberation we work for. Of course I am in tears as we sing the songs of peace and struggle and solidarity with African Americans, Palestinians, queers, women, and children. There is an opportunity to call out the names of folks we'd like to have join us and I call out the names of my grandma, Berta; my mother, Mini; my aunt Peg; along with Rosa Luxemburg, Emma Goldman, Mother Bleur and Mother Jones, and others as they come to mind. Kleenex is always available!

My searches into "my Jewishness" amused and puzzled my dad. And so, it was very meaningful when he presented me with my first menorah, a traditional gold-colored candelabra for the lighting of Chanukah candles, and even seemed pleased with my explorations.

Heritage

My childhood lessons came from the stories, oft-repeated, of constant danger: of pogroms faced by my grandparents and their parents, of the harassment and threats from the Czar's police because of my grandparents' radical activities. As a child in the '50s, I absorbed the fears felt by my parents and their friends, hearing words like McCarthy, Smith Act, HUAC, the Hollywood 10, J. Edgar Hoover. The message was clear: Danger was everywhere. We mustn't be conspicuous, targets. Who we are and what we believe must be hidden.

As a fat child these warnings and lessons were reinforced daily by the hostility I faced in my world: at home, in school, and with play-mates. Required always to be less than we were: less Jewish, less radical, less fat. Best to be invisible, protected from the probable taunts and the possible arrests. Fearing discovery and reprisal, hiding is part of my heritage. In our fear, giving up our power to those who would silence us as Jews, as Reds, as lesbians, and as fat angry women.

No longer! My heritage is also one of resistance and defiance, hard work to bring about a better future, and lots of laughter.

But the question remains, do I have an FBI file, and thereby will I make my parents and grandparents proud and avoid utter humiliation before my peers? Time will tell.

Baby Laura, 6.5 months. 1946

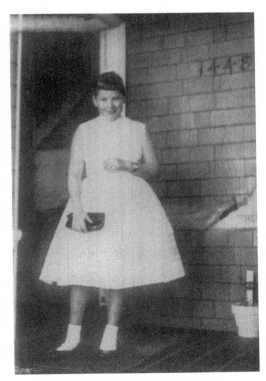

Laura's grammar school graduation day. 1957

Junior High graduation day. 1960

Lowell High school Graduation yearbook photo. 1963

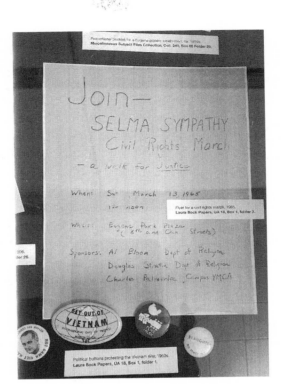

University of Oregon's Knight Library display case featuring some of the
Laura Bock archives in special collection. 1963-1967

Menorahs: the traditional one was a gift from Dad,
the other in front a gift from Laura's friend Sandy Jack.

4

Blue Skies, Troubled Waters
1945 – 1970

AUTUMN HAS ALWAYS been my favorite season—starting the school year; brittle, melodious leaves underfoot; and the two best dates of the year, October 4 and October 31.

On my birthday and Halloween I was a princess, adored, spoiled, feasted, gifted, the center of all good attention without a moment of judgment, criticism, or angry voices.

As a little girl I could choose my birthday menu for my party, whatever I wanted (one year it was hot dogs and coconut cake), and my parents went all out decorating (including a huge crepe paper bow on the back of my chair at the party table). Once my dad even made up verse clues for a neighborhood scavenger hunt for my friends and me, and for another birthday, Mom and Dad took my friends and me to a puppet show in a real theater with two stages where, for the first half, the seats faced in one direction, and for the last half, swiveled to the opposite side.

Then there was the year I turned eleven or twelve and knew I would grow up to be a teacher. I would spend hours in my playroom earnestly and enthusiastically "teaching" to my pretend class full of eager pupils. Somehow Mom got access to a school textbook repository, where teachers and administrators chose which schoolbooks to use and the teachers' manuals that went with them. I got to pick out teacher's editions for several textbooks, including ones for social studies and English. Mom and Dad bought me a blackboard and chalk and I was blissfully happy "teaching." Funny thing, as I completed each grade in school, I was certain that was the very grade I wanted to teach when I grew up.

When I turned sixteen, their present to me was to let me totally re-decorate my bedroom from the frilly pink and white little girl room to a tailored grown up "study." I chose the carpet, wallpaper, and all the furniture in shades of rich browns, beige with splashes of vibrant orange, gold and tweed accents.

Halloween was equally anticipated. I got to dress up as someone else, fussed over and admired. I was permitted to bring home my bag of candy and eat it as I chose, whenever and however much I wanted. There was no judgment from my father, no mean words, no scowls, no disgust, and Mom was relaxed and not needing to be the buffer. The rest of the year, it was a different story.

Autumn, in more recent years, is a time I relish and anticipate for the quickening and falling of the leaves, for the growing chill, for the coming of the darkness, for the smell of winter on the way. A cozy time, no seasonal disorder for me. Gladdened, not depressed by the change in light and temperature.

I always yearned for a sibling to play with, to be on my side in disputes with Mom and Dad, who would take some of the brunt of my parents' riveted attention, their fears and anger, off me. Naturally I idealized such an imagined sib. We would be dearest of friends for life, always in each other's corner and sharing memories of our growing up. Yes, yes, I know! But all I need to hear about is one such relationship and the other ninety-nine percent of stories of mutual disinterest and even rancor between sisters and brothers just slip away.

Desperate
Written for MotherTongue Feminist Theater's sister script

"Desperately seeking a sister."

Good start, now what?

"Older, younger, I don't care."

So far, so good.

"Ability to tolerate two overanxious hyper-vigilant parents."

I can't do this alone anymore. "Be careful, watch out, why, why not, are you sick, are you breathing?" I need a break.

"No goodie-goodie please. You must have issues, problems they can get their teeth into to distract them from mine."

It's not as if they haven't had time to develop outside interests. They are fifty-five.

"So if you're an orphan or never had doting parents and want a sister too, this is a chance of a lifetime. Please call, soon."

Mother had had several miscarriages before my birth on October 4, 1945. I was brought home to 420 Collingwood Street, a magical little house in San Francisco, perched on a steep hill near Twin Peaks, right above the Castro District. I remember knotty pine walls, a big front porch to play on, a neat scruffy back yard, a view of "all" San Francisco, and, in the living room, a big old fireplace. My dad rigged up a swiveling rack on which to bar-b-q special dinners.

My parents had built a beautiful knotty pine room for me as an addition to the back of our little house. The new room was large, with lots of warm wood that covered the walls, the floor, and the shelves under the windows to hold my toys and all my stuff. The windows looked out on our back yard, and from one of them I could reach out and touch a large and leafy tree. It was a special bedroom for a beloved daughter, an only child.

Before I went to bed each night, my dad would come into my room to say goodnight, and at my insistence would check in the closet and under the bed for dreaded Trotskyites so that I might sleep peacefully.

I don't remember how old I was—perhaps two, four or six, when I would wake up in the night terrified, hearing creaks, groans, moans, footsteps—eerie, frightening noises. A sound from over there, then suddenly from that corner there. Creaking from inside the closet, outside my closed door, all around me from everywhere. When I could not stand it one minute longer, I ran to my parents' bedroom screaming "Daddy, Daddy, monsters!"

Finally one night my dad put me in bed with my mom and went to sleep in my knotty pine room. The next morning he came staggering into the kitchen groaning, "I didn't get a wink of sleep, the wind, my god!" After that, my parents emptied a large walk-in clothes closet in the front of the house and put in my little bed and a small dresser. There was a window facing the house next door, and I loved this modest little quiet, contained room. No dark corners, no monster sounds ever again. And my beautiful knotty pine room became my playroom for daytime use only.

In 1955, we moved to a big old 1906 Edwardian on Willard Street in Parnassus Heights. Dad was doubtful about the place, for it was in bad shape, I'm told. But Mom could see all its potential and proceeded to repair and renovate with lots of avocado green paint ("the" color that year) as well as forest green carpets and furniture. Our dear friends, the Citrets, lived up the hill one-half block away, and within several years the Northcotts, also old family friends, moved in next door to us and we had a veritable compound, always in each other's houses for playing (the kids), cocktails (the adults), and impromptu meals. As an only child, it felt good to have this "family" nearby. This was the house that, many years later, after my mom's and dad's deaths, I turned into Bock's Bed and Breakfast, operating it for almost twenty-five years.

Mom organized a Brownie troop and became our leader each week as we met in our neighborhood library to work on our badges. The girls loved her enthusiasm and creativity as she planned our activities and kept us riveted. We learned about Harriet Tubman and put on a play about her for our families.

Then my activist mom started in a fight with the San Francisco Board of Education when she discovered that the schools only served us whole milk with our graham crackers at snack time. I had been put on a diet even in grammar school and she insisted that skim milk be offered as an option. Naturally, she succeeded. Several years later, she charged into the principal's office at my junior high to demand I be given a different French teacher because the one teaching my class was autocratic and scared me. I was transferred. Was she a totally involved parent? Yup. Did she have my back? Absolutely!

I was cherished, and I have a slew of photos to prove it. My grandparents, Berta and Morris Karasick, had moved up to San Francisco from LA and lived in an apartment next door to Grandma's sister on 17th Street and Sanchez. Pictures show me in their arms, as well as adorable shots of little Laurie on the couch sucking her thumb; on the front steps holding tightly onto my daddy's hands; in my tutu on the way to a ballet recital; playing in the backyard; on my tricycle in front of our big-finned Buick convertible; at parties; playing dress up; and with Mom and/or Dad gazing at me with amazement and love.

I grew up with books everywhere and being read to all the time, with much pleasure on both sides. Though I have few memories before the age of ten, I know I had a library card by that time and happily frequented the Park Branch of the San Francisco Public Library as often as I could. I know I would read long into the nights, under the covers with my flashlight. I know I got books as presents for my birthday and Xmas and that I was thrilled. I know I used my allowance to buy every Nancy Drew mystery as they came out in print, and I know I didn't like the Cherry Ames, Student Nurse books as much. I know I knew the Hardy Brothers series was for boys and I knew I could always "go away" into a book and find distraction and riveting stories.

Ten Books Remembered From Childhood

1. *Madeline*
2. Nancy Drew mysteries
3. Iris Noble's biographies for children (especially "Nellie Bly, Girl Reporter"). Iris was a family friend.
4. The *Cherry Ames, Student Nurse* series
5. *Uncle Tom's Cabin*
6. *The Owl and the Pussycat*

7. Hans Christian Andersen's *The Little Mermaid*
8. Dr. Seuss
9. *The Borrowers*
10. Archie comics

I loved the descriptions of the tiny world in *The Borrowers*,[24] a world parallel to that of the giant humans, with whole families and furnishings made from found items from the big world, like an empty spool of thread for a table and a matchbox for a bed. The creativity was amazing—cast-offs used to meet the needs of these tiny folk. I worried for them. What if they were discovered by the giants? It was an entire world in miniature—engrossing and beckoning.

The real world of giants was frightening, filled with illness, anger, scarcity. It was undependable and off balance. So I lived in books, and, in *The Borrowers*, was a ghostly visitor to the little perfectly ordered world, except for the occasional threats from "*them*." It was my preferred universe.

Books remain for me, today, my refuge, my distraction from things scary, anxious, painful, and my favorite recreation and one of my most enjoyable topics for conversation. For at least five years my partner Suzanne and our housemate Gail and I invited friends to join us for monthly writers' salons on Willard Street. We'd choose an author (mostly women) each month and read all we could of her work and about her life, then gather on a Sunday afternoon to nosh delicious food, read bits of her works, and talk, talk, talk and laugh too. To name just a few, our authors included Willa Cather, Emily Dickinson, Marge Piercy, June Jordan, Audre Lorde, Tillie Olson, Elizabeth Alexander,

---

[24] By Mary Norton

and Grace Paley. Now I am reading the authors and the books missed over the years, taking an author and reading all I can find by her as well as learning of her life. What bliss.

Besides books piled everywhere in my childhood homes, there was always music in the house, singing around the piano and the dining room table, and on the hi-fi.

Songs and Singers

As a child, I adored:

> Mom's lullaby
> The Weavers
> Pete Seeger
> Paul Robeson
> "Ballad of Joe Hill"
> "The Internationale"
> "Solidarity Forever"
> Opera (*La Bohème, Madame Butterfly, Carmen*)
> Mahalia Jackson
> The music of *Carmen Jones*

In my teens and twenties were the sounds of:

> Harry Belafonte
> Frankie Avalon
> Paul Anka
> Brenda Lee
> Rock and roll
> The Beatles

Joan Baez
Bob Dylan
Tom Paxton
Phil Ochs
Progressive folk music
"We Shall Overcome"
Miriam Makeba
Civil rights songs
Odetta
Buffy Sainte-Marie

Mom and Dad took me to concerts by Harry Belafonte and Judy Garland, and to operas and The Nutcracker at the elegant San Francisco Opera House. Mom and I traveled by train and bus to Ashland, Oregon several summers for the Shakespeare festival, staying at the Marc Anthony Hotel and having tea at the Ann Hathaway Shoppe. What a wonderful way to experience Shakespeare for the first time!

We went on annual family driving vacations, one time up through Oregon, Washington, and into British Columbia. This trip included dressing up and going to the very grand Empress Hotel in Victoria for high tea. I think these two working-class socialists loved it as much as I did. On this trip and others I was allowed to invite a friend to come along. One such vacation was that trip, in 1955, when we went to Disneyland in southern California for its grand opening and my father talked our way into having a hotel room.

Most summers I was sent to camp for several weeks, usually to ones run by the Recreation Department of San Francisco State University. They were up in the Sierras and mostly I was lonely and miserable, a fat, shy, self-conscious kid, not good at sports (except for swimming), or crafts or making friends. I never told my parents nor asked them not to send me away.

There were cherished pets as I was growing up, Scottish Terriers, to be exact. "Albert, *stop*. Pull over. Look there!" Mom would shout to my dad with urgency as we drove down the street. And he would indeed slam on the brakes of our family car, the Buick Roadster convertible. My mom had spied a Scottie playing in a front yard or walking down the sidewalk with its human. We would leap from the car to greet the hapless person and stoop down to pet and rub and scratch just above the tail of the little black or brindle Scottie, admiring her upright ears, exclaiming over his perky tail, lovely coarse coat, bright eyes, diffident manner, and inimitable Scottie walk. You would have thought we were Scottie-deprived, but we weren't, for we had one of our very own at home.

Why this devotion to one breed, first by my parents and in turn adopted by me for my entire life? Was it due to Fala, the beloved Scottie of Eleanor and Franklin Roosevelt? He lived with them in the White House and went everywhere with FDR. Roosevelt referred to him in speeches, in fireside chats, and his photo was often in the press alongside Franklin or by himself. He was in Warm Springs, Georgia when the President died there in 1944 and, as the story goes, Fala was bereft with grief and sorrow. Some years ago, I found among my parents' papers two photo portraits, one of Fala and the other of Eleanor holding the little black Scottie. They must have sent for them, and I have kept them to this day.

We got our first Scottie when I was quite young. His name was MacDuff and he came to us from another family across town. For some reason they needed to find a new home for him and so he came to join us on Collingwood Street. His short stay with us was painful because he kept running away, actually finding his way back by himself across town to "his family." Eventually, they accepted him back.

Then our good friends, the Andersons, who lived in the Seacliff area of San Francisco, offered us a puppy from the next litter of their Scottie, Penny. I was perhaps seven or so. Mom named him "Hail Heathcliff O'Seacliff." This seemed to be a strange choice from a working-class communist activist but I can explain the Heathcliff part. Mom adored everything Scottish, in particular Robert Burns, and chose Heathcliff for his name from Emily Brontë's classic novel *Wuthering Heights*, not remembering that book was actually set in England. He became Heathy and the three of us adored him for the twelve years of his life. He died while I was away at college at the University of Oregon and I mourned him by myself in my dorm room.

Then came Ms. Pokie McTavish. She had been with a family who had acquired an infant and suddenly no longer had room for her. They had purchased her "on time" and we paid her off and brought her home to Willard Street around 1968. By then I had graduated from college and was living in Berkeley but came home weekly to see my parents and Pokie and do laundry, of course. When I returned from grad school at the University of Massachusetts in 1973, I moved back into our Willard home and the four of us lived together. My mom died in 1977 and my dad in 1979 and then there was Pokie and me, devoted to each other. In my future there would be Rosie, yet another beloved Scottie acquired as a puppy, and we lived together for eleven precious years until her untimely and premature death.

I somehow knew from an early age that learning was essential and I did well in school, excelling in expected subjects like reading and vocabulary (if not spelling) and social sciences, and struggling in a few areas that girls, at that time, were not expected to do well in.

Math

Written for the Old Lesbian Memoir Writing Group

Addition, subtraction, multiplication, and division made sense and I knew these skills would be important. Even some basic algebra in junior high was fun as I moved elements around an equal sign until balance was achieved. I was a Libra, after all. But geometry, plain or solid and anything more advanced? Egads!

In college I listened, mystified, as I heard friends speak of a geometric theorem as beautiful; how math was philosophy, music, art; how formulas would solve a word problem or algebraic puzzler; or how shapes, and one or two or three dimensions, could lead to poetry. As Joanne and Greg, both math devotees, waxed eloquent about their research and the classes they took and, eventually, taught, I remained puzzled and unconvinced. It was all so abstract, this math business, and I was a "concretist," feet on the ground and head nowhere near the clouds.

To my utter surprise, years later I actually had a lovely math experience. My friend Maggie hired me to do her bookkeeping and her former "keeper" trained me in her single-entry system. I was very skeptical and anxious. As it turned out, I took much pleasure in numbers. I ended up working for several self-employed clients. I meticulously entered income and expenses, balanced checkbooks, used one ledger for the monthly totals and another for the annual computations. I took great satisfaction in finding the discrepancies of just a few cents and making everything balance. I felt competent and happy having free reign and being paid to do what I was good at: making order, searching for and finding answers, closing the books each time having successfully completed my tasks. Would that the rest of life fell into place so accommodatingly!

Math was not so bad after all, although I never did find the "poetry" in it and I still assert that memorizing geometric theorems is useless.

As a child, I was taken to ballet class, taught piano by the wizened woman who lived in a dark little tucked-away in-law apartment down the block, and tennis lessons—joining the Whitman Cup Club for Girls, playing twice a week on the courts in Golden Gate Park. Our coach was a middle-aged woman who walked from court to court, wearing a formal suit, nylons and heels, gloves, a hat sporting a little pull-down veil, and, around her neck, a weird fur pelt with the leg pieces hanging down!

Then there were the swimming lessons early on. There was the enormous Fleishhacker Pool out at the beach near the San Francisco Zoo. It was at least three football fields long—or maybe two—filled with salty, briny ocean water, and we kids were outdoors even in the fog and drizzle. We went for lessons and cavorting and screaming and romping.

There was the indoor pool at the Jewish Community Center on California Street. Around the age of ten I went there for lessons. Entering the building I smelled that stale, stuffy, chemical indoor pool smell and felt anxious and didn't want to be there.

There was Letterman Pool in the Presidio, where one summer I took lifeguard training from Mrs. Green, who was also my homeroom and English teacher at Roosevelt Junior High and whom I loved. In her shapeless, tweedy skirt, big loose plaid flannel shirt, and good sturdy Oxford shoes, she taught us to diagram sentences that looked like spider webs going off every which way and to fling ourselves off the diving board. I was entirely at home in water.

Then I didn't swim for twenty-two years. From the age of thirteen until the age of thirty-five I never entered a pool or sat on a beach in a swimsuit, self-conscious and hating my fat body.

In the early 1980s, I was overcome with amazement and pleasure the first time I went to the new fat women's swim in Richmond, saw all these beautiful big bodies, and felt the luscious water welcome me back. As a result of my weekly participation at that swim, I gradually transferred my appreciation of the fat bodies of other women to an acceptance of and pleasure in my own. If they were beautiful in all the diversity of their curves and roles, I must be beautiful too! It was transformative.

For twenty-five years I happily swam twice a week at the Koret Pool in San Francisco. After moving to Mill Valley in 2013, I found a pool nearby at the College of Marin. I will never be deprived again, if I can help it, of the magic of moving in water. It is my fervent contention that gravity is overrated and, given our first nine months swimming contentedly in our moms' wombs, we were made to live in water.

I was always a good little girl, a girly-girl, playing with my dolls, one of which was an adorable black baby doll, except that she didn't look like a real black person at all, but a white doll with brown-painted skin and curly short hair. I played endlessly with paper dolls, played squares in the garage on a "court" painted by my dad, and had friends on the block to play with. I did not play in dirt, did not climb trees, did not rip my pants with roughhousing or tumbling, and I tried hard not to worry Mom and Dad because they had enough to worry about.

Mud Puddle
Written for the Old Lesbian Memoir Writing Group

I was a girly-girl, clean and tidy. Yes, perhaps making a mud pie or two—but a tasteful one, and well contained. I played dolls and tetherball and tennis and blind man's bluff. Scraped knees and torn clothes were at a minimum. No climbing trees or rolling down hills.

But the thing is, I didn't know that I was missing anything until a day, perhaps a year or two ago, when Suzanne and I and Bailey the dog took a walk around Holly Park in San Francisco. It had rained hard and the grass smelled better than chocolate. We had a lovely walk—Bailey romping everywhere, meeting and greeting other dogs and humans and chasing his tennis ball like the zealot he was.

When it was time to go, Suzanne put Bailey in the car and I made my way along the hilly grassy edge adjacent to the curb next to the car. Suddenly I was down on my butt, slipping in the wet, and the more I tried to gain my feet, the more I sank-squished in the goopy mud. I started to laugh and laugh and laugh as I wallowed, as my arms and legs flailed helplessly, as my footing reached for a moment, was lost again and again.

I was covered in mud and I loved it. This is what I had missed— the utter abandonment and fun of not being in control—of being a messy, dirty, mud-covered, happy, anything-goes kid. Delighted and not contrite.

Do I want another such experience?
Absolutely.

Mom and Dad worried about me a lot. Perhaps this stems in part from the fact that I came after several miscarriages and also due to the time when my horrified dad, I'm told, dropped me on my head as a baby! I did my best to take care of them by not doing anything scary. But this meant that trying my wings and learning independence could be problematic.

I went off for my first day of junior high in September of 1957, feeling quite mature and trusted by my mom and dad. I was taking three buses, and having to transfer twice, to get to Roosevelt Junior High all by myself. No problem.

It wasn't until years later, to my embarrassment and dismay, I found out Mom had followed the buses in her car—for several weeks. Is independence always an illusion?

As a teenager I was encouraged by my parents to volunteer during summer vacations. I was a "yellow pinafore girl" one summer at Mt. Zion Hospital, delivering flowers and reading material to patients and supplies to staff, and for several summers worked in children's centers helping the teachers and supervising the kids. I felt good about these jobs and always received rave reviews from the staffs.

At Lowell High School, I excelled in English and social studies, and had a favorite teacher, Mrs. Wallach, who taught advanced composition and who complemented the content in my themes but despaired at my spelling. I worked hard for the election of John F. Kennedy as president and most of all to defeat the right-wing Barry Goldwater. During my senior year, I organized a multiracial lunchtime discussion group in an empty classroom, where several of us talked about the Civil Rights Movement and issues of race.

For my high school graduation, Mother and I went to Europe for six weeks — the first time for each of us. It was the grand tour, staying in *pensiones* and small hotels. It was my high school graduation present, and I had taken my finals early so that we could leave and I would miss the embarrassment of not being invited to the prom or any parties. In Paris, Mom and I found the old Jewish neighborhood, where, without knowing any French, she was able to communicate in her minimal Yiddish. And, of course, given my mom's proclivities, we made a pilgrimage to the offices of *Humanité*, the venerable Socialist newspaper, and to the headquarters of the French Communist Party, where the only word they had in common was "tovarich," Russian for comrade, but there were broad smiles all around! All in all, it was the trip of a lifetime.

That fall, in 1963, I walked purposefully down the curving path, resolved not to look back even to wave. Mom and Dad were still sitting at the table on the veranda of the Student Union of the University of Oregon, watching me leave. We had exchanged good-byes and they were to drive back to San Francisco. All three of us were excited and scared. I was almost eighteen and a newly minted college freshman, away from home for the first time.

That first term at college, I met Carolyn McFadden, who became my new friend. I joined CORE and the Young Democrats, gained twenty-two pounds, and got ridiculed by my PE teacher in front of the class. I joined Carolyn and other dorm-mates in our shock at the assassination of JFK, navigated my classes and assignments well enough, suffered through several engagement or "just pinned" ceremonies in the dorm lounge, and came back one day to find my roommate had moved out and up to the third floor. Feeling self- conscious because of my fat body, I started taking showers in the middle of the night so no one would see me in the open collective shower room, and went home for the holidays with my dirty laundry.

Finding independence from two very protective and worried parents was essential and necessary, but not easy or comfortable and took longer than one term. I had taken the first crucial steps as I left my parents that day in September 1963, acting as if I was full of confidence and ready for anything. Acting "as if" has been a useful tool throughout my life. I recommend it!

Not Bad, Dad
Written for the Old Lesbian Memoir Writing Group

You were at your best, Dad, when ...

* You stirred up a political tempest at dinner parties, enjoying the fallout.
* You relished some tasty tidbit and took pleasure in our common enjoyment of it.
* You took me for our annual December jaunt downtown to buy Mom's Christmas present (yes, this is being Jewish), selecting a gardenia from the street vendor and pinning it to my pretty dress. After our purchase, taking me to brunch at the Sir Francis Drake Hotel. I felt your pride that day.
* You read Descartes as I was failing my Philosophy 101 class and loved it and did your best to translate the abstractions and demystify the concepts for me.

* You bought me my first menorah when I was in my early thirties—showing me that rather than belittling my search for my Jewishness, you appreciated it.
* You balanced Mom's communist trust of leadership (the vanguard) with your anarchist's distrust of leaders. Both positions helped me formulate my own perspective.
* You punned up a storm or wrote your hilarious verses for birthdays or anniversaries or for life in general. I am now known for my hilarious limericks on such occasions.
* Your astounding intellect was in full swing and you were into one of your research and writing projects.
* You parked our two family cars outside on the street the night before 49er games at Kezar Stadium down the hill so that I could sell parking places and earn my holiday money.
* You took me to a few of those 49er games and we sat in the end zones and you hollered like the dickens for the opposing teams, creating havoc among the surrounding crowd, embarrassing the heck out of me, but bought me hot dogs and soda.
* You let me push you back up the steep hills after the game.
* You brought wine and cheese and glasses out to the front porch for people (friends and strangers alike) trudging up the hill from the game so we all could have a jolly party even if the 49ers had lost.
* You showed and told me how much you loved me with your words and your laughing smile and your twinkly eyes.
* You respected my growing self-possession and assertive voice and my setting boundaries with you, and we could finally treat each other as peers.

* Your mischievousness and ability to speak with and not be intimidated by anyone—whatever their class or position, modeled a
  way of being in the world.
* You eventually overcame your hostility and disgust of my fat
  body and buried your "Mr. Hyde" once and for all, and I didn't
  have to be afraid of your rages any longer.

For this and more, not bad, Dad!

Troubled Waters

At one of the meetings for the OLMWG the exercise was to write a
memory of being young (under 12). What came to me was a list.

1. Fat
2. Shy/introvert
3. Commie family
4. Not good at kickball
5. Didn't know how to ride a bike
6. Didn't skate
7. Only child
8. Didn't go to church
9. Severe constipation
10. Old parents
11. Taken to a psychiatrist
12. Family adored Scottish Terriers
13. Sucked my thumb until twelve

There has always been a shadow hanging over me and threatening, ominously. Why do I have so few memories before the age of ten? What am I blocking, what am I forgetting? But perhaps Mom's cancer, diagnosed when I was five, McCarthyism, the fear and anger in the house, and my shame about being fat are quite enough to have wiped out most everything else.

I do remember how scared I was of so many things. Of my parents dying and knowing I couldn't live without them and they were so old and could die and leave me at any time and I knew I would perish. I know it was the height of the McCarthy period, and I was terrified of Joseph McCarthy and J. Edgar Hoover and the FBI taking my parents away to prison or killing them like the Rosenbergs.[25] I know I pulled myself in tight, cringing and clenching, and I got severe constipation and was terrified of the daily trauma in the bathroom. I know I was given frequent enemas and that I dreaded them and was embarrassed and ashamed and humiliated that I had this problem, and was terrified of my bloody poops and screaming in pain. I remember that once after such an episode my mom invited her friend Helen, who was visiting, to come into the bathroom and take a look at what was in the toilet bowl. I know I wanted to die. I avoided spending overnights at friend's homes because I broke toilets.

I know I was given amphetamines at a young age so that I would eat less and lose weight, and that they cranked me up so that I was talking

---

[25] Julius and Ethel Rosenberg were arrested and convicted of espionage, of stealing nuclear secrets and giving them to the U.S.S.R. The international left-wing organized ferociously for their release and exoneration. They were put to death by the United States government.

a mile a minute and trying to climb the walls, as the story goes. I know my parents were afraid I was fat even when I was still in my highchair.

I know I was afraid of my mom's cancer and my dad's rages. I knew there would be hell to pay if either Mom or I raised our voices in anger, especially at Dad, because he would not tolerate it and then he might leave us.

And I was afraid of Trotskyites too.

Bedtime

Written for the Old Lesbian Memoir Writing Group

"Time for bed, Laurie. Come on, brush your teeth and scoot under the covers and I'll be in to tuck you in."

"Okay, Mommy, but then can Daddy come in and check everything?"

"You bet."

Later....

"Daddy, make sure you check under the bed and in the closet, all the way in the back."

"All clear."

"Are you sure?"

"Absolutely!"

"Okay, good night Daddy."

Monsters? Vampires? Boogie men?

No, Trotskyites! A somewhat unusual childhood? I suppose so. It was 1950 in San Francisco and I was five years old. The nightly ritual had been going on for a while and would continue for a few years to come. Given my parentage and grand-parentage, I could have been equally afraid of the FBI or the Cossacks hiding in the dark to frighten me, to grab me or my parents and take them away from me.

I was an only child. We were comfortably middle-class. We were Jewish, I suppose, but I played with the kids on the block, most of whom were Irish Catholics, and I sometimes went to church on Sundays with my best friend, Gail. I had swell birthday parties and a great backyard to play in. So far, so good. My mom and dad had a bunch of friends to laugh with and talk politics. It was like an extended family for me. Mom and Dad were really old, forty years older than me, but all my friends envied me because they were so terrific, and funny and lively.

But I was afraid and there was no one to talk to about it. I was told that if my aunt and uncle were taken away to prison, my bossy cousin Gene would come to live with us. I know I heard talk of so-and-so "going underground," or how one or another of our family's dear friends was "fighting deportation," or that my uncle Gene was in prison. And I shouldn't tell anyone about anything, because bad things may happen to us.

At the same time, I was terribly proud of my heritage—who we were and what we believed in, and the risks and activism undertaken by my grandparents and parents to bring about a more just world. To this day, I take no credit for my politics. They came as my birthright and now I proclaim it to all without hesitation and with pride.

I recently met a woman with a similar left-wing background, but with one significant difference: As a child, she would ask her parents to check under her bed at night for communists. Her family was Trots and Progressive Labor!

Fears and anxiety of future loss have been with me since early child-hood and continue to this day. It's my default setting. There were the early fears of McCarthyism, parents jailed, fat taunts, Mom dying of cancer, poverty, other people, Daddy's threatening to leave us, the deaths of Mom and Dad leaving me helpless, Daddy's unpredictable moods and rages (I never knew if he would be Dr. Jekyll or Mr. Hyde), and anything but normal pooping. I have since added to this list. It now includes illness in general, sudden death, the "what ifs," home-grown fascism, dentists, getting cancer or having a stroke or heart attack, my partner's health and losing her, the "other shoe dropping," further hear-ing loss, and dementia. Oy!

And the result of those childhood fears included, but were not lim-ited to: nail biting, nightmares, thumb sucking until I was twelve, ex-treme shyness and isolation with my books, binge eating, self-hatred, hiding, and severe constipation. As far as the latter, my parents, in des-peration, first took me to a child psychiatrist and eventually a proctol-ogist/ventriloquist, Dr. Jerry Feigan, who, with the help of his adorable "dummy" and a regimen of medication, helped me lessen the trauma, pain, and shame in having a bowel problem.

Photo–Mom and Me

Written for the Old Lesbian Memoir Writing Group

We are side by side; she is sitting in a wheelchair and I am standing beside it. She is wearing some flowered, long robe. I am wearing a favorite "go visiting" dress with a high empire waist and skirt ending just above my knees. I don't know the colors of our clothes. The picture is in black and white. I have on my white socks and black Mary Janes. My hair is cut like Buster Brown and looks as if a bowl had been used as a template. Neither of us is smiling. Mom is holding a lit cigarette in one hand. We are out of doors in a garden. We are not holding hands or touching in any way. We are not having fun.

I have no memory of this occasion, but I can guess it was after my mom's radical mastectomy while she was recovering at a hospital. I was four or five. Dad would have brought me to visit her. Dad must have taken the picture. We looked grim, scared, worried, and awkward with each other. Nothing was normal.

There must have been joyful relief for both Mom and Dad when she reached the first five-year survival date and breathing could commence.

The late 1940s and early '50s were such anxious times for our family. There was mother's cancer in 1950, Dad's fear of her dying and having to raise me alone, their concerns about my being fat and desperate attempts to deal with my severe constipation, the McCarthy period and possible and actual arrests of family and friends. I was so afraid and very shy and took care of Mom and Dad as best I could. But sometimes Dad could get so mad at me, for being fat and for being clumsy and tipping over my milk glass at dinner when I knew he was watching every mouthful I ate. He yelled and yelled and called me names like "fat pig" and "fat slob." Mother tried to buffer. At other times he was so loving and funny and affectionate and brought me little gifts, even chocolates. I never knew which Daddy he would be at any moment.

Nail Biting
Written for the Old Lesbian Memoir Writing Group

It's a large bedroom, long and narrow, with windows at both ends. There are twin beds, each with a white headboard and a white nubby spread with a pink ruffle at its edges. There is a child's dressing table with a round stool in front. Both have a skirt of the same material and pink ruffle as the bedspreads. There is a desk and chair, a small white bookcase displaying a collection of dolls sent from around the world, each wearing their national costume, and a collection of Nancy Drew mysteries. It is a lovely room for a cherished and lucky little girl.

The room is dark, it is night, and there is a child about eleven in one of the twin beds. She is on her stomach under the covers, with her arms fully extended over her head. The door to the bedroom is closed. She is whimpering.

"Ow, ow, ow—it hurts so bad. I can't think, I can't sleep. The pain is throbbing and traveling up my fingers and hands. Help, help! I'll just shove my hands down in the little tight space between the headboard and the mattress. Okay, a little better, the squeezing helps numb them a little."

Now she can sleep. Tomorrow early, she will wipe the blood from the headboard.

She is not a cutter, she is a biter. In the morning she will wake up with her nails down to the quicks and her cuticles and adjacent skin torn. She will try to hide her hands at school from taunting kids and appalled teachers. She wants to be dead.

"I don't know why I have to do it. I can't talk to anyone about it. It's just that I feel so awful inside and it's like all this pressure building up inside and I concentrate on my little stubs and I find a tiny ragged edge and grab hold with my teeth and pull and then keep the nail bit in my mouth for a moment tasting it and softening it and then I spit it out. But then the leftover fingernail isn't smooth and I have to try to smooth it out so I find other ends to bite and tug and rip. It doesn't hurt when I am doing it. Not 'til later on. If there are no nails left I can grab hold of my skin and pull that. I hate myself—I am fat and ugly and Daddy gets so mad at me. I want to turn off all feeling like a switch in my head—there, gone."

She has learned to "go away" from her body and life with her parents. She has learned ways to numb out from the anger and hostility coming at her—the disgust of her. She's getting better and better at it. She sucked her thumb until she was twelve but then they shamed her into stopping, as well as painting her thumb with Mercurochrome and other nasty products. She was scared of being found out and hid her thumb with the bump in the middle.

She was scared and ashamed of stealing money to buy sweets to be gobbled in secret. She can use sugar: binging on bags of cookies and donuts and cupcakes and candy, which worked to damp down her anxieties but made her somewhat sick to her stomach. And her allowance didn't usually cover such purchases and so she would steal coins from her mom's purse and her dad's pockets and then eat in hiding.

Nail biting is yet another way to escape from her feelings of shame and loathing. Of course, then there is the physical pain and mortification the next day. She was so nervous and scared and wanted to die. Biting her fingers somehow helped calm her.

"All I needed to do is find the switch in my brain which controlled bad thoughts and switch it off. I'm getting good at it, but I have to be alone in my room and in the dark. If I get one of those awful feelings, I just picture the switch and flip it off. But I can't do it at school or other places very well yet. When some of the horrible stuff comes at me, I know I just need to get home into my bedroom and then I can 'go away.' But it is scary even there because I have to listen real hard for footsteps coming close."

The problem is, after one of her frequent self-soothers, she feels worse than before—filled with self-hatred and humiliation. And she needed to keep her hands hidden in public, away from the disgust and judgment of others. On the other hand, this little girl found a way to live, in a fashion, and did not kill herself and did grow up. Unfortunately, when she flipped the switch in her head, she cut off all feelings for a very long time, including anger and pleasure.

In her mid-thirties she decided to choose one finger to grow a nail and she would not bite it, comforted that she would still have nine others to bite. She chose the index finger on her right hand so that she would no longer have to be embarrassed when she could not pick up a coin in public. After a year or so, she decided to add another fingernail and chose the index finger on her left hand.

One by one she has added to her collection of unbitten nails, and now she has only two bitten ones left, the two pinkies. For years now she has been able to get along okay with these two, not freaking out anymore, and keeping the others, for the most part, off limits. She is proud of herself and has other tactics now for dealing with her anxiety. She stopped eating sugar in 1977. Now she reads a lot, takes therapeutic naps, and swims regularly. She is no longer ashamed or self-hating.

After decades of hard work she has shed these burdens. She has no intention of trying to stop biting those two little nails. And she is fine with this. Oh yes, and she has, over the last thirty years, found her anger and learned to express it.

She has never painted her fingernails but thoroughly enjoys a pedicure once in a while.

It is only in hindsight that I understand that the extreme physical pain of the severe nail biting was easier to take than the emotional pain, and that the one was able to push down the other, temporarily bringing relief—until the next time.

It was at night that the terrors so often gripped me. In that beautiful pink-and-white, ruffly room, I would lay in bed on so many nights unable to sleep. I was listening so hard. I heard the creaks of the stairs, certain that someone bad was slowly coming up the steps and would creep down the hall to my room and would slowly open my bedroom door. I didn't cry. I didn't yell for Mom or Dad. I just listened and waited, so scared. This was night after night for years.

I had other ways to soothe myself growing up. Besides sucking my thumb, books, binging on sweets, nail biting, and practicing "flipping the switch" to numb out, I went to the ocean.

Ocean Beach to be exact. I went by myself. I took the N-Judah streetcar west to the end of the line. It seemed to take forever and I could barely hold back my tears or contain my urgency. I was not looking forward to the walk through the long, dark, dank, eerie tunnel under the Great Highway to get to the sandy shore. It was scary, with an uneven surface, echoing sounds, and shadows with who knew what lurking. But once through the passage into the light, I was finally there and could breathe deeply, feeling the relief once again.

I brought my despair and self-loathing to the ocean. I brought my tears, my loneliness, and my isolation to the beach. Dim, overcast days were best, for they were devoid of sunbathers and the gaiety of others. I brought my silence to the sound and fury of the surf, the foamy waves hissing as they receded back into the ocean. I found relief in the release of my torment. I discovered how I fit into the grandeur, the immensity of the ocean's forces.

I was enveloped by the sounds of the seagulls' repeated cries, the pungent smells of salt and fishy surf, the feel of the gritty sand beneath my feet as my toes flexed and played in the grains. These ever-present gifts captured my attention and insisted that I be present, there and then, helping me know that my despair was a mere speck in the expanse of it all.

After several hours, I felt a measure of calm and could face returning home, taking the N-Judah the fifty blocks back into the fray, knowing the ocean would be there for me again.

I was twelve and thirteen and fourteen and fifteen. Now I have entered my eighth decade and the ocean is still here for me, ready with her gifts, which give me exactly what I need, no matter how much grief or loss or despair I bring to her. Each time as I leave her I feel tranquil, knowing the bounty in my life, and having gotten "lessons," having decided what steps I will take, what shifts I will make on my path.

In 1960, when I was thirteen, Aunt Peg came to live with us on Willard Street, and for the first time I had an ally, an adult to witness what was happening in my home and how I felt. Her husband, my uncle Gene, had died of lung cancer and her son was off to the University of Wisconsin as a freshman. She was grieving and rootless and found a home with us. The strife in our home did not stop, but I had Aunt Peg to love me as I was, no matter what.

Often, we would go off to Ocean Beach together to find a respite from our torments, and I found acceptance in her company. She played this role for me through my teens and twenties, and it wasn't until I was thirty-six and came out to her as a lesbian that she began to distance herself from me. It was wrenching to lose her. We never were close again. And any opportunity for reconciliation was lost when she had her stroke.

I was ever on the outside, yearning to be "normal," to fit in, to be wanted, to be thin. I was a fat kid unchosen for teams, a fat teen unchosen for dates even though I taught my girlfriends how to dance—the bop, the swing. Wanting to die. My parents and I started seeing a psychiatrist when I was in high school. I saw him twice a week while they saw him only twice a month, so it was obvious to me that I was the big problem. I refused to talk to him about anything besides books and movies. This lasted a year. Dad said it helped him when the doc suggested he think of me as ill or with a broken leg. Then he wouldn't feel so angry, if he saw his daughter as ill.

When it was time to think of college, I considered my options. I could stay at home and attend San Francisco State University. I could go away, and with my parents I visited several campuses, including Chico State and UC Santa Barbara. My fearful self cautioned me to stay at home with Mom and Dad, but I knew I had to get away from my dependency on them. Away, but not too far. I decided upon the University of Oregon in Eugene. I chose the University of Oregon because it was away from home but not too far away—knowing I needed to find independence but also aware that I could indeed take courageous steps if they were small and well considered ones.

When Did You First Leave Home?

Exercise written for the Old Lesbian Memoir Writing Group

At age seventeen, I am preparing to leave home for the first time. I am going to the University of Oregon in Eugene to live in a dorm, without knowing a soul, to fly, perchance to sink, to live without my parent's watchfulness, their safety net, but also without their anxieties and my dad's rages and judgments of me.

They are driving me and my stuff up, to leave me on my own. Well, not exactly. They are paying for everything.

That summer, I had spent two weeks at St. Luke's Hospital in San Francisco, fasting to lose weight so that when I went to college I would be thinner and, as a result, more confident and less shy and self-conscious.

This is huge. I know I must go away and learn how to be independent from their fears for me. But I also learned my lessons well— that I probably can't live without them and, since they are forty years older than me, this means my life will be significantly shortened. I have got to give myself a shove out the door, but I am so scared. I choose Oregon because it is 700 miles away, far, but not too far. And I ask if I can still get the *San Francisco Chronicle* because I need, as an anchor, that link to my city, to what is familiar, like the local news and columns by Herb Caen and Art Hoppe.

It's the end of August now. We are leaving in ten days. What to take? My zillion stuffed animals? My statue of David that Mom bought for me in Florence? My Torpedo typewriter for sure. My posters of Baez and Dylan, my peace sign?

I will be sharing the tiny dorm room in Collins Hall with a stranger. I don't meet people easily. I will be alone and lonely and socially inadequate.

Five days to go, into the breach, something I must do, off a cliff.

They were triplets: loneliness, self-hatred, and depression. The result was hiding. Hiding and covering up the terrors can be lethal. I wrote the following in 2001 for MotherTongue Feminist Theater collective.

Cover Ups

Cover Ups 1

We met in college—classmates, comrades, roommates, best friends for life. Joanne died at forty, breast cancer. At the end she confided bitterly that she knew why she had gotten it. It was the stress of an unhappy and abusive marriage and the secrecy she had felt obliged to maintain. Never told me. Never told her mother. No one. Ashamed. Cover-ups can kill.

Cover Ups 2

At twenty I am thinking of killing myself. God it was hot, unbearably hot. Summer in Eugene at the University of Oregon. Nineties every day, and every day I wore a big billowing coat when I had to leave my cave and go out, and every day I sweated. (Ironically, it was called an all-weather coat). I told everyone I had a cold, all summer long. I despised every inch, every ounce of my fat body.

Mortified, so I lied and sweated and hid. And I rarely left my darkened apartment. I did not go to classes. I ate junk food—there was a McDonald's steps from my back door, and I watched soap operas all day. I almost flunked my classes. Dad's stroke saved me. I had to fly home and was allowed to drop my classes that semester without penalty due to the family emergency.

When I returned to Eugene I forced myself to go to the student health center and ask for a counselor.

Cover Ups 3

"I'm fine, just fine, thank you."

I'm not. I'm sobbing inside. Despair fills every crevice. Every breath is an effort. Help, help.

"I'm fine, thank you."

Cover Ups 4

I was living in Berkeley, California in 1968, and working as a substitute teacher for Children's Centers in Berkeley, Oakland, and Alameda. I was counting pills, not leaving my third floor apartment on Euclid Street. I was binging on junk food to numb the pain and writing dark gloomy poetry in my journal. I was hiding, tiptoeing. And crying.

One night, in desperation, I got myself to the twenty-four-hour Safeway on University and filled my cart with ice cream and cookies and Hostess donuts. As I headed to check out, ready with a story about a last minute party, a commanding voice came over the loud speaker—"Shoppers, please vacate the premises immediately!" I left my basket and drove home, embarrassed about the melting ice cream and someone finding the cart's contents, reacting with disgust. How ironic that I had been foiled in my desperate need to self-soothe by a damned bomb threat!

I was reading Doris Lessing's *The Golden Notebook*. This desperation went on for three months. I had to make a decision: life or no life. Doris's words, as well as finding myself sobbing in the bathroom at work, moved me to find a psychiatrist, a Freudian no less, start antidepressants, and force myself to reach out to a friend.

Cover Ups 5

I am twenty-four living in Amherst, Massachusetts and attending grad school at the U of M. I am lonely, have no friends, counting pills. Do I have enough, just in case? Pills are my only security. I am in the attic studio apartment of a carriage house on Sunset Avenue, living above my landladies, Miss Irene and Dr. Charlotte. I pull the shades, draw the curtains. I pretend that I am okay in my letters to Mom and Dad and Aunt Peg and to friends back home. I am lost. I am in darkness. I get myself a counselor at the student health center and live on.

Cover Ups 6

Dad warned Mom and me. Friends won't keep coming around unless we're cheerful, entertaining, upbeat. Mom's struggling with cancer, inch by inch. Don't talk about it. Anyone ever heard of a breast cancer joke?

Solitude has played an important role in my life. It has been in those very times of torment and despair that I have needed the time alone to feel the miseries and find lessons and make decisions, forging steps, little by little, to make changes, however overwhelming, to reach out, to live. And do I believe in therapy? You bet!

Partly Cloudy, Gentle Waters

One of the very beneficial aspects of looking back and writing memoir is that one can find lessons in the most unlikely places and times. Both Mom and Dad modeled chutzpah and acting "as if" entitled, and demonstrated planned risk-taking for a "good" goal. At any age, I was the envy of my friends for the cool parents I had, as they drew people of all ages into their circle. Dad taught me how not to take an initial "no" for the final answer. Both taught me how to problem-solve and that if one route does not work, take another, and then another. Mom showed me how to be organized, to budget, and to teach myself what I needed to know if there was no one else available to show me. She modeled how to tell a good story dramatically, embellishing as required for effect, and I took this lesson to heart when later I joined two theater companies. They taught me to find people to be resources and teachers and facilitators. I learned from them how to speak publically, in crowds small or large, to let my humor out, enjoying and provoking hearty laughter in others with my words and storytelling. From Mom I learned research tools so that I can speak or write authoritatively and take action with confidence. And I learned from my dad important and useful life axioms: that courage is being afraid and acting anyway, and that in a dispute with some bureaucrat, take a position that leaves room for escalation!

The following two pieces were exercises written for the Old Lesbian Memoir Writing Group. Until I wrote these pieces, I hadn't realized the important lessons learned at those times.

Mother's Shoes

She would drive miles for a shoe sale, and when she found a pair she liked, she would buy four or five pairs, in different colors. This did not break the budget, for she shopped at Gallen Kamps and other "cheap" places where shoes cost her only six or seven dollars a pair. Dad would tease her a little because of the money she had spent on gas to get the sale shoes. But I admired her and to this day will "shop around" for the best price even if it is across town.

Knitting

I was living in Berkeley in 1969, when I decided to learn how to knit and crochet. This was a rather unexpected resolution for me. Mom and I had been convinced that neither one of us could do anything with our hands. It took special talent and we did not have it.

My maternal grandmother had sewed and knitted and crocheted exquisitely. In her younger immigrant years, she had worked in the shirtwaist sweatshops of New York City's Lower East Side, and continued in the needle trades when the family moved to Los Angeles. I still treasure the lacey doilies, sweaters, and doll clothes she made for me. She refused, however, to teach her daughters these skills. She fervently believed that handwork contributed to the enslavement of women in low paying jobs. She insisted that Mother and Aunt Peg learn valued and powerful skills—those using the intellect. As a result, Mother and I decided we were too clumsy to do handicrafts of any kind.

Back to Berkeley. It was September, money was scarce, and I was worrying about giving gifts in December. Making them was an answer, so I found a small yarn shop on Telegraph Avenue where the owner would teach me to knit if I bought her yarn. To my surprise, I had fun!

To protect myself, I told no one—family or friends—what I was doing, just in case. Ultimately, I anticipated and thoroughly enjoyed their surprise when they opened the gifts and learned I had made them myself.

There had certainly been times in my life when learning something new had not gone well, but this particular learning experience was a good one because the decision to try something new was mine alone. I wanted to do it. Second, because it felt risky, I protected myself in ways that helped me feel safer. Third, the learning situation was friendly, supportive, and social. There were four or five of us around the table, learning, helping each other, and kibitzing. I made four or five caps, a poncho for my mother, and began an afghan. And fourth, I received loads of wonderful recognition for my work. I felt competent and pleased with myself for meeting a challenge I had set in spite of being convinced I would fail.

So, what happened to the afghan? I chose day-glow bright colors and started crocheting tons of squares. Before long, this lost its appeal and I ended up taking six months off, eventually completing a twin-size afghan several years later. Satisfied to have it completed, relieved it was finally finished, and a bit dismayed at the anything-but-restful colors I had chosen. And the twin-size, when I had a big bed? Enough was enough!

Mother had taught herself to mend the hems on my skirts, sew buttons, and even use my grandma's old White electric sewing machine with the metal knee bar. She figured out how to wind bobbins, and sew backwards by inserting the needle, pulling up the clamp, and reversing the fabric. Although, to my grandma's horror, she took satisfaction from her efforts.

All of us hang onto some of the lessons we learn as children, reject others, and probably should reject even more. Many of my lessons from my family have suited me well over the years. But what did my family expect of me and what paths did I ultimately choose for myself? The following was an exercise given at the Old Lesbian Memoir Writing Group.

Expected	Chosen
Education	Education
Activist	Activist
Be arrested	No arrests
Radical	Radical
Thin	Fat & proud
Public speaker	Performer and public speaker
Minimally Jewish	Progressive Secular Jewish identity
Getting Masters	Incomplete
Marrying	Not for me
Having children	Choosing no children

Dependent, needing to be cared for	Independent and self-sufficient
Avid reader	Avid reader
Clumsy because of being, fat—bull in a china shop	Graceful, great dancer
Shy and quiet	Extrovert
Straight	Lesbian
Good Speller	Accepting myself as non-speller
Smart	Smart
Scared to risk	Take measured risks

Yes, I had been shy. To put it mildly—
Yes, scared of my shadow—for real
Yes, hiding my body and spirit—no kidding
No longer!

I lived with two amazing and volatile parents, smart, articulate, incredibly informed, supreme conversationalists, adept at witty rejoinders, fast talkers, fast thinkers. I could not get a word in edgewise nor did I have the courage to try. I was extremely shy, especially with my contemporaries, anxious and fearful.

So, what were the steps I took which ultimately led to finding my voice and confidence? They weren't under a rock or around the corner. They weren't buried ten feet below or twelve fathoms deep. Mostly, I suppose they just hid out. It took pushing myself, reaching down, finding grit. I was determined to change my life, setting a small goal, and taking little step by little step.

Given how important the ocean has been to me, its presence ever-providing me with solace, balance, lessons, tranquility, and a reminder of the bounty, it's no wonder that what saved my life and largely helped me find my voice and my confidence was the coming of "The Second Wave"!

420 Collingwood, Laura's first home in San Francisco.

Grandfather Morris Bock with infant Laura at 9 months. 1946

Laura with grandparents, Meyer and Berta Karasick. 1946-47

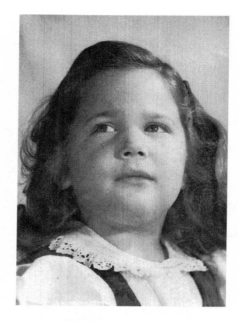

Laura portrait. 1949

Laura with parents after her mom's mastectomy. c 1950

Ballerina Laura, on the way to a recital. 1951

Laura and Mom in their Buick Roadster convertible. 1951

Willard St. family home from 1955 until Laura sold it in 2013.
She ran Bock's Bed and Breakfast in it from 1980 to 2005.

Laura with mom and beloved Scottie, Heathcliff, on Willard St. deck. 1957

5

Ridin' High on the Second Wave

AS AN ONLY CHILD, I had absolutely no experience when it came to sisters and sisterhood. So in 1999, when I joined the MotherTongue Feminist Theater Collective's new project, "Sisterspeak," the script was to be about sisterhood as well as about biological sisters. I thoroughly identified with the former. I wrote and performed the following three pieces:

I Want One

(July 1999)

I want one, just one—I'm not greedy.

Okay, maybe two.

You all who have three or four or more,

Have you ever heard of sharing? Really.

Hoarding is not feminist.

I read that in the Feminist Manifesto, Book 53, Chapter 2,

verse 16.

Look, you'll never miss just one.
You probably can't keep track of 'em anyway.
I'll let you choose: size, color, age, creed, no problem. A little
   more of this, a little less of that.
I'll be thrilled, no kidding.

Listen, I come with references.
Anyone can tell you
I'm reasonably bright, good conversationalist, recovering
   co-dependent (mostly),
Amusing, an all-around nice person,
Judgmental, opinionated to be sure,
But pretty good with limits and boundaries according to my
   therapist of fifteen years.

So, what do you say?
We got a deal?
Do I get a sister?

(After one performance, a woman actually came up from our audience
declaring, "I am applying to be your sister"!)

Personal Ad

(April 1999)
SISTER AVAILABLE
Fifty-three, no prior experience but eager and a quick study.
   Amusing, comforting, a good listener, somewhat
   judgmental, but good with limits and boundaries.

Available the second and fourth Tuesdays,

Fair weather, not foul.

For richer, in health, 'til aggravations do us part.

Call, it couldn't hurt!

Congratulations

(July 1999)

"Congratulations, Miss Bock, you have a brand new sister."

"Thank you doctor, but..."

"She's just fine, a big beautiful bouncing healthy girl—
   length sixty-eight inches,

weight 250 pounds, curly hair, hazel eyes. She's just perfect."

I'm thrilled, emotional, speechless,

and labor wasn't even that bad!

A *sister*—now what do I do with her?

I knew I should have taken those classes in new sistering
   skills.

Hi, I'm Laura.

Listen, I'm new at this, so I may mess up some.

I better fill you in on family matters.

Mom and Dad are old lefties—for that matter, so were our
   grandparents. Mom's a commie,

Dad's an anarchist. This makes for frequent and loud political

disagreements, with everyone talking at once.

Let's see...

We're Jewish, Mom and are I fat; Dad hates fat.
Dad has a temper.
Welcome to the family!
I've been waiting for you.
I just know we have everything in common.
We'll talk for hours, never fight, stick up for each other,
always be supportive,
never competitive, ever protective, never judgmental.
We'll never feel alone, whatever the geographic distance.
Eventually we'll have adjoining rooms at the Jewish Old
    Folks Home.
Two old curmudgeons thoroughly enjoying ourselves and
    making trouble wherever we can.
And they'll shake their heads and say, "Those Bock sisters..."
Watch out!

So how does one go from utterly sisterless, from an ultra-shy, self-hating, depressed young woman to a flaming feminist radical activist in a community of sisters of choice? Only with a heck of a lot of help, good timing, good people, and a prime location. At least that's what it took for me. It took more than friends, more than a family, more than gumption and determination, and more even than a good therapist.

It took a movement.

Brady Street 1975

Written for the Old Lesbian Memoir Writing Group

Where in the hell is 63 Brady Street? The notice said, "Come to the Women's Center for a fat women's support group." And how am I gonna get myself there? I'm not talking about which bus or train. I'm not worried about getting lost or never finding this unheard-of street in San Francisco. I know it is some narrow alley off Market Street near Gough.

The barriers I faced in reaching this address were not physical or about my blindness. They had to do with courage and possibly turning my back on a lifetime of beliefs about myself. How do I take such a big risk as an overweight, self-hating woman? I hid at home and was as inconspicuous as possible out in the world—wearing loose, sedate muumuus in brown, navy or black, definitely no big flowered or horizontally striped prints. And meeting new people—strangers! I wouldn't fit in (literally?).

The messages I had learned so well and taken to heart over the thirty years of my life included:

1. Being overweight is a character flaw.
2. Being overweight is a choice anyone can do something about.
3. Being overweight means you have failed at every diet you've tried.
4. Being overweight means you haven't tried hard enough to lose weight.
5. Being fat means you are unhealthy.
6. Being overweight means you are ugly.

7. Being fat means no one will ever want to be with you romantically or sexually.
8. Being overweight means you are out of control and think very little of yourself.
9. Being overweight means you are a slob and eat enormous portions of food, not to speak of the wrong kind of food entirely.
10. Being overweight means you should feel humiliated and mortified about existing at all.
11. Being overweight means you will not be hired for a job because you are a health risk to the company.
12. Being overweight means you will be unable to get any health insurance because you have a preexisting condition.
13. Being overweight means it is all your fault.
14. Being overweight means you are abnormal.
15. Being overweight means you are stupid and should not be believed about anything.
16. Being overweight means you should hide at home so as not to offend anyone with your mere presence.

At thirty, my lifelong shyness prevented me from speaking up in public and "public" was any place with more than one other person. Yet I was desperately unhappy and looking for something, anything, to help. I was at the end of my tether. Nothing had worked.

For several days before the meeting at the Women's Center, I did what I always did before taking any new risk. I dieted. Because only then would I have the necessary confidence and self-respect to step off into the unknown. So off I went, quaking but determined.

The Women's Center was a modest, cramped storefront on Brady Street. I entered timidly into a noisy room filled with women chatting and laughing and looking purposeful. Even with my tiny bit of vision in one eye, I could tell the walls were covered with bulletin boards that were filled with flyers and announcements and lists. This modest den of female activity was a part of the new women's liberation movement also called "the second wave," as I was to discover.

The diet I had put myself on for those few days would turn out to be the last diet I would ever attempt. I had spent a lifetime dieting, including Atkins, hospital fasts, Weight Watchers, the grapefruit diet, and hundreds of others. My parents had even put me on diet pills—*amphetamines*—when I was a toddler, to curb my appetite. Each of them worked for a while and then I would regain the lost weight and more.

Over the next few years, following that first meeting at the Women's Center, and to my utter amazement as I stopped dieting, I also stopped binging, secret eating, and hiding, and began to peel off the thick layers of self-hatred, depression, and isolation I had experienced since early childhood.

I walked into the room that day in 1975, feeling hopeless and terrified. The center was supplying a facilitator for the first few sessions of the support group. That first meeting was a blur. I remained silent, shy, withdrawn, and clearly out of my element as I listened to stories from other fat women. At that time, of course, I did not use the word "fat." I had yet to redefine it and claim it, first as an objective, descriptive word rather than an epithet, and later as a banner, a defiant celebration of who I was and what I stood for and against.

Gradually, I began to talk as the group meetings continued. This support group was one of the many consciousness-raising groups that were being organized all over the country by and for women to learn about each other and ourselves. These groups would eventually lead to a level of activism unprecedented in its influence on the mainstream political, social, and economic systems, as well as in transforming the lives of individual women. Our motto became, "the personal is political," and I learned what this meant as I heard my story repeated over and over in the words of others. And I started to understand something else was working here—something systemic, having to do with patriarchal conditioning and domination and not about my own flawed character. As I learned this, I began to feel angry for the first time, and felt a compelling need to *do* something about it.

How did this dramatic turnaround happen for so many of us? In that amazing support group, we talked, we listened, and we made connections:

I learned that my feelings of personal humiliation and mortification and self-hatred were voiced by other women and this was not a coincidence.

I learned that self-hatred was not just a personal character flaw; it was widespread and universal among women. And that suggested that other forces were working to indoctrinate and disempower us.

I began to understand the phrase, "the personal is political," and in that group I could release my own guilt as I got angry on behalf of other women.

I found my voice, my tears, my anger and indignation—I became articulate; I could speak to groups of a few and even to an entire room.

I found my power with my dad—and for the first time set limits when it came to his fat-shaming remarks. Eventually, as I grew stronger and began insisting on his respect, we found a new, easier rapport with one another.

That support group lasted for years, meeting at each other's homes, adding new members, and changing our lives. I became one of the continuing organizers and facilitators—discovering I had natural skills and was learning new ones. In that group I began and continued my healing, and took my first steps towards becoming a fat activist, angry, joyful, not dieting or binging and ready to take action to change the lives of fat women. But this total transformation took time, and happened step by step.

Getting out of huge formless muumuus and into pants was a giant leap. Marge from the support group said she would go with me to Rochester's Big and Tall downtown to buy my first pair of pants. I was scared and tentative and extremely self-conscious. It was a big day, literally and symbolically, and she and I will never forget that shopping trip. I could make these changes and take those risks because of the support of so many other women making similar changes and taking their own risks. They had my back and I had theirs. No longer would we try to diminish ourselves in any way. Little by little, I stopped hiding my body until eventually it became easy to be as big and shapely and colorful as I wished. Bring on the form-fitting pants and flowery printed and striped shirts, tucked in, of course! And no more hiding.

In the late 1970s, we heard that a couple of feminists were coming up from Los Angeles to speak at the Full Moon Café bookstore, a women's space on 18th Street in the Castro district. They were to give a talk about something called "fat liberation." We crammed into that small room to hear amazing words — "fat politics," "fat oppression," and eagerly paid the pittance for a multi-page document with an orange cover boldly entitled "The Fat Underground." The words, concepts, facts inside, were ground breaking and left me breathless and exhilarated.

Soon after that momentous meeting, I became involved with a collective of women in organizing, planning, and presenting three public meetings on the subject of fat politics from a feminist perspective. My assignment was to write a paper, a talk to be given at the meetings. The collective read the paper, commenting and critiquing it in a supportive manner, suggesting changes and some modifications. The plan for the meetings called for a showing of a videotape made by the Fat Underground, my speech, and a general discussion. Two of the meetings were for women, one would be open to men as well.

I was terrified. I was taking another giant step coming out of my shell. I was about to unpeel my layers, take down my walls, go out on a limb, and talk about what it was like being me, *in public*.

The first meeting was at the Artemis Café, a women's coffee house on Valencia Street. The room was packed with eager women. I was scared and excited. I started to speak, my voice quavering, and I sensed that the people were with me, learning, identifying, and starting to make connections. They laughed, gasped, and affirmed. As I finished my talk, I was blown away by the resounding applause and cheers. A few people even suggested I publish the paper.

We all sat in a circle discussing some of the issues raised, and I could see that the vulnerability I expressed to them in my talk gave some of the women encouragement to tell their stories and bring up additional questions. The discussion was excited, emotional, and transformative as women listened and shared their own stories and thoughts, grateful for the chance to be together, amazed at our courage to speak openly, and hungry for the revolutionary perspective we were offering them.

All three meetings went well, were well attended, and our audiences were very responsive. The programs were, for me, such a positive experience because the right ingredients were present. I was well prepared. I knew that I had important things to say. I was well supported by the collective, and I was validated and appreciated by the audiences. And I was so pleased to see people stimulated to further thinking. These events were groundbreaking for all of us.

I had traveled an enormous distance, dieted my last diet, shed most of my self-hatred, found my anger and my voice. I would never be the same frightened, hiding, mortified person again.

From my first introduction to the second wave of the women's movement in 1975, there followed more than twenty-five years where I was in the thick of extraordinary activism, culture, ideas, and sisterhood, addressing every issue in the social justice panoply from a feminist perspective. They say location is everything and I was lucky enough to live in the San Francisco Bay Area, which turned out to be a beehive for this feminist flowering of culture, organizing, and politics.

Spaces and Faces
Written at the Old Lesbian Memoir Writing Group

It was 63 Brady Street—a hole-in-the wall storefront in an alley off Market, where the San Francisco Women's Centers opened, where I found my first consciousness-raising group—a fat women's support group, and found my voice, and body, and community.

It was Cogswell College in San Francisco where the first Women and Violence Conference was held over several days in 1979, with amazing workshops, solidarity, and anger, and where we took to the streets one Saturday night in the first "Take Back the Night" march, after a rousing, fearless speech from Andrea Dworkin, her fiery exhortation sending us out into the night feeling safe and strong in our numbers and in our outrage at pervasive violence against women.

It was 3618 18th Street where the San Francisco Women's Building[26] opened in 1979, in an historic large hall. A group of courageous women decided we needed an entire building to house our movement and they took a tremendous risk to raise money to purchase that four-story building. It housed women's organizations like BAWAR (Bay Area Women Against Rape) and Options for Women over Forty, and where we went for concerts and readings and talks and classes like self-defense and assertiveness training, and to be with our family of women. It was there that the annual Women's Crafts Fair happened every December, where the most amazing and creative art and entertainers sparkled and where I had my first and only psychic reading and found out about a past life. My friend Sarah was from a Hungarian Gypsy background and threw her sticks to focus her mind. She informed me that once "I" was an Amazon leader of my community of women, always faithful to my duties and much beloved by my people. One day a dashing woman outsider came through and, throwing all responsibilities to

---

[26] Years later, in the late 1990s, I had the opportunity as a volunteer archivist to process the extensive collection of the San Francisco Women's Building for the San Francisco GLBT Historical Society. The history of the building and of the women's liberation movement in the Bay Area was thereby preserved for future researchers and historians.

the winds, I left with her. As a result, I have had to work out this guilt in subsequent lives by being the most dedicated, organized, loyal, and self-sacrificing friend and leader. Oy!

It was the Full Moon Café on 18th Street in the Castro, a tiny bookstore and women's space, where I heard about the Fat Underground for the first time from some visiting Los Angeles lesbians discussing something called "Fat Politics."

It was on Valencia and 23rd Street, the Artemis Café, a women's café with a small performing stage, where I met friends for lunch, had tea by myself, and, with other activists, gave a workshop on fat and feminism.

It was Eureka Middle School on Church Street where the first Jewish Feminist Conference was held in 1982. It was where I met a woman named Sally, who would become a lifelong sister-friend, who had organized a workshop for Red Diaper Babies. For the first time, after years of training to be discreet and secretive about my family's politics, I came out as an RDB and hung on every word as we went around the large circle telling our stories and then singing the old songs. It brought me to tears. At this conference, the Fat Lip Readers Theater performed in public for the first time, to cheers. I was in the audience, too shy to be on stage yet but happy and proud to be watching Judith, Leah, and Judy in their magnificence. It was being there with my first lover, also Jewish, and meeting women who are dear ones to me today.

It was 19th and Holloway at San Francisco State University where I audited two classes in the Women's Studies Department. One was "Women and Appearance," the other "Jewish Women"[27] taught by Ricki Sherover Marcuse. In her class there was mind

---

[27] See Appendix I, page 305, for my class paper

opening and voice-finding, and after the last class I found myself walking down Holloway with tears streaming down my face, so sad that this class was over.

It was on MLK in Berkeley at KPFA, a community radio station with progressive programming, where there was a Women's Department producing and hosting myriad women-centric programs, music, discussion, and writers. I was interviewed on one of those programs about fat politics and feminism, and Fat Lip Readers Theater was asked several times to do unlearning and sensitivity trainings for their interns.

It was Amelia's, a women's bar on Valencia Street, where one evening a bunch of us fat women invaded that thin crowd and danced up a storm, making a stand and enjoying "throwing" our weight around, to the jaw-dropping amazement of all present!

It was Osento, a women's hot-tub and massage center on Valencia Street where we could go for a soak and to relax with friends and strangers, and where we rented the entire place before or after public hours for the most fabulous private parties. I had a birthday party there one year and it was bliss! There were fat and thin women everywhere, naked, unselfconscious, soaking in the tub, dunking in the frigid cold water barrel, lounging on mats, enjoying the most delicious non-diet foods, and relishing each other's company.

It was Women's Crafts West on Valencia Street, which sold exquisite arts and crafts by women artists and where I bought my first labrys[28] to wear on a chain around my neck.

---

[28] The labrys is a double headed ritual axe. It is found in ancient Minoan depictions of the Mother Goddess, where its symbolism is related to the labyrinth. The word "labrys" is Minoan in origin and is from the same root as the Latin

It was Old Wives' Tales, a woman's bookstore next door, where we could binge on books, and where we gathered for countless readings by feminist and lesbian writers, and where Fat Lip performed (me included). It was where I purchased my "Sisterhood is Powerful" enameled pin by Judy Stone. It was round, with a woman's symbol and a fist inside the circle. I chose a red one, of course. Carol Seajay, the owner of this most wonderful store remembers me—a fat, blind woman holding a book an inch from her face, trying her damnedest to read the print.

There was Operation Concern on Market Street near Guerrero. This was a gay and lesbian counseling center and where I attended a coming-out group, and a disabled lesbian support group led by Ricki Boden, which lasted for years, and where, finally, with their support, I faced my blindness and found and expressed my grief and anger. And found friends for life, like Silvia, and Dina, and Melinda, and June, and Jean, and many more.

There was Valencia Rose on Valencia near Market, a performing space where so many singers, actors, comics, and ensembles entertained us, and where I too performed with Fat Lip.

It was New College on Valencia, a progressive- and feminist-accredited school offering many programs, including a feminist therapy credential, and where Fat Lip performed our outrageous sex script in the auditorium. I did a striptease!

It was magazines like *Ms.* and *Broomstick* for older women. It was *Plexus*, a Bay Area monthly lesbian newspaper with articles, calendar, controversy, and columns for women.

---

labus, or lips. Use of the labrys has been documented on medieval charms used to attract women. Today, it is often used as a sign of identity and solidarity among lesbians.

It was women's bars like Ollie's in Oakland, and Maud's and Peg's Place and Clementina's in San Francisco, where we could meet and dance and cheer amazing performers, be our wild wonderful selves. It was at Ollie's where I heard Silvia Kohan sing for the first time. She was up from Los Angeles and we had heard about this gorgeous big woman with a phenomenal voice. She sang "Fat Girls' Blues" for the first time and I was in awe. She wore a gold lamé jumpsuit and red sneakers but I was far too shy to go up to her after the show. We would later become the best of sister-friends for years until her death.

It was heady and risky, it was breaking ground and being embraced. It was cultural workers like Holly Near and Chris Williams and Meg Christian filling us up 'til we spilled over. It was Ronnie Gilbert, and Malvina Reynolds singing her "I Can't Stand the Men." It was women musicians, drummers, the Women's Philharmonic performing unknown women composers. It was concerts where we were serenaded and roused by groups like the lesbian chorus Voices, and Sweet Honey in the Rock. It was Alix Dobkin's first album, *Lavender Jane*, and feminist songwriters/performers like Judy Small from Australia and Motherlode from Oregon. It was women like Diane Sabin producing women's concerts, and gatherings, and teaching other women to do the same.

It was new feminist publishing companies printing and distributing authors whose voices would never have been otherwise heard. Companies like the Feminist Press and Aunt Lute Press and journals like *Sinister Wisdom* and books like *This Bridge Called My Back* and so many others. It was feminist bookstores in Oakland and Berkeley like A Woman's Place and Mama Bears, where feminist authors, poets, and thinkers presented their works.

It was demonstrations in favor of the Equal Rights Amendment and Pro-choice, for safe and affordable contraception, equal pay for equal work, addressing issues of race and class and immigrant rights. It was learning the new skills we needed to write the articles, flyers, and broadsides and to "market" our ideas, getting the word out and organize, organize, organize.

There were galleries and exhibits dedicated to showcasing women artists, like the Vida Gallery in the San Francisco Women's Building, where Zoe Moskow showed her glorious photographs of fat women, and where, each Friday of that month-long exhibit, there was a different performance, including Fat Lip.

There was the Berkeley Feminist Therapy Collective, women's spirituality gatherings with Starhawk and Z Budapest. There were lesbian and feminist covens, and solstice rituals, several of which even I attended and found to be lovely and women- and earth-centric. I figured had I not been a third generation committed atheist, I might have looked to this tradition for a spiritual practice.

There were national organizations like NOW (the National Organization for Women), Black Sisters United, and the Feminist Majority, as well as the Black Women's Caucus, Women Against Violence in Pornography and Media, and so many others. There were women planning strikes, guerrilla actions against billboards, organizing conferences and workshops to help us learn skills essential to the movement, how to write résumés, and resource centers, to help us find jobs and housing and child care.

It was the opening of women's shelters for battered women and their children, like La Casa de Las Madres where women in jeopardy could find safety.

It was addressing the basics of the English language, which excluded women, claiming that words like "history" and "chairman" and thousands of others meant everyone. They did not. It was thinkers and writers like Mary Daly who started developing new language that was either truly neutral or women-centric, like "Ms." and "herstory" and "chairperson" and so many others. This was huge.

It was taking charge and listening intently. It was shouting when necessary, being outraged frequently, insisting we be heard and that our issues and needs be addressed without delay.

It was community. It was culture. It was our higher education. It was a movement struggling to embrace the diversity amongst us.

And as we marched we chanted and sang songs like, "*We are the Women/And we are marching/Bella ciao, bella ciao, bella ciao, ciao ciao/And we are marching for liberation/We want our revolution now.*"

It was the forming of consciousness-raising and hundreds of support groups for women sharing affinity of all kinds, like coming out, study groups, how to interrupt internalized self-hatred and racism and class hatred. There were support groups for grief, breaking up, for taking risks. They allowed us to tell our truths, support each other, and move forward, taking risks to empower ourselves.

I had been sister-less (and sib-less for that matter), yearning for family, the ideal, of course. And I found it, my sisters of choice, in these support groups. With the encouragement and support of other women, I discovered my voice, my anger, went out on a limb time after time, taking risks, speaking truth to power (including to my dad) and learning how to love another. I found out I could trust these women to have my back and hold my hands. I learned how to show affection and be held in turn.

My friends teased me about being such a committed "groupie." Whatever my problem was, I looked for other women dealing with the same issues.

Junkie

Written for MotherTongue Feminist Theater Collective script "Sisterspeak," October 2000

"But Laura…"

Look, I know you mean well, but your concern is really misplaced. Yes, when I'm dealing with something difficult I do get desperate and panicky and need a hit—perhaps once, even twice a week, but truly I have it under control.

"What sets you off?"

Anything, really—coming out, body image, grief, class angst, ageing, illness, breaking up, menopause, disability issues, sexism, being Jewish, politics, a hangnail. You know, the usual.

"For how long?"

Oh, I don't know—probably since the early '70s. I begin to hyperventilate, obsess, get sweaty, become sleepless and agitated, and I know there is only one thing that will help me cope. I know where to go, I know who I need to ask, and when I find my connection and get the hit I need, relief will come and, along with it, understanding and enlightenment.

"We're worried about you."

Don't be. I am *not* in denial. Look, I'm an old feminist, what else am I supposed to do? It's not as if I do drugs or alcohol or sugar.

"But…"

All right, all right, I'll confess. Are you satisfied? *I'm a woman's support group junkie. I can't quit. I won't quit. So turn me in.*

Well, perhaps I do have a problem. I *can* face it, with *your* help. I just need a group!

Because I'd had no sibs with whom to fight while growing up, it was in the women's liberation movement that I learned about wrenching "family" fights when there were the inevitable misunderstandings and hurt feelings, and ultimately even issues that divided us to the quick (SM, racism, disability, classism, lesbianism, ageism, separatism). There was deep disappointment when eagerly anticipated sisterly camaraderie wasn't there, like when my friend Miriam Weber and I started a Jewish Women's Study Group and I discovered that, even among feminists, issues like Israel brought us to what were apparently unbridgeable differences. What an unhappy awakening.

In retrospect, I believe there was something extremely positive that resulted, even from our painful splits and anger at each other. Growing out of the anger and frustration and invisibility of so many women in the predominantly white middle-class and straight women's movement of the second wave, feeling unheard and unrepresented, so many women left "mainstream" feminist groups to form their own. And this added to the richness and diversity and influence of the movement in the end. Women of color, and women of the poor and working class, as well as lesbians and other communities, started their own organizations and publications and stimulated these women to write and publish and perform and do their art and organize in activism, reflecting and representing their concerns and unique and vital herstories. Our diverse groups frequently worked in coalition with each other for shared goals, while maintaining our independent affinity.

I also learned that part of sisterhood is loss and grieving when sister-friends died. I talk to them when I go to Sharp Park on retreat, calling them my committee, and I miss them with every corpuscle. And there was the grief and loss when any feminist icon died and left us behind to live without her. Never met, but the loss is personal nonetheless.

Bygone and Lost Forever

Written for MotherTongue Feminist Theater Collective's "Sisters-peak" script

Joanne, Stella, Sheryl, Anne, Maggie, Silvia, Susan, Tita
Sisters mine
Bygone and lost forever
Agonizingly, inch by inch, or sudden departure
Cancer, seizure, suicide, coronary, cancer, heart failure, cancer,
    coronary
Sisters by choice, by joyful discovery
Sisters for life
Taken from me, from themselves
Leaving tears
And fears of future sister loss
Bygone and lost forever
Splendid sorrow, sisters mine.

And there are my sister-friends now. At various times we are sisters or mothers or daughters to each other. Sometimes our paths are bumpy and we take a little time out for a while, trusting we will return to one another. Sometimes, sadly, there are breaches and we say a painful goodbye to a sister-friend.

I have had a bounty of sisters, having chosen each other with care or with sudden intuition that this will be a sister-friend to grow with. This only child has lived happily and gratefully in a huge extended family of women who have enriched my life immeasurably with their presence.

While the second wave of the women's liberation movement started in the mid to late 1960s, for some unfathomable reason I was clueless until 1975. I was blooming at the age of thirty! Speaking my mind, dancing my spirit, flirting, playing, touching, feeling my emotions and my body, coming out into a circle of cheering women, writing, acting, producing, being interviewed, appreciated, doing the unthinkable, the unpredictable, making out, "going all the way," hamming it up, finding my voice, and what's more, not shutting it up. Kicking up my heels, my mind, my wit, my spirit, my activism to change this fucking world, I had found a home. This only child found more sisters than she could have dreamed of, ebbing and flowing around her, teaching and learning and fighting and loving, and demanding with each other.

Thank you feminist movement, second wave; thank you, consciousness raising groups, coming-out groups, disabled women's groups, study groups, support groups, and groups galore. Thank you. Thanks to the Fat Liberation movement and Fat Lip Readers Theater in particular. Thank you to "Take Back the Night" demonstrations, and all the artists, musicians, writers, and thinkers who inspired, incited, informed, and connected us. I had been green in the ways of the world but in the second wave I found my *wild* side. Bye-bye shell. Bye-bye silence. Bye-bye self-hatred and hiding.

Hello *Laura*!

Lest you assume that now, at the age of seventy, my feminism has mellowed, that my anger over misogyny and patriarchy has receded, here's a story for you:

Recently I got one of those phone calls from a nonprofit looking for donations. The exchange with the young woman on the line followed an all too familiar pattern—

"Hello, is Mrs. Bock there?"

"No. She's dead."

"Oh, I'm sorry."

"She's been dead for thirty-five years."

"Is Mr. Bock there?"

"He's dead, too."

"Very sorry."

"Is there a first name on your list?"

"Yes. Laura."

"Good, you've got her. Please don't assume I am married and go by a 'Mrs.' in front of a husband's name.

"Well, I think that is a safe assumption."

"It is not, and it is offensive. By calling a woman by her husband's name you diminish her into an appendage of him. Many women choose not to marry and many women marrying choose to retain their own last names. Please talk with your manager and rewrite the script to ask for someone by their first and last name, regardless of their gender."

We both hung up at the same time. What is appalling is that this young woman is not unusual. She and many other young women have no clue, are unaware of history, and have not one feminist bone in their bodies. This woman was heterosexual, assumed everyone was straight, and assumed that whether or not a woman was married she would be complimented by the assumption.

Not long ago I heard of a woman who, when writing her paper for a college creative writing class, chose not to use the word "feminist" because it was, she said, "combative."

What has happened to all our hard work and hard-found victories of the second wave of the women's liberation movement during the '70s, '80s and '90s?

I need to wear a button with the words, "An Old, Combative, Feminist—And Proud."

Laura on San Francisco Bay ferry. c 1985

Laura with group of dear Friends l to r starting in back:
Nadine May, Silvia Kohan, Sally Goldin, and Laura is sitting in front. c 1985

Dear friends, from l to r: Sally Goldin and Kate Northcott. c 1987

6

Life in the Fat Lane

WE WERE TEN FAT women sitting together in an Oakland living room in 1981. We were strangers to each other, having walked diverse paths to get to that moment in that room. Our host, Louise Wolfe, had been active in NAAFA[29]. There were Karen and Cathleen, a lesbian couple who were witches (my first!) practicing the Wiccan tradition. There was Elena, a doctoral student in psychology at UC Berkeley. There was Judy, a long-time activist in social movements. There was Cath, who worked for the phone company and had a lovely singing voice. There was Judith, who had years of performing experience with Mother-Tongue Feminist Theater Collective, as well as her alter ego "Prosciutto," a clown character she developed. There was Leah, studying to be a chiropractor. There was Nancy, a survivor of abusive mental health practices who was organizing in support of other people victimized by that system. We were one straight woman, eight lesbians, and one unknown (me).

We were in that living room because we had responded to a call for fat women who wanted to actively advance a fat liberation and feminist

---

[29] National Association for the Advancement of Fat Acceptance, a national organization.

perspective. I had been in a fat women's support group for six years, had helped to organize and present at three public meetings on the topic of fat oppression, and I wanted to find additional ways to be an activist in solidarity with other fat women.

One idea proposed that night was a speaker's bureau, but when a theater company was suggested, in the fashion of the much-respected MotherTongue Feminist Theater Collective, we jumped at it. What better way to spread our radical views and work on behalf of this new movement than to entertain folks in the process of informing them! We chose the name Fat Lip Readers Theater as a bit of a take-off from the MotherTongue name, as well as a double entendre on "fat lip," as in "Ya want a fat lip?" Or, "Everything about us is fat, even our lips!"

We became a sisterhood of Fat Lippers, with a deep connection between us. We were zealots in the cause of celebrating women's bodies whatever their size, and confronting the oppression and discrimination targeting fat women. Together our work promoted a fat liberation feminist analysis, and we performed unflinchingly honest pieces and scripts about our lives and about fat politics.

The first year, we wrote at our weekly meetings. As we got to know and trust one another with our stories and our secrets, we became family beyond the work to which we were so committed.

At the start of our second year, we held our first performances in front of selected, invited guests to test the waters and get our feet wet. We had several women-only shows and one for fat women only, which was a little tricky when it came to deciding who was fat enough to be in that audience. Most women felt fat no matter their size.

That same year, Leah, Judy, and Judith performed to cheers at the first Jewish Feminist Conference in San Francisco. I was not yet brave enough to perform. By the following year, at the second Jewish Feminist Conference, I was up there with them, although backstage before we went on I was trying not to throw up from nerves. I asked Silvia Kohan, who was waiting for her cue, "Do you actually enjoy this?" She replied, with enthusiasm, "You bet, honey!" For the next eighteen years of performing with Fat Lip, my modus operandi was to stay in the bathroom until the last moment, willing my body to calm down. Once the show started, I was just fine.

Fat Lip caught on with our audiences, who were hungry for what we had to say, as well as audiences beyond our feminist communities. In the following years we were invited to perform in Santa Cruz, Los Angeles, Palo Alto, Seattle, and Sacramento, all around the Bay Area, at meetings like the Women in Psychology Conference, at universities, and on radio and television. The *Phil Donahue Show*, an immensely popular national interview show, invited us and flew us out to Chicago. Again, I was way too shy but Judy, Nancy, and Louise appeared. At one point a member of the audience, a man, baited them by asking in a sneering voice, "You mean to tell me, you fat people have sex?" Judy retorted, "Buddy, you should have it so good!"

We provided training workshops for nonprofits, "unlearning" workshops at women's centers, and were interviewed by the print media locally, nationally, and internationally. At one such interview for a foreign TV program, we were asked why we did this work. I declared with fervor, "The lives of our daughters are at stake!" I definitely had inherited my mom's passionate soapbox style!

We performed on street corners, on proscenium stages, in classrooms, and conventional theaters. We performed locally at women's bookstores and performing arts venues like the Valencia Rose and the

Women's Building in San Francisco. We did street theater in the Castro and at Halliday Plaza in downtown San Francisco for a number of annual International No Diet Days. We were on the local daily television program *Good Morning, Bay Area*. By that time my internal ham had taken over and I too was on that show! We eventually made a video to enable us to extend our reach, despite our severely limited financial resources for touring. It is called *Nothing to Lose*.[30]

Fat Lip was active for eighteen years and I was in for the duration. We learned to write for theater (no footnotes!), act, direct produce, manage, cope with inevitable differences between us, do outreach, and learned so much along the way. It was where I took risks to extend my reach, knowing I had this family on whom to rely and to encourage me. With their support, I could perform on stage or in the streets, on TV or radio, be interviewed by the press, give workshops and trainings, write pieces, learn to block a script and direct, and even do a striptease as part of our sex script! What happened to the extremely shy and very inhibited girl-woman I had been?

Over this long period, our membership changed from time to time, some of the original members leaving and new ones coming on board after a careful interview process. An early priority was to find a sign language interpreter to join us, and we lucked out when Susan Williams, a fat woman herself, became part of the collective. We were committed not only to fat liberation but to having our work fully accessible to disabled folks. This included a list of requirements given to outside producers before we agreed to appearances. In addition, we insisted that all venues be wheelchair accessible and that all media an-

---

[30] Fat Lip Reader's Theatre Presents Nothing to Lose: http://amzn.to/1Reijxy

nouncements and flyers include the info that our performances were to be perfume- and scent-free so people with environmental illnesses could attend.

The first ten members of Fat Lip were entirely white and in time we felt strongly about bringing diversity into our work. We did outreach and, over time, four African American women became members: Chupoo, April, Peggy, and Shanju; along with one Chinese American, Bernice; and a Palestinian American, Sema. They added their stories, their wonderful writing, and unique perspectives to our work. As in other feminist second wave groups, we struggled with our differences on race and class, as well as whether or not to let in an s/m dyke—we did, and whether to do outreach to more straight women—we did. Becoming diverse wasn't easy, and learning to work together with all our differences was at times challenging and painful. Meanwhile, the hard work continued as we strove evermore for new material, including songs and inventive and hilarious choreography to spice up the scripts and keep our performances entertaining.

It is my belief that after eighteen years of incredibly hard work, we were so tired we just could not work through additional issues that divided us, specifically around one of our members transitioning from female to male, as well as hard feelings around race. It was not an easy or happy ending; however, this does not negate the tremendous impact we had on women's lives (including our own), on unlearning our self-hatred about our bodies, and on furthering a feminist agenda and analysis.

Over those years, we received so many comments, letters, and cards from women thanking us for our work, our bravery, and the ways in which we had made such a difference in their lives. During our shows, we were met with cheers, tears, and a few jeers—and even some folks walking out, from time to time. We were having an impact, in any case!

For me, it was transformative. Being a Fat Lipper took me from a shy, introverted, scared, fat woman to a self-assured and confident teacher, performer, director, writer, and rabble-rouser.

Following are many of the pieces I wrote and performed for Fat Lip during those eighteen years, from 1981 to 1999. They primarily resulted from group writing prompts. I have occasionally added a comment or two, but I think most stand up well by themselves, describing my life as a fat child, a fat teen, a fat woman filled with self-disgust, and the genesis into a fat, proud fighter against women's oppression. In addition, there are a few pieces I wrote for the Old Lesbian Memoir Writing Group between 2009 and 2014, as well as for several Mother-Tongue scripts done between 1999 and 2004. These will be noted as such. Additional Fat Lip pieces appear in other chapters of this memoir. Many were performed as group pieces.

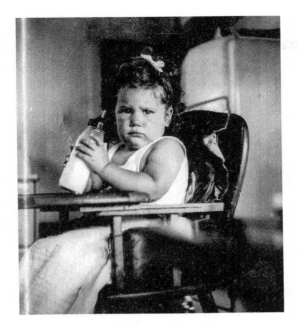

Laura in highchair at 13 months. 1946.
Notice attitude. It went underground soon thereafter for 30 years!

Little Laurie Jane (January 1980)

Little Laurie Jane.
What a good girl,
Such a help to her mom and dad.
At dinner parties—quite the little hostess.
Such an intelligent child,
Reads all the time,
And gets those grades you can be sure.
So quiet and polite.
Has her grandmother Lena's lovely complexion,

Says the most amusing things,
So poised with adults...

Such a pity.
What a shame.
A constant worry for poor Min and Al,
They've tried everything,
Sparing no expense—
diets, psychologists, hospital fasts, Vic Tanney's,[31]
At their wits' end,
They love her so.
So worried about her future—friends, husband, security.
Such a pity.
What a shame.
And such a pretty face.
If only...

Daddy Says

Daddy says, "Look at her, she's as fat as a pig!"
   Mama says "Shhh, she'll hear you."
   Mama's friend says, "Don't worry, she'll grow out of it."
   What will I grow out of?
   Dad was thin but always insisted he had to watch his weight.
He wanted an athlete for a daughter, a tennis player: fleet, strong,
svelte. I tried my best and at times I felt his pride, but his outrage
and shame was lurking just behind, ready to explode.

---

[31] A chain of gyms

Mama was the buffer, protector, explaining one to the other. She was fat, struggling with diets off and on her entire life, and trying to make dieting a game for me, an adventure.

I learned my survival skills at home, not in school: thievery, sneakiness, lying, techniques of search and seizure.

It was a game: let's hide the cookies and see how long it takes Laura to find them and then Dad can blow up and Mom can look worried and disappointed.

Being watched all the time. The only privacy, in my bed at night. But those crumbs. All those damned crumbs!

Dad's anger and Mom's concern. I got so much bad attention, I wanted to disappear.

Bicycles Etc. (Written for the Old Lesbian Memoir Writing Group)

I never learned to ride a two-wheeler. I have never told the truth about why this was so. It was not because I lived on a very steep hill, although I have offered this explanation with earnest regret. In fact, there were plenty of other kids on the hill who rode their bikes with daring and joy. I have never shared the real reason for my avoidance before. I was a fat kid, very self-conscious and hating of my body. Everything and everyone around me taught me to hide myself—in oversized, un-patterned clothes, navy, black or brown, avoiding attention because it would result in taunts and ridicule.

I could not face the learning part—the trying, the falling off, the looking awkward and foolish, bringing even more attention and ridicule onto me. Neither did I learn to roller skate, use the pogo stick, and always I offered to be one of the turners for rope jumping.

Hopscotch was doable if I was playing with just one other girl, and no audience, but dodge ball was out of the question. Now, blind man's bluff was okay because we stood still, and the attention was on the "blind man."

Do I have ambivalent feelings about playing sports? You bet. Now that I am sixty-eight, the only bike I ride is stationary, but I do swim up a storm. Hang the looks of distaste and judgment! I can't see them anyway.

Fat Child (Written for the Old Lesbian Memoir Writing Group)

I wanted not to see their looks, hear their taunts. I avoided looking in shop windows—avoiding my reflection. Wanted to be invisible when I was anything but. Was shy, wanting not to be noticed, was humiliated by my body, mortified by my size—hated and ridiculed by strangers and my father.

Why couldn't I be like Carol, an "overweight girl" in my class, but who strutted and flaunted—was the life of the party—popular, sought after—wore bright colors and patterns not designed to be slimming. I was muted in what I wore, navy, black, brown, my voice meager, my gait tiptoeing.

I wanted, yearned to shine, to dance out in the open.

The irony is that now, with little sight or hearing, I can't see others' reactions or hear others' comments, or see my reflections. And yet now I revel in my big, powerful, colorful, loud self and strut with the best of them.

Dear Carol (May 1985)

Dear Carol,

When we were seventeen, I watched you a lot with such astonishment and disbelief and a touch of envy. You were fat, quite fat, but you didn't act like me at all. You wore bold colors and tight sweaters (and you were big-breasted) and flare skirts that weren't designed to be slimming. You flaunted and jiggled when you moved. You weren't shy and quiet. You were exuberant, boisterous, and sometimes even brassy. And you got asked out on dates a lot, and at parties you danced up a storm. Everyone wanted to dance with you.

At the time, I judged you. How come you never dieted, you didn't hide, you weren't afraid to let loose?

Now, Carol, I've followed you, and I love the memory of you.

Signed,

A Fat Sister

Class of '63

Livingston Brothers and Me

Well, ready or not, there I am, reflected in my mirror. I've never tried harder in my sixteen years to look okay. I think I can pass. I mean, I feel almost thin, really, even pretty. I'm wearing my most favorite dress; it is form fitting and takes at least thirty pounds off my hips, and even though it's plaid, the checks are small and the colors subdued so it's permissible. Underneath I have on my long-line bra and my long-legged girdle, so I'm cinched from my shoulders to my knees. No part of me should jiggle. If only the bulge around my waist doesn't pop through and show beneath my dress. Please God! My nylons are in place, my black heels on my feet, a little bit of lipstick. Rather sophisticated, all in all. Okay, I'm ready for the job interview with the manager of Livingston's Department Store.

I want this job. My first paying summer job and I know I can get it. Mr. Livingston is interviewing me at the request of a friend of Dad's and if I don't make some major flub I'm sure the job will be mine.

Mr. Livingston is thirty-five-ish, well dressed, aloof but cordial. He gives a cursory glance at my application as I picture myself behind the counter of the haute couture department selling finery to Pacific Heights' matrons.

"I'm sorry, Laura" ... (*Shouldn't I be addressed as Miss Bock?*)... "you really don't have the look we require in our sales personnel."

"But I don't have to work out in front of everybody. I can work in the back, in the stockroom. No one will see me!"

"Yes, well, perhaps in a few years."

I leave trying to hold in my tears of disappointment and humiliation. As I make my dignified exit, I can feel the stays of my longline bra digging into me, the welts forming, and the legs of my long-legged girdle rolling up. I know by the time I'm home I'll be chafed and raw between my legs.

It all would have been worth it if only I had gotten the job. I know better now than to feel good about myself. I can never pass.

Freshman P.E. (Written for the Old Lesbian Memoir Writing Group)

Exercise: Tell me of a time you were in trouble in class:

Every incoming freshman coed was required to take a P.E. class called "fundamentals" at the University of Oregon. At the start of the term, dressed in our skimpy P.E. garb, our full-body pictures were taken, frontal and profile, and our weight was recorded. This was done in front of the class. At the end of the term, once again, our pictures were taken and weight recorded. In between we exercised the usual calisthenics. That summer, before going to college, I had worked hard at reducing my size. This included a two-week fast at a San Francisco hospital. I was a shy and self-conscious, self-hating, overweight girl and knew I would feel more confident about starting this new chapter away from home if I was half my size.

That first semester, I felt scared and lonely much of the time and gained weight, as usual after dieting.

As the time came for the final reckoning in front of the teacher and my classmates, I was so terrified that I made myself go to talk with my teacher in her office and, in humiliation, ask that I be photographed and weighed in private. She begrudgingly agreed.

At the final class of the term, we were sitting on the gym floor as our teacher summed up the class. She said, "You all did very well except for one of you. She, on the other hand, has gained over twenty pounds in these three months!" There were gasps and disbelief and horror among my classmates as they looked around to find the miscreant.

I wanted to kill myself.

Hey, Teach

It was 1968, my first job after college, and it was work that I had planned for ever since I was ten years old—to be a teacher. I Weight-Watched for a year, dieting down to what I felt was an almost acceptable size for being interviewed.

I was hired by the Alameda Children's Center as a substitute teacher. My work seemed to be appreciated and I worked steadily.

There was a young woman, on permanent staff at the center, who was fat, very fat. She had a wonderful rapport with her kids as well as with the other teachers, but I never had much to do with her. Somehow I wanted to avoid associating with her, feeling relief that I was no longer that fat.

As time went on I inevitably stopped dieting and, just as inevitable, began to regain weight. It did not seem to interfere with my work nor my relationship with my supervisor or other staff members, until the director of the center returned after an extended leave of absence. She called me into her office for what I expected to be an evaluation of my work. She said, "Laura, you know we already have one obese teacher on staff. You really can't expect us to carry two of you."

I soon left that job. My anger at her remains today, perhaps because I could not bring myself to feel, let alone express, it at the time.

Tell Me about a Swimsuit

Mom and I had to go to Lane Bryant's downtown to buy my clothes—this time a swimsuit. Back in the '50s, clothes for "big girls and gals" were gross and designed to hide as much of the wearer as possible.

First the color—navy, brown or black (slimming, don't you know).

Patterned? No horizontal stripes or big flowers. If striped, must be vertical to accentuate your height, not your width.

Skirt—absolutely necessary to hide the bulging inner thighs and it must be voluminous, designed to drown you as you attempt the crawl.

A successful shopping excursion was the purchase of such a garment. I was a fat girl, a fat woman. I covered my body to within an inch of my flesh. The image of a burqa comes to mind. I know that from the age of thirteen until the age of thirty-seven I never entered a pool or sat on a beach in a swimsuit, self-conscious and hating my fat body, becoming expert at hiding.

But I *so* missed swimming, yearned for that first bliss of skin touching water. Dreamed of once again doing the crawl, my arms wind-milling, my legs scissoring with ease, propelling me forward. I found it again in the 1980s at a weekly fat women swim at the Richmond Plunge.

A group of fat women had organized this weekly fat swim at the beautiful Richmond Plunge in Point Richmond, California. It was a huge indoor pool that even had a fountain in the shallow end. Fat women gathered in pleasure, in acceptance, in delight with our bodies.

The first time I went, I was filled with great trepidation. I had bought a bathing suit—black of course, to diminish my visibility as much as possible—and took myself there on a Saturday morning.

The locker room was—*egads*—open and communal, and filled with fat women in various states of undress, even naked. I didn't dare look. Keeping my eyes to myself, I focused on getting into the pool lickety-split.

On one end of the pool there was a rollicking volleyball game going on, and on the other were lap swimmers, and in the middle were the dunkers and kibitzers. There was a board for diving as well.

As I started down the steps, feeling that cool water at last, I felt tears of relief, as if I had been holding my breath. Then I was in, up to my neck and beyond, my body remembering the moves, the strokes, the grace of moving without gravity holding me back.

Within one or two weeks I, too, was easily naked in the locker room, relishing all those fat bodies, the rolls, the creases and crevices, the expanse of the upper arms, the voluptuous thighs. And finding beauty in all those fleshy women, I started to discover it in my own body. If they were beautiful in all the diversity of their curves and rolls, then perhaps I must be beautiful, too!

Soon, I was looking at myself in mirrors without cringing. Soon, I bought a bright purple bathing suit with a zip-down, sexy bodice. Soon, I had found a community of fat women to play with, to romp with, to splash with, to go out to lunch with after swimming, entering the restaurant as boisterous, joyful fat women ready to enjoy our food and each other, whatever the judgmental looks, and be gloriously full of our selves. This was liberation on so many levels.

For the last twenty-five years, I have happily swum laps twice weekly at the Koret Pool in San Francisco, and I will never be deprived again, if I can help it, of the magic of moving in water.

No more hiding! Last one in is a skinny fool!

Uncoverings (Written for MotherTongue Feminist Theater Collective)

I asked Marge to go with me. Excited, nervous, oh yes! A shopping expedition to buy my first long pants, at age thirty-two. No more hiding beneath tent dresses and muumuus. This fat body was about to show off its rounds, its curves, its rolls and swells, thighs, butt, and belly for all to see. I've come a ways—my fat women's support group cheering me on. I'm comin' out. (Deep breath.) Maybe I'll just wait awhile to tuck in my blouse!

Compulsives? (1984)

My friend Deb went to a compulsive eaters workshop based on "Fat Is a Feminist Issue." All the women there were thin.

One related a story about a pregnant friend whose doctor told her that if she didn't lose some weight she would jeopardize the health of her baby. She admitted that it was hard for her to lose weight but he insisted and put her in the hospital on a 750-calorie a day diet. After one week she had lost only a quarter pound. He accused her of cheating and put her on a 500-calorie a day diet and had her watched twenty-four hours a day. At the end of the second week she had again lost only one-quarter pound. He finally believed her and let her eat.

The women at the workshop heard this story and exploded—outraged at the male doctor, astounded and horrified at his misogyny, and concerned about the health of the baby after two weeks of starvation.

Then Deb told them about me, a fat—very fat, woman who, she said, never eats more than most other folks, never eats sugary foods, never binges or diets, and has maintained a steady weight for years. The women listened to Deb and didn't believe her, insisting that someone who doesn't sneak eat or eat lots of sweets would naturally lose weight. Nothing Deb could say would convince them.

How come they could see the doctor's prejudice, but not their own?

Hey, Look at That Fat Woman (October 1995)

Hey, look at that Fat Woman
She's walkin' like she owns the streets
She's sittin' like she don't care how much space she takes
She's talkin' like she wants to be heard
She's dancin' like the wild thing she is
She's lovin' like there's no tomorrow
She's tastin' like life is sweet
She's ragin' like a righteous woman
She's smilin' like she *knows* the secret
She's me.

Flying High (1989)

"Ladies and gentlemen, our departure has been unavoidably delayed due to an unexpected miscalculation. The aircraft is overweight."

Jeez, this airplane is packed. Did we all bring too much carry-on luggage?

"Our captain has instructed your flight attendants to ask each of you your weight and tabulate the result."

What!?! This can't be happening. Oh no, they're going down the rows and we have to say *out loud* what we weigh. What will I do?

"Ms. Bock, what is your weight?"

I can't say the true number. "One hundred seventy-five pounds" said in a quiet voice. (I shave off 100 pounds.)

"Thank you for your cooperation. We are now ready for departure. Please fasten your seat belts."

We're moving. Will my lie prevent lift-off? Thank God, we're off the ground!!

"We are at our cruising altitude. Lunch is now being served."

"No thank you, I'm not hungry." I can't eat, it would only compound my lie! What if the airplane crashes? I could be responsible for the deaths of 125 people! Maybe if I sit very still, hardly breathe..."

We landed at San Francisco International Airport on time. As I deplaned, the flight attendant said, "I hope you had a pleasant flight."

It's been twenty years and the memory still haunts me.

Musical Chairs

Talk about not fitting in. Take chairs for instance. Relaxing, inviting, comfortable. Are you kidding??

When I first enter a room I furtively survey the possibilities. Any chairs without arms? Any chairs that look fragile (perhaps a family heirloom)? A beanbag chair? Oh shit! Gravity can get me down into it, but not even "the force" can raise me up.

A classroom chair, with that nasty little desk coming round the front to sock me in the gut. I gasp. The teacher beams because she thinks it's her lecture.

Going Greyhound for a restful sojourn? Be early to board. Grab a double seat and quickly dump all your belongings on the seat next to you and start to snore! If sharing's a necessity, hope for a skinny. If your seatmate is anywhere near average-size, you're in trouble. You'll spend the entire trip adjusting your seat. When she's upright, you're laid back, and vice versa. You'll gain an inch or two. Rubbing shoulders is one thing, but this is ridiculous!!

A straight-backed chair that's so straight-backed that when I sit down I end up leaning slightly forward and lose half my lap. These chairs seem to be most prevalent at buffet dinner parties.

Flying the friendly skies? Will the arm rest go up so I can smoosh over? Will the seatbelt buckle? If only the next seat is occupied by an infant! Can I bribe the airline official who assigns such honors?

Dining out? This could be hazardous when the only seating available is in a booth. Hold my breath, as I try inconspicuously to squeeze in between the unmovable table and the bench—a space big enough for Twiggy. And then savor my meal with the table edge jammed into my ribs. Or try the swivel seats at the counter, with no room to swivel or put my butt or hang my arms. Is heartburn worth all this?

The question is how to look nonchalant just after you've broken a chair.

Theater seats, car seats, seatbelts...

Look, the truth is this fat-hating world just doesn't make room for us.

What? Oh, no thanks, I think I'll stand.

Kaiser Korner (January 1990)

Facing a brand new internist at Kaiser, I thrust out my hand for a shake (to make her acknowledge me), and took a deep breath.

"Doctor, I am looking for a new internist and want you to know a few things about me and then we can decide if we want to work together on my behalf.

"I am a lesbian feminist, fat liberation activist. I don't diet because I agree with the studies that show diets don't work and yo-yoing in weight can be dangerous to my health.

"I need to work with a physician who, while she may not agree with me, will respect my position and not subject me to hers. Are you that person?"

Much later I had occasion to order my chart from Kaiser. In her notes for that visit, the doctor had written, "Patient refuses to diet; calls herself a 'fat freedom fighter.' "

Right on!! (Fist raised)

Robust and Rowdy

A number of dances called "Robust and Rowdy" were organized at various community halls for us fat women, to prance and dance, dress up or down, flirt and strut our ample stuff. We had been taught to minimize ourselves by dieting, by our submission to a fat-phobic and judgmental world. On those nights, we threw off that mantle and were ecstatically robust and rowdy to our heart's content.

I was exploring the femme in me, and at one of these dances I wore black silk flowing pants, a black sequined top with plenty of exposure, and lipstick! I didn't have one shy cell in my body that night and danced with abandon—giving over to the music and to my partner of the moment.

The room was filled with gorgeous fat bodies, gyrating wildly or coasting sedately, and I loved the ways in which all our pounds moved and swayed to the music.

To top it off, on that particular night I won a raffle prize to be on the Fat Dyke Float at the Gay Pride Parade.

Talk about being on display to all the multitude. The float was on the rear of a large flatbed truck. In the center was a very large *papier mâché* sculpture of two big fat women wrapped around each other. Silvia Kohan, in her gold lamé pants suit, sang her heart out, including her signature song "Fat Girl Blues." I waved my queenie wave and our float won the "Most Outlandish" prize. They got it wrong! We weren't outlandish, we were outrageous! What a hoot.

Nervy (January 1989)

"You fat people have a lot of nerve! Who do you think you are to tell me what to think?"

You want nerve, lady? I'll give you nerve!!!

Nerve is applying for a job when you are qualified…and fat.

Nerve is being on the street and hollering back when some jerk mouths off.

Nerve is being a fat teenage girl going to a dance.

Nerve is eating in a restaurant and glaring back at the gawkers.

Nerve is swimming in a public pool, or joining a gym, or walking or jogging at the park.

Nerve is a fat student requesting an armless chair in her classroom.

Nerve is riding the bus and taking up your space.

Nerve is saying to your doctor, "No, I won't be weighed."

Nerve is going to a family feast and not pretending you're on a diet.

Nerve is being a fat woman and interrupting the inane and incessant diet talk at the office.

Nerve is performing on stage with Fat Lip in front of a thin audience.

Nerve is a fat dyke asking women to dance at Amelia's.

Nerve is a fat child going out for the team.

Nerve is doing just about anything in this world that's reserved for thin people, and that's just about everything!

So What (1992)

So what!

So what that I'm almost fifty and acting fourteen.

No, it's not immaturity. It is not menopause.

How could it be the second adolescence when I never had the first?

And that's the point.

I was a fat kid, a fat teen, ridiculed, ignored—never dated, never kissed, never went to dances (though I taught all my girlfriends how to dance so they could impress their dates), never flirted, never desired, never hoped.

I was the mature daughter, the best friend, the good student, helpful, supportive, nurturing, amusing—sobbing inside.

Now I want everything I missed:

I want flirting and dating and necking at drive-ins.

I want picnics and dances and parties, more than I can count.

I want to be romanced and courted and wooed and...

I want flowers and candy and love notes and surprises just for me.

I want to sit by the phone in agony—wondering and hoping, and...

I want to be giddy when it finally rings.

I want to giggle with my girlfriends comparing suitors.

I want to spend all afternoon deciding what to wear for a date and...

I want the excitement and butterflies just before the doorbell sounds.

I want my head to swim when I'm kissed and...

I want to be breathless and scared and thrilled with all the attention.

I want what my thin girlfriends had and what I read about in *Seventeen* magazine.

Well, guess what...I'm having it all.

And if I'm acting fourteen,
So what!

I did not write the following piece, but it became known as "Laura's Soapbox." I performed it in an evangelical preacher style. It was written by Judith Stein, with a few additions from me.

Laura's Soapbox

Ladies and gentleman, fat oppression hurts all of us. Fear of getting fat, or getting fatter, keeps women preoccupied with how we eat instead of the sexism and misogyny oppressing us all. Fear of getting fat keeps women who are within social definitions of thinness terrified about what they put into their mouths.

The idea that the body is some wild beast, only held in check by some act of willpower and grim determination, otherwise to grow and grow, is a notion that keeps all women focused on our eating, our food, and the size of our bodies.

This idea is not only biologically false, it reeks of that puritanical ethic that claims that the body, and most especially women's bodies, need firm restraint and tight control. This stems from a fear of the feminine, the innate power of women.

Men have devised many ways to control women's bodies and women's sexuality and keeping us terrified of what would happen if we just "let ourselves go" is merely one more bridle around our necks. Most probably if we let ourselves go, some of us would be fatter than we are now and many of us (fat and thin alike) would be about the same size.

It is an illusion that controls us, sisters, a deep-seated, man-made hatred and fear of fat, purposefully distracting us from our true persecutors.

Reflections (MotherTongue Feminist Theater Collective, 1999)

The assignment was to look at myself in the mirror and write about the feelings that come up. I didn't do it. It's not as if I didn't think about doing it...often. It's just that glass isn't my thing.

Look, I'm liberated enough. If I had no hang-ups left, how could I relate to people? One needs goals left to strive for, hills and valleys to traverse. So mirrors are mine.

I'm a fat and sassy, fat and reasonably happy, fat and pushy woman who swims, dances, makes love, runs a business, performs, and all the rest. That will have to do for now.

So Sorry

A. "Sorry, I'm afraid you're not suitable for the position.

"But I have my certificate to teach in children's centers."

"To be honest, we feel you would not be up to the physical demands of the job. Look...you're too fat to run after the kids, okay?"

B. My dear friend is in the hospital—two weeks since her surgery and still so sick, with daily crises: edema, phlebitis, reactions, migraines, bowel obstructions; struggling to live to fight for herself, to maintain hope in the face of pain and unresponsive doctors and uncertainty. No food for two weeks, fed by a tube through her jugular. A doctor comes in and offers the comforting thought—"Well, at least you've lost a few pounds."

C. I awoke one morning with a new body shape—was it something I dreamed, something I ate the night before? Perhaps I had forgotten my vitamins yesterday. Anyway, I don't like it—I'll return it for credit, a refund or, better yet, an exchange. It came with a ten-day free trial offer but I don't want it around for that long. It must be a second, a nearly new—came with the lumps and rolls and gets in the way when I sit and when I jump up from a prone position. It's stiff and ungraceful. It's old and wrinkled and at times unsteady. It tends to move side to side instead of confidently forward and, when observing it from the side, it has a truly unflattering design.

All in all, I liked my old model and I want *that* one back. It was fat and graceful and moved with delight on the dance floor. It was *me*.

Did anyone lose their body? I found it—no reward necessary.

I'm closing this chapter with two pieces. One is a dream of a future utopia. The other is a song we sang at the conclusion of our scripts and for an encore.

Reversal Fantasy (January 1989)

I simply cannot conceive of living in a fat-loving world where I was the one envied, catered to, extolled, and thinnies excluded, decried, and exploited for profit. I am too accustomed to being an outsider. I've been fat since I was a kid and my survival skills have been honed. I'd flounder in the mirror image world. Needing to ally with the oppressed in order to feel comfortable, I'd probably be helping the skinnies organize a militant resistance.

On the other hand, I can imagine a lesbian world where we were the ones honored and cherished. Perhaps the difference is that I've lesbian-identified for only eight years and I don't have a lifetime of internalized homophobia to overcome.

I think if the world changed tomorrow and fat paid off, I'd be scared it would all change back in an instant and life would so much harder, having had that taste of freedom.

This one, a song, was written by founding Fat Lip Readers Theater member, Nancy Thomas, and frequently was our encore number.

"Fat Is For The..."

(Sung to the tune of "M is for Mother")

> *F* is for the fine fat friends it gave us
> *A* is for the audience applause,
>   Applause.
> *T* is for the theaters we played in
> *L* is loving women, which we are,
>   Which we are.

I is for the images we're changing
P is for the politics we hold,
    We hold.
Put them all together
They spell Fat Lip
A group that's worth its weight in gold!

Fat Lip Readers Theater photo, from l to r:
Karen Bourque, Sherrin Lloyd, Bernice Soohoo Lee, Judith Masur,
Nancy Thomas, Laura Bock, Cath Thompson, Louise Wolfe. c 1987

Fat Lip Fan, image created by member Judith Masur
and fan by member Ada Grenoble. c 1990

Fat Lip reunion Flyer. July 24, 2011

7

Coming Out Loud

"GUESS WHAT? I'm a lesbian!"

"But how do you know you only like Italian food if you've never tried anything else?"

This was the exchange around 1982 between my dear friend Nadine and me in two of the cassette-taped letters we sent while she was living in Paris. I confessed my big news to her, that I was a lesbian and had a crush on a woman. At the time, I was stunned and so disappointed at her reaction. She would never have posed that question had I come out to her with the big news that I had a crush on a man for the first time and thought I was straight! But to be fair to her, knowing my history, or lack thereof, in the romance department, it was not an unreasonable question.

Somewhere Around Puberty
Written for Fat Lip Readers Theater

I mustn't think. God, don't let me feel, the pain or anything. I'll numb my mind. My bloated, inflated body won't exist. And when

189

those sudden, unpredictable flashes of feeling come–pain or pleasure–I'll learn to flip the switch in my mind and turn off. I'll protect myself from the external taunts and disgust from Daddy and strangers, as well as the internal voices blaming, condemning, warring. And when the panic fights through, I'll eat some cookies or cake and push it down again. And I won't feel anything.

I must be in control no matter what. Numbness is freedom from pain; liberation is the absence of feeling. If I can't cut myself off from my grotesque body, I can cut myself off from all feelings. I won't exist below my chin. No one look... Don't anyone touch me. Don't come near. Excitement and fear feels the same in my gut. Help! No, don't! I'll be amusing, intelligent, helpful, concerned, politically active. I'll keep my distance.

For twenty-four years, I've kept to that decision, until recently. I didn't know why I was different from everyone else. At times feeling a freak, envious, relieved. I was everyone's confidant and counselor–giving attention to others, deflecting it from myself. After all, I just didn't have sexual needs, I was asexual or something. I never talked about it to anyone. I suppose it was assumed that since I was fat I had no intimate experiences to share anyway. But a lot of it was because I set the barriers, the limits of how close others could come. I identified myself as straight so that at least I could call myself something. But I had no feelings for anyone. At the age of thirty-six, I'm coming out of it now, like from a long drugged sleep. It's terrifying and exciting. It would be easy to go back in–back to feeling competent, controlled, orderly. I hope I stay out. If this is a fairy tale, it's *Sleeping Beauty* with a twist–without the prince. I've awakened myself and it's up to me.

This was the piece I wrote one night in 1981, as ten women sat in a circle in Louise's Oakland living room. We had named ourselves Fat Lip Reader's Theater and we were completing our first year of writing, writing, writing, and finally we were ready to write about sex and being fat. Throughout that first year, we all had written the most wonderful, funny, and heartbreaking pieces as we wrote about every aspect of our lives as fat women. We planned to weave these stories into scripts and, along with additional pieces written by ourselves and others, we would end up performing them for the next seventeen years.

As in all our previous meetings, we wrote first on a chosen topic and then went around reading our pieces aloud for feedback. In the piece I wrote that night, with shame and embarrassment I revealed for the first time to anyone my most hidden secret.

I had been feeling an attraction for the first time ever, and the object of my stirrings was sitting next to me on the couch. Breathing was difficult. As my turn came to read, I said in a quaking voice that I just couldn't read what I wrote, it was too intimate, too scary. She said, "Laura, do you want me to hold your hand?" I screeched "No!"

She was adorable and talented and a wonderful dancer and performer. It had hit me like a ton of bricks: had I gone from an unfeeling, celibate, unidentified nothing to a crushed out—lesbian? Egads! Help! Was I sick, was I being influenced by all the other lesbos in Fat Lip? She was in a long-term relationship, thank goodness, because I needed to deal with my new feelings by myself.

Then began a journey to find my sexuality, after thinking I never had any to begin with. What an earth-shaking development!

At some point during that year, I had begun having dreams filled with imagery about being on busses, sitting near the back, not knowing where

I was going, and being driven forward with no control. And I must say, for me being in control is a personal value of the highest import.

I knew I needed help facing these foreign feelings, and so I discretely made some calls. I timidly asked the UCSF Human Sexuality Program for a lesbian therapist, and they referred me to Marnie Hall. I was terrified before that first appointment. I had to find the words and the courage to tell my secret, to reveal how weird I was. I was thirty-six and had had no intimate experience with another human being. I had weekly sessions with Marnie for months, and it was the hardest work I'd ever taken on. As she discovered, my preferred way of making changes was "little step by little step," and so she gave me embarrassing homework each week.

When I admitted to her that I had never even masturbated and didn't know what to do, or where to do it, she told me to go to a shop in San Francisco called Good Vibrations. There I would find two picture books on masturbation. One was called *I Am My Lover*. I was to ask the owner, Joni Blank, for the books, take them home, and start touching my body in the ways the books indicated.

The shop was a little hole-in-the-wall in the Mission District. I went at a time I thought few shoppers would be there. Haltingly, I approached the counter and, in a whisper, asked for the books. With an enthusiastic booming voice, Joni bellowed, "Oh yes. Those are just the best books on masturbation!" I thought I'd die. I grabbed them, threw some money on the counter, and fled.

My next homework from Marnie was to borrow a vibrator from my friend Maggie. While Marnie did not advocate the use of vibrators, in my case she wanted me to experience what an orgasm felt like. It was all new, all overwhelming emotionally, all overpowering physically, and all unbelievable. Except for Maggie, I told no friends what was happening to me.

And then, about four months after starting therapy, I took another huge step.

Time Warp

Written for Fat Lip Readers Theater, February 2002

It was 1963, at the University of Oregon, about eight p.m., in the lounge of the freshman women's dorm. In a circle, all voices hushed as the lights dimmed and a candle, beautifully nestled in a bed of fresh flowers and with a ring placed on the top of the narrow taper, slowly passed from girl to girl until it was blown out by the girl who was announcing her engagement. Then, the lights were turned on and screaming, cheering girls surrounded the "lucky one," hugging her and each other. I pretended, I smiled, tried to be a part of them. I felt alone, so out of it, again.

It was 1981, in a living room in a Berkeley apartment, women of various ages sitting around in a circle, the meeting of my feminist theater collective had begun check-in. I made sure I went last. One by one, each woman spoke of her week, the highs, lows. I could hardly breathe. At my turn, I whispered, "I think I'm a lesbian." Pandemonium, an eruption of shouts, cheers, all jumping to their feet, clambering around me, embraces, kisses, thumps on the back, it went on and on. And then came what I was later to understand was part of the tradition: being grilled with questions:

"How do I know..."

"Did you meet someone?"

"Who is she, are you dating, have you held hands, kissed, necked..."

"How far..."

"What did she say..."

On and on. I was in an eight-day blush and I loved it, loved them. I had come out and I had come home.

Among those ten women, there was one straight, eight lesbians, and me. No one could have dreamed of a more wonderful coming out. They were so happy for me, not just that I was a lesbian, but because I was experiencing sexual feelings and for the first time. I am certain that, were it not for the year of writing and sharing and support from those fat women, I would not have turned that switch back on.

During this time of astounding change and emotional upheaval, the strangest thing happened. I had been legally blind since 1971, unable to read more than a line or two of print, relying on readers and Books on Tape. Now, I wanted to read lesbian novels in the worst way and not with some reader between me and the exciting prose. These books had not been recorded for the blind, needless to say. I somehow ended up reading seven books *by myself* including, *Patience and Sarah*,[32] *Beebo Brinker*,[33] *Lesbian Woman*,[34] *Rubyfruit Jungle*,[35] and *Desert of the Heart*.[36] I was thrilled. Ever since, I have remained unable to read

---

[32] By Isabel Miller

[33] By Ann Bannon

[34] By Del Martin and Phyllis Lyon

[35] By Rita Mae Brown

[36] By Jane Rule

the printed word. It was a miracle of sorts, coming to this secular athe-ist, non-"woo-woo," new lesbian.

I wrote about some of these "firsts" for the Old Lesbian Memoir Writing Group.

First Date, I Think

What was her name? Maybe Barbara. She was newly relocated from Chicago and joined our fat women support group. We had been meeting together weekly since 1975, to share our stories, listen to others' and, in the process, shed our old self-hatred and loathing, accepting our beauty whatever our size. It had been transformative for me.

I should have picked up her vibes at that meeting. For one thing, she was thin and had had a fat lover in Chicago. What was she doing joining our group? Probably an FA (fat admirer) looking for a new girlfriend, but I didn't have a clue at the time.

I did my B&B host thing, "Hey, welcome to San Francisco. Let me know if you need help orienting to the city."

So she calls me and asks me to go out to dinner. I say, "Sure," getting ready my spiel on San Francisco sights, sounds, communi-ties, etc. A day or two before, she calls and asks me if I like red or white wine, because she wants to bring a bottle with us to the restaurant. I'm not much of a drinker, I say, but she could choose.

She comes to pick me up and asks me if I can see how nice she looks (she knew I was legally blind), that she is wearing a handsome jacket. I think, "Huh?"

Then arriving at the restaurant, which she had chosen, she asks me a few foodie questions, and then orders for me. "Huh?"

Then she proceeds to tell me all about her Chicago ex—how uptight and non-frisky she is and that she could tell I am very different—open, experimental, playful. "Huh?"

Over salad she says, "You know I'm hitting on you!" I choke on a baby green. Huh?

Over the entrée, I manage to tell her I'm just coming out and in a coming-out support group and seeing a lesbian therapist to help the process along. She says, "You don't need a therapist! You just need a good lover!" Oh geez!

After dinner, she asks me what I want to do and, scrambling and panicky, I think, "Stay in public," and suggested going to Peg's Bar nearby, never actually having been to any lesbian bar yet myself.

The bar is crowded and, to my horror, I see folks I know. I am definitely not "out" yet to anyone but my nearest and dearest. Yikes! She insists we sit with them and asks me what I'd like to drink. I say, "Soda water." She orders me a bourbon. I am silent, numb, passive in disbelief.

I feel her hand on my knee, moving her hand on my leg, as she leans closer and I lean away. She finishes her drink and orders another for each of us, even though my first drink remains untouched.

Finally, I somehow find my voice and say I want to go home. In front of my house I say goodnight and bolt from her car and am inside in a flash! About ten minutes later, I'm in my nightgown. The doorbell rings. Her car won't start, can she call AAA? I let her in. But she doesn't call, sits down in a chair and asks if I'm really not going to have sex with her that night. I manage to say, "No." We sit there in the foyer and I don't seem to know how to end this impasse.

It must be around midnight when I hear my blessed roommate, Susan, coming out of her room and head for the stairs. I greet her with relief and a degree of enthusiasm hitherto never displayed before toward her.

At the door, to add to the surrealness of the entire evening, Barbara says, "So maybe we can go down to Monterey next weekend." Huh!

Sleepless the remainder of the night, I am shaking all over and feel sick to my stomach. If this is what it is like to be an out lesbian, maybe I'll go back in.

Sobbing, I call my therapist at dawn.

First Kiss Ever

I remember my first kiss (at the age of thirty-six, a slow starter!).

Sometime in early childhood, I learned how to switch off all feeling and really got quite good at it. Except for fears. I did not feel joy, pleasure, desire, happiness. They got lost at the same time I turned off emotional pain, shame, humiliation. It seemed to be part of the deal. And if and when one of the bad feelings crept in, I'd picture flipping the switch. Sometimes I would need to supplement with chocolate and other sweets to aid in this obliteration.

I have few memories from before I was ten. The years between 1945 and 1955 were undoubtedly filled with fears—of the FBI, of my mother's breast cancer, of McCarthy and HUAC, of my constipation and the pain and embarrassment of it, of my dad's threats to leave us, and of his rages at me for being fat. Perhaps all this has crowded out all other day-to-day memories of that time.

And then came a day in 1982. I remember that first kiss with MJ. Tentative, teeth tapping. Not the kiss of my dreams. My learning curve was just fine with her, however, as I experimented with sweet and slow and when to breathe, and gradually felt an opening up and taking pleasure in body sensations.

Little by little, I began to switch back on.

First Lover

She came to the first Fat Lip performance, in a Berkeley studio. It was 1982, and after the show we put on music for dancing. It was glorious, a room full of fat women twisting and twirling, jiggling and laughing. She asked me to dance. Soft butch, around five-foot-two, light brown hair to her shoulders, a dynamite smile, dark eyes, round, pear-shaped body, wore men's cords and a polo shirt. She was about a head shorter than me, very cute. She became my first lover ever and I called her MJ. She was creative and imaginative.

We were together for nine years.

Both of us were Jewish, not religious — shared progressive feminist politics and a love for our dogs. From the beginning, she was attentive, besotted with me, and utterly accepting of my need to go slowly, and I mean tiny step by tiny step. I knew nothing — how to kiss, how to make out, how to touch, how to receive touches. I was without experience and was very scared. I wasn't sure about the anatomy — was that bump the clit? What was I to do with my hands, my mouth? What was an orgasm, and how do I give her one, and how will I know if I get one?

What would it feel like to touch skin to skin with my body parts that had never known another's touch?

What would it be like to hold each other close, breast to breast, naked?

Embarrassed and self-conscious, I told her the truth—my history and fears. I wanted to come out as a lesbian and as a sensual being, but I had to go slowly and needed support and understanding. She gave this to me. At first light kissing, sitting next to each other on the sofa—bumping glasses and noses and getting the hang of it and wanting more.

Then, fully clothed, lying side by side on a queen mattress, holding hands, sleeping together, and wanting more.

Then, in bed without clothes above the waist, touching a little, and wanting more.

Then, unclothed, in bed, kissing and holding, and wanting more.

She taught me about my body and how to explore another's. She taught me to relish the feelings, and I gradually lost the fears. I went from imagining, for years, what it might be like and of envying other "normal" people, to an actual, sensual, sexual being myself!

After six weeks of touching, I had sex for the first time, and in six months, I presented her with a key to my house. I grew to love her, to make love with her, and to love my own big body as I relished hers.

She was the perfect choice as a first lover. I had a girlfriend—at last, someone who wanted to be with me romantically and thought I was terrific and beautiful. She said she was so proud to be with me.

After two years, I was ready to agree we were partners. Step by step—big toe, little toe, heel, ankle.

The first four years were wonderful. The last five—increasingly awful. And then, one dreadful, wrenching night it was over—torn asunder.

Thank God.

Still, she was perfect for me to come out with—to discover my body with, to discover my feelings with. We were two fat women, relishing each other's curves, rolls, valleys, and crevasses. And when we stepped out, we strode, hand in hand, arms around each other's sumptuous backs, bursting with blatant pride, pleasure, and purpose. With her at my side, I marched in my first Gay Pride Parade, striding down Market Street, thrilled to be with her and thousands of others, declaring ourselves a joyful and righteous movement for civil rights.

Within a few months after MJ and I broke up in 1991, I started dating again. I had known Betty for some years and knew she had had a crush on me for a long time. She, too, was a soft butch, funny, fun to be with, and it was wonderful to feel wanted and beloved again. And then Theresa came into my life and I attempted to date both of them, having had absolutely no experience with this lifestyle! Soon, Betty opted out, and I concentrated on this new, big, fat, ultra butch.

Not only was she a stretch for me—she was an S/M dyke—but lo and behold, my inner "ultra femme" came bursting out. Who knew she had been there at all! I went to Walgreen's to buy lipstick—the first since I was a teenager—bought feminine blouses as well as frilly lingerie and even, for goodness sake, a garter belt! It was 1993.

She introduced me to some of her "playthings": whips and handcuffs, etc., and I pushed myself to give it a try. My old friend Nadine worried about what would happen to me if, let's say, there was an earthquake or some other emergency and Theresa was injured and I was left handcuffed to the bed posts unable to save myself!

We were together for about two and a half years, and during that time, I wrote the following pieces for Fat Lip Readers Theater.

First Time Around

Here I am, a fat liberation activist for more than fifteen years, a founding mother of Fat Lip, have accomplished major, affirming changes in my self-image, and can see my experiences within a larger political framework. I'm a ham on stage, give workshops, write articles, and field interview questions without a second thought.

But the old buttons are still there, and they are getting pushed again.

You're my first—my first lover smaller than I am and I've got feelings. I'm taller, I'm older—no problem. This is different.

You're fat, I'm fatter.

You've got what I got, just less of it.

My hips are wider.

My arms are thicker.

My folds are bigger.

Your shoulders are more defined by bone and muscle, mine by fat.

My chins, thighs, calves, fingers, everything is 4X to your 2X.

I can surround you fully, hands meeting and holding behind you. You embrace three-quarter's way around me, uncompleted.

And I've got feelings.

You're new to this movement, new to the life-altering ideas that eventually transform isolation and self-loathing into anger and celebration of survival. I already see the changes in you, the opening, the eagerness. But I'm mistrustful.

How can you appreciate and enjoy my body when you have such trouble with your own: your belly, your breasts, your rolls? How can I believe your pretty compliments when we are both products of the same hateful indoctrination that still triggers me?

Sometimes I can't. Perhaps we're not so different.

Yes, I am that fat liberation militant, but when those old, tenacious tapes get going, especially when we are naked in bed together, then, once again, I'm that fat, lonely little girl, hating herself and knowing no one will ever love her or think she is beautiful. Not really.

Big and Butch

I like 'em big and butch
But I'm not picky.

Could be one of those soft cuddly teddy bear show butches—
not much good for anything but kissin' and lovin.'

Could be one of those muscley, take charge, struttin' around,
    practical butches—
the kind that knows how to build a fire, or jump-start my
    motor and likes gettin' her hands dirty.

Either way, one thing is certain...
They all have to have plenty of nooks and crannies
And lots and lots of places to hold onto.
I like them big and butch.

The following four pieces I wrote in late 1992 and performed for Fat
Lip's sex script, "Fat and Sexy."

Fat Feet

I try not to let on
Carefully moving them just out of reach
Catching my breath and muffling a gasp when they
    are inadvertently brushed.
Embarrassed about my secret—
This oh-so-kinky erogenous zone.
Sole, toes, heel, instep—stroked, rubbed, licked,
    kissed, bitten, sucked—
Drives me wild
Don't tell!

Junk Food Baby

Baby, you're my junk food
    sweet like layer cake
    sticky like cotton candy
    salty like french fries
    smooth like a chocolate shake
    chewy like a juicy burger

But you're forbidden fruit for us health-conscious
      California fat gals.
    You make me dizzy, give me
    a sugar rush, make me short
    of breath, make my heart
    race. You lower my
    resistance, you raise my
    blood pressure.

And woman, like junk food, the more of you I eat, the more
      I crave
    fried and greasy
    well done or raw
    bland or spicy
    hot and sour

Many say I should avoid you—you're not good for me. I say,
      "To hell with tofu and brown rice!"
    Sometimes only junk food will satisfy.

Hole in One

Wanted: Fat woman with belly button for fun and games. What's the big deal? We all have one! I'm looking for a woman who will let me have hers!

Get the picture: I want to search the curves and caverns, the folds and valleys, with my fingers. And when I find it hidden there, waiting for me, I will circle it with my tongue, getting closer and closer.

Then I'll insert a finger, ever so slowly, deeper and deeper, rotating, feeling the warmth and moistness, until I reach its depth.

I'll move my finger gently up and down and then gradually pull it out, bringing it to my nose for a sniff, then up to hers for the same.

It's time for my tongue to enter, at first teasing and then thrusting and tasting as I grab her big voluptuous stomach with my hands and bury my face in her button.

So, *wanted:* Playful fat lesbian with an innie dying to be discovered and explored (lint optional).

Fat Slut (Performed while doing a striptease!)

I'm a woman with a secret—deep dark yearning, a fantasy, an aspiration if you will, and I must confess it—just between you and me.

But first, a few words of background (is this procrastination?)

I've been fat all my life and either invisible or discarded as a potential object of romantic or sexual desire. I did not date, masturbate or have sex until I was thirty-six. Before that, I just wanted an orderly, well planned, and hard-won predictable life.

A success story.

Oh yeah, the secret...

I want to be a slut—bed-hopping, cunt-teasing, sweaty, panting, anything-goes, card-carrying Fat Slut.

Oooooooooooooo baby, here I come!

Theresa and I broke up just before my fiftieth birthday, and it was very sad. Lack of love was not the problem. I wanted more and she was not available. During the next five years I put out a few personal ads:

1. Flirting....*Yes*! I'm femme, fat and forty-nine. I'm looking for distraction. Am I looking for you?

2. My Dream Butch

    She's big and fat and likes her femmes the same. She's forty-three-plus, has progressive and feminist politics and is playful and adventurous. She loves to laugh and kiss and cuddle and make love slowly, letting it build. She's strong and tender, lets her emotions as well as her opinions out, and "feeling" is not an alien concept for her.

    She's of any race and cuts quite a figure on the dance floor (leads, of course). She's expressive and empathetic and can acknowledge and validate as well as ask for what she needs. She doesn't smoke, drinks little, and thinks Scotties are adorable. She knows how to treat and appreciate a very special femme. She lives in S.F. This is a fantasy. Some of the above are optional. Call and find out which!

3. Headline: PERFECTION, NOT!
   But dating, laughing, dancing, playing, cuddling, kissing, flirting....*Yes!* I'm femme, fat and forty-nine. I'm looking for distraction. Am I looking for you?

4. Fifty-four-year-old woman, looks fifty-three, desires to meet another neurotic. Can be any age, but must look fifty-three.
   Must eat tofu, miso, seaweed, but not discuss it.
   Need not be affectionate, but expect eye contact.
   Can be cranky. Must wear erotic socks.
   Sagging butt? No problem! Protruding gut? I'm into fat liberation!
   Drooping spirit? I have extra Prozac!
   Hate people, music, and animals? Who's perfect?
   Sentence diagramming skills optional. Old, bald, lavender seniors preferred.

I dated once or twice in the late 1990s, and the following was written for the Old Lesbian Memoir Writing Group.

Date with a Cheese

It was quiet in my house—my roommate, Elise, was out or in her room. Margaret and I were on the comfy couch in the living room. We had gone to see a theater performance about Mary Ellen Pleasant, starring Louise Teisch and another actress. I had very much wanted to go because I had named one of my B&B rooms after the former slave and notable San Francisco entrepreneur and Underground Railroad activist. The audience had been filled with well-dressed black straight couples and a few others like us scattered about.

Afterwards, I invited her into the house for tea but we never did have any.

She was a stone butch—fat and black and had not one shy bone in her body. I was fat and "femmish" and white and self-conscious. She said she had thought I was stuck up because I had never been very friendly to her. I said I thought she was out of my league.

I told her my relationship with Theresa had ended some months past and that I put out a personal ad because I wanted to date. She had answered the ad.

She had quite a reputation—as a top, as best friends with Joanne Loulan (a notable speaker and book writer on lesbian sexuality). She was a poet and, along with Gloria Steinem, co-founded and published Ms. magazine.

I was a bit off-balance the entire date. Way out of my element. As we sat in the audience awaiting the start of the performance, she looked around and said, in a very audible voice, "God, I can't stand the black bourgeoisie!" I was one of the few whites in the room and reacted to her outburst with embarrassment and further self-consciousness, looking around hastily for reactions from those around us.

After the play, my date introduced me to Louise Teisch, who seemed to be her bosom buddy, and I felt tongue-tied as I usually did with "cheeses." I tend to gush or freeze.

Back at the house—there we were on the couch, perhaps a couple of feet between us. Suddenly, she lunges—her arm around my shoulders, kissing me on the face, her tongue inside my mouth. What happened to foreplay? I knew I was not in charge.

Now, ordinarily I'm a gal to go slowly—and I mean at a snail's pace. Then I felt the buttons on my blouse coming undone from top to bottom and a hand slipping into my bra.

This was the fast track and I had no wits about me. Yikes!

And then without warning she was standing up, saying, "I'm getting in too deep emotionally and you're not done with your ex." And she left, leaving me with blouse unbuttoned, one breast out of its cup, tongue hanging out, half reclining on the couch, stunned with her sudden departure. I was nonplussed to say the least!

Margaret Sloan Hunter died from congestive heart failure in 1994. Our memories and her powerful writing remain with all of us.

In about 2000, I came to a monumental decision to expand. For the past several years, I had done some healing from a broken heart and got to thinking about what I wanted in a girlfriend at that point in my life. I had done this list from time to time over the years, and it, of course, changed according to my needs of the moment.

Up to now, I had only been attracted to butches—soft, medium or hard. (I sound like I am talking about boiled eggs!) Now, this limits the pool of potential girlfriends. So, I decided to expand my criteria. Why just lead with the heart? How about the head, consciously deciding to review the other possibilities? There were also femmes—girly girls, lipstick lezzies, power femmes, and those in between on the butch-femme continuum. And there were what we called "androgynous"—a bit butch, a bit femmy, a bit of a tomboy. Perhaps I could learn to be attracted to these others if I just left myself open to the possibilities. I'd give it a try.

I found her in MotherTongue Feminist Theater Collective. She was a poet-writer looking for writing opportunities (and a girlfriend?) and I was a writer-performer missing Fat Lip Readers Theater and wanting to get out in front of a crowd again.

I'd say she was a tomboy or androgynous, who at times wore little earrings with her boots. She had been a softball player on lesbian bar teams and loved baseball, her dog—Amber Rose, red wines, and her VW bugs. She had a knockout smile and dancing eyes. Her handshake was firm (a must for me) and even though she was slim of build, she obviously had no problem hugging a fat woman, and hugging her hard! So far so good.

I liked to laugh and bring others to laughter, moving folks with my words, whether on or off the stage. I loved my Scottie, Rosie, and needed a woman who was a dog appreciator as well. I consumed Books on Tape, and talking about books was a must for me. I was politically a radical and could not be with anyone to the right of "progressive."

She was a voracious reader, radical feminist, and had been a member of SDS—Students for a Democratic Society, and the Weather Underground briefly. She was five years older than me and had known she was a lesbian early on.

We were no carbon copies. We had differences in background, assumptions, knowledge, and, occasionally, in politics, and this was enough to add spice, and sometimes to lead to hurt feelings and disagreements.

I was a talker, easily hurt, hard to come to anger. She was a recluse, easy to anger, covering old hurts from childhood. I was afraid to fight;

she was frustrated that I backed away and got scared. She flew off the handle, got over it, and was surprised that I remembered every word she'd said during one of her meltdowns, holding onto my wounds. I was a nice, good girl. She was an acting-out bad girl (in her family). What a learning opportunity for both of us. With her, I took my first, tentative steps in learning how to express my anger. The shoe didn't drop, the world didn't come to an end, and she didn't leave. And now, expressing my anger comes easy to me. I'm a natural!

We have been together for more than fifteen years and while it was, at times, rough for the first years, we now understand each other's melting points and give each other space to freak out in our own ways and come back to the center while the other one waits at a comfortable distance.

She's my family, my dear one, the best kisser in the world, my co-guardian with our dogs, my support, my critic, my rock, my play partner. We each want to die first so as not to have to outlive each other. Time will tell on that one. Her name is Suzanne Gary.

What I know now is that hard thinking outside the box and my decision around 1997 to expand my options was the best one I ever made. Look what I turned up—what a bargain!

My coming out as a lesbian was exciting and scary and so very much easier than it is for so many others. My parents had already died, so I did not need to address their reactions. I had my friends in Fat Lip to cheer me on, and a wonderfully supportive and loving first relationship. I did, however, have one very painful coming-out experience, which I wrote about for my Old Lesbian Memoir Writing Group.

Aunt Peg

Her name was Margaret and sometimes Reggie and sometimes Reg and then Peggy or Peg, depending on her age, the age of or connection with the person addressing her. She was Aunt Peg to me and came from New York City to live with us after her husband died and her son went to college.

It was around 1960, and I was almost fifteen. She became my one and only witness to my treatment in my family. She became my refuge, my solace—the adult who affirmed me and confirmed how bad it was in the house.

I would go into her room to watch, mesmerized, as she took out the hundreds of pins from the crown of braids atop her head and let them trail down her back. Then she would unbraid each and shake out her hair, so long she could sit on it. She let me brush it and then slowly she reassembled the entire edifice—transforming herself into a proletarian queen in her tiara of braids.

On particularly bad days, we would go to the ocean together and walk and talk and sit on the sand in the comfort of each other's company. She was a lifesaver for me.

She would want to know how *I* felt, what *I* thought—making room for me as I was, in my volatile family.

After a year under our roof she moved across the street—still bearing witness from a small distance. We remained close—talking on the phone and writing letters during my college years in Oregon. We traveled together to Helsinki to the International Peace Congress in 1965, she as a journalist and I as a student representative. I went to her with my distress as the "outsider" within my youth delegation. I was representing the Young Democrats of the U of O, while the others, representing the DuBois Clubs or the Young Trotskyites, were suspicious of me.

We traveled by train together to Moscow—she to visit with her eldest son and grandson and to write dispatches for the *People's World*, and I to tour with my delegation.

Upon graduation, I moved into her Berkeley apartment on Euclid as she left for a year traveling throughout the world, writing.

She was a pillar in my life and a friend and my first non-judgmental adult.

Then I came out to her as a lesbian. Everything changed. She never spoke the words, just started moving away emotionally, farther and farther—removing herself from my life, and her life from me. I knew why, but it was years later, after her death, that my cousin, her son, confirmed her homophobia. She said to him, "I will never think of that woman as Laura's partner." Her eventual death had little impact on me since I had lost her so completely years before. My cousin reminded me that communist doctrine posited that homosexuality was a product of capitalism. When the latter was brought down, the former would die out.

In spite of her distaste for my lesbianism, she did give me one last gift, one I will always treasure. She told me a story. Before my mom's death, these two sisters were talking together about their kids. My mom said to Aunt Peg, "I want Laura to find love and I don't care if it is with a man or a woman."

I suppose she didn't have to relate this conversation, given her own rejection of my "choice." So, for that, as well as for the role she played in my life for so many years, I am grateful.

As I went about San Francisco and also traveled a bit throughout the world, I walked proudly as a lesbian—and a blind lesbian, at that. I trained many friends how to walk with and assist a blind person, and I coined a term that I bestowed on them, to their merriment and pleasure. I realized one friend, Sally, needed further training when, on a trip to British Columbia, I was following her closely down a covered sidewalk and she easily walked beneath a hanging planter. Forgetting that I was taller, she neglected to warn me and my head collided right into it! Oops! I fired her on the spot as my "Seeing Eye Dyke"! But I rehired her immediately, realizing I needed to expand my "S-E-D training syllabus" and do it in a hurry!

There you have it. I chose the road less traveled but, nonetheless, it was one crowded with so many others in the Bay Area walking that path. I was so lucky to have a group of cheering Fat Lippers to come out to in 1982, Marnie Hall to professionally help me into my future, and a wonderful coming-out support group at Operation Concern, the GLBT counseling center, to aid the process. It is likely that if I lived in Podunk, USA, and not in the San Francisco Bay area, coming out would have been far more troubling and painful. It was the right time and the right place for me.

And my friend Nadine, who asked me that question about Italian food? Well, I wasn't the only one evolving. She became an ally extraordinaire. Some years after that conversation she gave me a button, "How Dare You Presume I'm Straight!" and I gave her one, "Number One Best GLBT Ally." She calls me excitedly when court decisions come down in support of gay rights and to commiserate when they don't. She attends far more films at the GLBT Film Festival than I do, and we go to rallies and marches and demonstrations together.

And the object of my very first crush? She's still awfully cute and, to this day, thirty-four years later, she does not know what role she played in my coming out of that carefully constructed cave. This is one secret that's kind of fun to keep!

8

Lights Out, Sound Off, ACTION

Turning Point

Written in the Old Lesbian Memoir Writing Group

What if, in June of 1971, at the age of twenty-five, I hadn't gotten sick with severe nausea and a constant, searing headache? What if I hadn't landed in Springfield Hospital under the care of an absent neurologist? What if my eyesight hadn't started to dim? What if I hadn't been taken by ambulance, airplane, and ambulance to Mt. Zion Hospital in San Francisco? What if I hadn't lost 100 percent of my vision within five days? What if I hadn't stayed in the hospital for a month undergoing unspeakable tests? What if I hadn't gotten a final diagnosis of optic neuritis? What if, suddenly and unexpectedly, a bit of my sight had not returned? And what if I hadn't needed to spend the next six months at home recovering my strength, rehabbing, and learning how to be legally blind? What if I hadn't returned to Amherst, only to struggle with my new limitations, as I attempted to pick up where I had left off?

For starters, I would have picked up Mom and Dad at the Springfield Airport and driven them to their motel, the first step of our two-week visit together traveling throughout New England. Next would be a visit to old Sturbridge. We would be celebrating the completion of my first year in grad school and the fact that we had all survived ten months apart.

At the end of the two weeks, we would have braved farewells as I put them on the plane. I would return to my little studio under eaves in the carriage house on Sunset Avenue to continue my adventure.

Later, I would have graduated with an MA in history, with a focus on American Cultural and Intellectual History, and found a teaching job in a community college, teaching history with a radical and ultimately feminist perspective. I would be a terrific teacher, stimulating and beloved by my students, of course.

Perhaps I would have bought an 18th century stone farmhouse in the Connecticut Valley and happily remained in New England with all its beauty. Would I have stayed shut down and shut in emotionally? I hope not. Would I have come out as a lesbian? Undoubtedly. Would I have had the very satisfying, if challenging, life that I have had? Don't know. Would I have met Suzanne and been partners with her for fifteen years? Unlikely. Would I have ever found a fat women's support group, learned to love my body and hate fat-oppression? Simply unthinkable. Would I have joined a theater group for eighteen years—writing, directing, performing our lives on stage, TV, radio, in print, on street corners? Sadly, probably not.

Back then, on that hot June day in 1971, we never did make it to Sturbridge.

Lights Out

ON A DAY in early June of 1971, I was driving south on the highway, following the Connecticut River toward Springfield, Massachusetts. I was on my way to pick up my parents at the airport, anticipating with excitement our reunion after ten months on opposite coasts. This was the first time I had lived so far away from them.

It had been an eventful year. I had arrived in Amherst after driving across country in the "racy" white 1966 Mustang I'd "bought" from my dad for one dollar. I dropped off my travel companions in Albany, New York, and proceeded over the pretty Berkshires into western Massachusetts. I had a studio to move into just two blocks from campus which Mom and I had found on a trip to Amherst that June.

My landladies, Miss Irene and Dr. Charlotte, were two old women who had lived together for decades and, while they did not identify their relationship, were devoted to each other. Dr. Charlotte, who was a retired osteopath, was a soft butch and did all the chores around the property. Miss Irene, a bit femmy, was less mobile and was the "lady of the house." She had been a public health nurse. Dr. C was a member of the Daughters of the American Revolution and Miss Irene lamented that she could not join because her people had been Huns!

I presented myself to them in August 1970, and I had no thoughts about lesbians or alternative choices, nor had I heard the term "Boston Marriage."[37] I was to live in a little attic apartment above

---

[37] The term "Boston Marriage" was used in late nineteenth-century New England to describe a long-term, intimate, monogamous relationship between two women. The women were generally financially independent of men, either through inheritance or because of a career. They were usually feminists, New Women, often pioneers in a profession. They were also very involved in culture and social betterment, and these female values, which they shared with each other, formed a strong basis for their life together.

them, in a converted carriage house. When weather was nice, they would go up to their "cabin" in southern Vermont where I once was invited to visit. It was charming and rural and was no rustic "cabin" as far as I was concerned.

They were most welcoming, although Miss Irene could be rather brusque and very opinionated about "those young people today," scowling as she listed "their" shortcomings, like short skirts, long hair, hippies, and so forth. As we sipped tea the day I arrived in Amherst with all my belongings, I politely listened to her rant while unobtrusively attempting to push my skirt down over my knees.

I was lonely that first year, too shy to make friends; I liked my classes but felt out of my league. My BA was in English, and here I was, a graduate student in the history department, trying to catch up. What the heck was "historiography" anyway? I was one of just a few women grad students in the department, and there were no female faculty. The men there, both students and faculty, easily connected with one another, intellectually and personally.

I loved studying American Intellectual and Cultural History, and I loved living in Amherst, in the Connecticut Valley. I felt like a kid in a picture postcard of quaint New England. I loved the fall colors, my studio with its view of a field and trees all around, loved winter snows and ice storms (although I had to learn about snow tires and how to come out of a skid). I quickly sought advice on how to tolerate summer's insufferable (from a foggy San Franciscan's point of view) heat and humidity with a window air conditioner (and something called BTUs). Then there was "mud season," something I had never heard of, during which I took my first trip to a "sugar shack" as winter waned, where folks were happily crowded into a room and given plates of snow with hot maple syrup drizzled over it. Even more curious were the bowls of sliced dill pickles on the long butcher paper covered tables. Yum!

My little white Mustang took me down back roads, where I found truck stops with fresh "native" produce from our Connecticut Valley, to the butcher in the woods for my local meats, to Frost Library in Northampton, and, as I strolled around the Amherst village, pausing to sit on the green, I had to pinch myself to prove all this was real. In the fall I had a delightful visit from my close friend Stella, on her way to England to marry John. Aunt Peg visited me for a few days and stayed in a wonderful little dormer room I found for her at the inn on the Amherst common. We had a good visit and I felt less lonely.

By that May of 1971, I had done well academically and was anticipating my parents' visit with the usual mix of excitement and anxiety. I had booked a motel for them for a couple of days and we would plan our route. I thought I'd like to see Old Sturbridge Village first. We would tour western Massachusetts a bit—perhaps up into the Berkshires, into Northampton and the Frost Library, a beautiful old building where I spent so much of my time doing research, and showing them all my discoveries along the way. We would go to dinner at the darling inn in South Hadley, driving down South Pleasant to the restaurant on the pretty little creek. It was quintessential, quaint New England. In the days to come, we would drive east to Boston and the Cape and up to Concord and Salem and north if there was time. We had two weeks to visit, to be tourists, and to enjoy a driving vacation together reminiscent of our summer car trips when I was a child, but this time I was all grown up and hosting my parents.

As I drove south to the airport that day, excited about the next two weeks, I reviewed the plan for the following day: Mom and Dad would have time to rest from their journey, then I'd show them around Amherst—the homes of Emily Dickinson and Robert Frost—walking around the village common, introducing them to and having tea with Miss Irene and Dr. Charlotte. I was a little nervous about what my dad might say to these two old women. He was a bit of a mischievous, witty guy, and Miss Irene was a bit intimidating, a very proper, rather formal "lady" who might not see or appreciate the twinkle in his eyes or his familiarity.

Life was good. Life was full. I had no idea that starting the next day my life would be forever altered as illness struck suddenly and accelerated dramatically.

A couple of days before my parents arrived, I had started feeling lousy—headachy, a bit queasy, but I carried on, of course. I was afraid I was coming down with a cold and it would spoil all our plans for a wonderful visit. By the end of that first day together, our plans had been postponed and I was experiencing searing head pain and rolling nausea. My folks took me to the university infirmary. We returned to the motel, where they had a rollaway bed set up for me in their room. I don't remember much of the next two days. I was getting sicker, screaming when I tried to lay my head down on any surface, even the softest down pillow. I guess my parents were in touch with the university doctor and it was decided to refer me to a neurologist who would admit me into Springfield Hospital.

He was concerned about meningitis, and I needed a spinal tap. My poor, dear parents, not familiar with the area at all, managed to get us to Springfield in my little Mustang, me into the hospital and themselves into a hotel nearby.

In the hospital, I remember being in a bed in a small cubicle with no window, being taken for tests, being unaware of much except that the lights in the room were so dim and getting dimmer. I was bewildered by it all.

I had been in the hospital for a day when my eyesight began to fade. I kept saying, "It's getting dark, aren't there any lights in the room?" I think I was there for five days, including a weekend when the neurologist was away and left no one on call in his place, and it was getting darker and darker. My parents were frantic about me and were going nuts trying to reach this specialist. (Months later, I learned my dad was so enraged that he thought about suing that doctor for malpractice. Somehow Dad got the doctor's home number and would call him from San Francisco in the middle of the night to harass him.) When I returned to Amherst six months later, the doctor sent a bill for his "services." I "declined" to pay, writing, "You've got to be kidding!" and returned it to his office. I never heard from him again.

At the end of those five days in Springfield Hospital, I was totally blind. My parents swiftly organized an emergency airlift back to San Francisco — by ambulance to the Springfield airport, by plane to the San Francisco airport, and another ambulance to Mt. Zion Hospital. Our family doctors had been alerted and the crisis team was awaiting my arrival, organized by our dear family friend Dr. Coleman Citret. And so the tests began.

In San Francisco, I spent four weeks in the hospital undergoing unspeakable tests to determine the cause of the blindness, nausea, and, further, facial nerve abnormalities I was then unaware of. These tests ranged from fairly innocuous to the mother of all, called a pneumoencephalogram. I had already had a spinal tap and other X-rays, and now they wanted to determine if I had a "pseudo" tumor. It seemed that young, fat women were found to get this sometimes. I was told that the pneumoencephalogram would take pictures of my brain after air had been forced into it. Yes, the doctor said, I would have some headache but that's about all. I was taken to radiology and yes, they did shoot air up into my brain. I thought I would pass out with the pain. After what seemed like hours, I was taken back to my room, in agony with pain and nausea, where I was given pure oxygen and slowly began to feel a little human again. Then, in an hour or so, an orderly came into the room and prepared to put me on a gurney. I asked him, "Where am I going?" He said, "Back to radiology. The docs wanted more pictures with the pneumoencephalogram." I said, "*No!*" They were in shock that I was refusing but I held my ground (or my bed) and raised my voice and repeated, "*No!*" Enough was enough. I understand that, subsequently, this test was discontinued because it produced few useful results and is considered barbaric.

Another test was in a surgical theater, where half my head was shaved and a surgeon drilled two holes in my skull. This test was to determine if I had intracranial hypertension. I needed to be awake for this and they had told me it would not be any different than being at the dentist. Yeah, but I heard the drill and smelled the burning and knew I was getting two holes drilled in my skull. Yikes!

Ultimately, all tests were negative and it was decided that some rogue virus had attacked my optic nerves. I had optic neuritis. A neuro-ophthalmologist ordered a series of steroid injections directly into my eyes. I later learned that my parents had been told that I would never regain my vision.

One day, in the hospital, I was dying to get some fresh air, having been in my hospital bed for so long, and I asked my dad to take me up to the roof garden. It was so reviving to be out there, breathing in fresh, cool San Francisco air, and I enjoyed myself. It was not until several years later that I found out, to my astonishment, that my dad was very anxious about our being on that roof because he thought I might try to kill myself by running off the edge.

About three weeks or so into my hospital stay, our dear family friend Coleman Citret was visiting in my room. He was standing between my bed and the window during the day. Suddenly I said, "Coleman, do you have your pipe in your mouth?" He did, and it was not lit. I could see the dim outline of the pipe and his profile, backlit by the window and the bright light of the day. This big, lumbering man ran out of the room to call the docs and my folks. Some vision had returned, a little bit, and I would thereafter be considered "legally blind."

I was never particularly upset, never freaked out about being blind or partially sighted. I didn't think much, dealing with the minute-to-minute challenges and feeling so sick. I think I was dazed and numb about everything that was happening to me.

At the end of that month in the hospital I returned home with my parents, where I spent the next six months recovering my strength and learning how to live as a blind person. During these months of forced exile from Massachusetts I was, however, pissed off. I had been derailed. My carefully considered plan to attend grad school, get my MA, and teach at a community college was out the window. This couldn't be happening. I was going to be a radical and feminist historian, teaching history from "the bottom up," amazing and stimulating my students. Someday, I would live in an 18th century stone farmhouse in

New England, plunging into the exciting primary resources located in archives within a stone's throw. I had started a major project on Paul Robeson and had looked forward, later that summer, to going down to New York City to the Schoenberg Collection of Black and African American History. Now I was trapped, stuck in San Francisco.

Before long I connected with the Department of Rehabilitation and they arranged for mobility training (using a white cane), teaching me Braille (it didn't take—I was pissed off about having to learn a new language, and instead of using the soft part of my finger pads to gently determine the dots I used the hard tips to "find the goddamned dots." Needless to say, I did not get very far with that course of study.) The Department of Rehabilitation wanted to send me to a residential program in El Cerrito to learn self-sufficiency skills with other "blinks,"[38] living there for three or so weeks. I agreed to look at it and turned it down flat. I didn't want to have anything to do with that facility. Angry? I suppose so. To prove to my assigned counselor that I was competent to cook for myself, I made a baked apple and took it to him!

Mostly, I focused my energy on how I could resume *my life* in Massachusetts. My counselor, Robert Nestler, who was totally blind, knew, of course, that my grad studies in history had been interrupted. He said the California Department of Rehabilitation could support me in going back to school—*if* I changed my studies to special education and if I returned to a school in California! I was shocked, confused and desperate. I told him my field was in history and he said he would take it up with his supervisor.

The next time I went in to see him, he started off by saying the Department of considered me unemployable at my current weight and

---

[38] A word for "blind," only used within the blind community.

therefore it would be a waste of their resources to support my studies. I did not tell them to go to hell but left his office humiliated, shaken, and hopeless. At that time, I had no weapons with which to fight back. In 1971, there was no fat lib movement and I had no consciousness about discrimination against fat people, nor a feminist analysis, and was still filled with self-hatred and thought dieting was the only answer.

My parents urged me to contact the Commission for the Blind in Massachusetts. After a number of calls and much paperwork, I was told it would be their pleasure to support my return to my grad studies in Amherst. They assigned me to a counselor, had no problem with my weight, paid my tuition and books and a stipend for readers and drivers, and hooked me up with the local Lion's Club, which rented me a large-print typewriter. My counselor was available to talk to me and meet with me to discuss my problems with adapting to my new situation as a blind student.

I returned to Amherst and my little attic garret in January 1972. Dr. C and Miss Irene had been so wonderful. For several months after my evacuation home they said to my folks that I did not have to pay rent for a while. I suppose they were horrified at what had happened to me. Then my parents started sending the rent and they held the studio for my return. So I came back to a familiar setting, white cane and all. I had useless vision in the right eye—there was light but no focal point; in the left eye I had good central acuity, corrected, but only a teeny visual field. It was like looking down a pencil point.

I was picked up at the Springfield airport by my neighbors, David and Ellen, who had been using my little white Mustang for the six months I was gone, at the request of my parents. I could no longer drive. Nor could I read print. Henceforth all letters to and from friends and family would be recorded on cassette tapes that were mailed free of postage as "matter for the blind."

Fortunately, I had a month before school resumed in order to get oriented and get some resources lined up. I hired Lorna, another student, to be my reader-driver.

It was a bumpy restart. Nothing was the same. My graduate dean welcomed me back with the comment that he had never heard of a blind historian. Navigating through heavy snow with a white cane was more than challenging—tapping was impossible and what visual cues I had relied on before had disappeared in the snow. Doing research, with readers between the documents and me, was frustrating. And most of all, I could no longer use my tried and true methods for absorbing, integrating, and creatively working the material into cogent and well-written papers using techniques that had hitherto been successful for me.

As a result, in June 1973, I finished the coursework for my masters with three incompletes. My professors were awaiting my papers. I was stymied. Finally my mom suggested I study for my oral exams that summer, take them, and then come back home. I could complete the remaining papers from San Francisco with her support. What a relief. A plan. I passed the exam with a high mark, arranged with Lorna to drive me and my stuff in the Mustang across country, said goodbye to Miss Irene and Dr. Charlotte, and headed home.

To my shame, I never completed the papers. I started a new research project, this time into *The Wasp*, a satirically political magazine from the late 19th century edited by Ambrose Bierce in San Francisco. Once again, no paper came out of this very stimulating work. I never got my masters. I know this made my mother so sad for me.

Is there a silver lining? Heck no. There has been, however, between then and now, a full life, including coming out as a lesbian; joining a fat women's support group and learning to love my fat body and to fight fat oppression; eighteen years in the feminist theater collective Fat Lip Readers Theater, writing, directing, producing, performing our stories and our politics. We were hot and we were zealots, and we were told, time and time again, by so many women that we changed their lives. The women's liberation and fat liberation movements transformed mine, for sure.

As devoted as I was to my fat politics and relished being out a lesbian, the issue remained: how to make a living as a blind person. After Mother's death from cancer in 1977, and my father's two years later, in 1979, I researched the idea of opening a bed and breakfast—something rare and new at the time—in our family home, and ultimately opened Bock's Bed and Breakfast in June of 1980. I operated this successful business for more than twenty-two years—expanding and learning and finding surprising ways to be creative (marketing!) and meeting so many diverse guests, many of whom came back over and over and became friends.

I must say it was somewhat tricky running a business while being blind and required careful planning. When guests first arrived, I told them where to place their luggage in the foyer and, moving around without my white cane, showed them the common rooms and their bedrooms. My intention always was to "come out" the following morning at breakfast as I pulled out maps and explained why I could not point to streets and sites with any accuracy. However, a couple of times, unbeknownst to me and to my embarrassment, they had moved their bags and I tumbled over them. Needless to say, at that point I had to quickly explain my vision loss so they did not think they had an inebriated host.

Once I faced a particularly tricky challenge with a new guest. He was arriving around midnight and was profoundly deaf. He was used to communicating with pad and pen. I, however, could not read! How was I to give him my usual introductory "spiel," which included a welcome, necessary information about his room, bath, breakfast, and myriad other details? I wrote everything out on index cards, the first one informing him that I was blind. As we took the tour, I would hand him the pertinent card.

Now, this guest was in San Francisco for the annual Folsom Street Fair, a mecca for the S/M community. It turned out he had won the title "Mr. Drummer"[39] of his region, a big deal, as I learned. I spent the rest of the night worrying how he and the other guests would communicate at breakfast in the morning. When the time came I had little pads of paper and pens arrayed around the table and hoped for the best.

It turned out all my guests that weekend were gay men, and they all had a wonderful time "talking" and laughing together and were excited to meet the new guest. They insisted he go upstairs and put on his winning costume (what there was of it) and model it for them. From the kitchen I heard cheers and whistles, and sounds of metal "accessories" jingling and jangling from his outfit. When I gathered their writing pads after breakfast I was surprised to read of an exchange between two of the guests. A preppie-looking guest had asked, "Did you go to the beer bash at the bar last night?" to which Mr. Drummer

---

[39] "Drummer" was a magazine for gay men who practiced S/M, and sponsored regional contests to choose "Mr. Drummer." At the Folsom St. Fair, a national Mr. Drummer would be "crowned."

replied, "No, I prefer fine wine." So much for my stereotype about rough-and-tumble SM guys!

For the first ten years of the business, I did all my own cleaning and quality assurance, hoping, but never sure, that I was doing a good job. For several years, I attempted muffin making until I discovered that my muffins were either burned or raw inside. After that, I gave in and relied on Just Desserts to supply me with their scrumptious offerings. I started using a bread-making machine and turned out yummy, fragrant loaves, getting more credit than I deserved.

My blindness did not prevent me from acting as a consultant with would-be innkeepers, speaking at conferences and panels, doing all the pre-computer-days paperwork necessary for booking reservations, keeping the books, ordering supplies, dealing with the city's require-ments for collecting hotel tax and the accompanying tedious reporting of it, writing a manual for my substitute when I eventually took a va-cation, and so on. Eventually, when I started having back pain and could not trust I was doing an adequate job on my own, I found inde-pendent contractors to assist me with the cleaning, repairs, and im-provements. I became an excellent organizer, a detail person, and managed to keep all the plates spinning, at least most of the time. Some of this was enjoyable because I relished feeling competent and finding out I was good at problem solving. My greatest pleasure came in relat-ing to my guests and finding ways to facilitate their relating to each other at the breakfast table and beyond. Some made lasting friendships and continued to be in contact after leaving, and even made plans to return to Bock's together. Somehow I figured out how to do all this as a person with low vision.

Being an innkeeper and running Bock's Bed and Breakfast became an essential part of my identity. I was proud of starting a business and making it successful. It also gave me some cachet in the GLBT community. Each June I donated several rooms to filmmakers who brought their work to be shown at the renowned Frameline GLBT Film Festival. It was fun for me and my other guests to meet these creative people, and each time a program began at the festival, Bock's Bed and Breakfast was one of the featured sponsors. One time I was sitting in the huge Castro Theater for a film and, when the Bock's name and logo flashed on the enormous screen, a number of people in the audience clapped and cheered. What fun!

For Pride Month each June I had rainbow flags artfully arranged around the house and gave all guests, whether gay or straight, a mini flag of their own to wave. Wanting to do all I could to have diverse guests comfortable with each other during their stays, I included the following info each time I had an inquiry from a prospective guest: "There is a diversity of folks who stay here, including gays and lesbians, and if you think this might be awkward for you, this is really not the place for you to stay. I'd be happy to give you several referrals to other B and Bs." This seemed to work quite well. However, one time I had a guest from Podunk, shall we say. At breakfast the morning after he arrived, he announced that he had been walking downtown and was "hit on" by a gay man. Each day he had a similar story. I, early on, concluded it was wishful thinking on his part. This was early in my running the bed and breakfast, when I did not come out first thing to my guests. So with this fellow, I impatiently waited until the end of his weeklong stay and at his checkout I proclaimed, "Well, when you return to Podunk, be sure and tell all your friends and family that you stayed in the home of an out-and-out lesbian!" He went pale in shock. I loved it!

Bock's Bed and Breakfast was a wonderful, all-consuming, and challenging way to make a living and I was passionate about it, but I wasn't doing history as I had dreamed of and worked towards in graduate school. How could I bring that back into my life? I found a way with the help of volunteer readers at the GLBT Historical Society. I processed the sizable and significant collection of the San Francisco Women's Building/Women's Centers, which reflected all the issues and activities of the second wave of feminism from the early 1970s. This took years to complete, but today it is available online and at the archives for researchers, and this herstory has been preserved. History has always been primarily written by wealthy white men, ignoring the events and lives and experiences of women, people of color, and the poor and working class. I am very proud of the work I did there and my contribution to filling in these gaps in the historical record.

By the way, on that first day of my visit with my parents in Amherst, we did have tea with Miss Irene and Dr. Charlotte. As usual, Miss Irene expounded on her distaste of hippies and young people in general—their unkempt appearance and bad manners. My dad closely examined a painting over the mantel of one of her honored ancestors, a formal portrait of a man with long hair. He said, "I see you had a hippie relative yourself, Miss Irene." I gulped. Miss Irene looked fierce, glanced at the portrait and smiled just a little bit (did I hear a tiny giggle?). I breathed again.

As a blind person I was subject to some of the most ridiculous and, later, amusing interactions with people, which I wrote about in 2002, for the MotherTongue Feminist Theater's script on disability.

Strangers

"What? No, an eye transplant won't work."

Move along.

"But, I didn't want to cross in this direction."

Move along.

"No, taking Jesus Christ into my life will not improve my vision."

Move along.

"Oops, excuse me." Shit, it was only a light pole.

Move along.

"Thank you, I'm fine. I fall all the time." Ow.

Move along.

"How many steps? Five?" Damn, there were six.

Move along.

"Hi, it's great to see you." Who the hell is it?

Move along.

"How do you do (extending out my hand)?" Egads, it was a breast.

Move along.

Committed

I am in a committed monogamous relationship with three others. Each of us with our own moods, needs, demands for attention. Me, her, my disability, her disability. Am I nuts? No, just in love. But, it is crowded in here.

Dream of Driving

For twenty-five years, I waited, I dreamed, I fantasized, I pleaded with friends and lovers, and I hoped. Yes, yes, they all assured me that someday they would be happy to let me drive again, perhaps in an empty parking lot at dawn.

I had been a crackerjack driver, and so cool with my 1966 Mustang, loved the freedom, the independence, the therapy of driving wherever and whenever. Taken from me, forever.

Well, not quite. Sally and I were tooling down a lovely little country road in the Paharo area of Hawaii's big island. An overcast day, the road newly blacktopped with freshly painted white lines along the edge and center. I said, "So, what if I drive?" fully expecting the usual reply.

The next instant, Sally pulls over, gets out of the car, marches around to my side, pulls open my door and says, "Your turn!"

I protest "Wait, wait, let's talk about this." She pulls me out, gets into the passenger seat, and closes and locks the door. What could I do?

I settled myself in the driver's seat, buckled up, adjusted the rearview mirror (?), and turned on the ignition. It all came back. I slowly pulled out—no traffic, the road was straight. I concentrated on staying between the white lines.

"Sally, I think I'm going too fast."

"Laura, you're going about fifteen miles per hour."

"Sally, there's a car coming up behind me, I'm pulling over."

"Laura, *not* here. Just keep going"

"Sally, the road ends, I have to turn right."

"You can do it."

I did. It was grand.

Finally, Sally saw a road sign announcing a narrowing of the road and thought it best we change places. I carefully pulled over — into a ditch, but not a very deep one, thank goodness.

All in all, I drove for about a mile. I had the time of my life. It surpassed any high, awards, degrees, sex, and the dream itself. Glad there was no traffic cop around. What would I have said?

Would I do it again? You bet!

(Sally and I told this story during our session with Story Corps, a federal program of the Library of Congress to record and archive stories all around the country. A very few selections are broadcast on National Public Radio and to my utter surprise and a little chagrin, this story was chosen to be on the air!)

Divorce

I've had it. I'm done with you. I've tried my best for thirty-one years to be supportive and accommodating and can't do it another second. Go make it with some other woman. Go and mess with her life. Tie her hands. Tell her what she can and can't do. I'm bored and frustrated and want to try something new.

So, my dear, dear blindness. *I want a divorce.*

Irreconcilable differences.

The following was written for Fat Lip Readers Theater. At times I found it hard to find the detachment I needed to perform it without sobbing.

Fat and Blind

"Tubby! Chubby! Fat ass! Tub o'lard! Porky Pig!" I grew up fat, enduring the street taunts and jeers coming at me all the time, doing my best to be invisible, unhearing, uncaring. But this was different.

"Hey, Mama, look at the blind lady!"

"Hey, lady, what's that white stick with the red tip for? You going skiing, playing pool, golf?"

I heard curiosity in their voices and then sympathy and pity. Before, when my fat was the target, I heard hostility, derision, and condemnation.

It was 1971. I was in grad school in Massachusetts when suddenly my vision dimmed. Within two weeks I was totally blind and back home again, in a San Francisco hospital undergoing a battery of gruesome tests.

"Hey, Mom and Dad, it's okay. No big deal. I'm just fine. The nurses and doctors are nice and I've been learning to find my way to the bathroom and back to bed dragging my IV pole! No sweat!"

The blindness was new and I was not ready to deal with it yet. Instead my worrying focused, as always, on my fat. How would they get me on the gurney, into the ambulance, up the airplane steps, carry me, lift me, push me?

The hospital dietician proposed a weight-loss diet. Since I was in the hospital anyway, why not take this splendid opportunity to lose some weight while the doctors were searching for a diagnosis?

They seemed to be focusing on a rare disorder called pseudo-tumor, which apparently only afflicted young, fat women. Before this diagnosis was dismissed, I lay in bed trying to grasp the horror that my fat had caused my blindness.

I eventually left the hospital without a diagnosis but with some of my vision restored. I was legally blind, and there were new skills to be learned. Braille, mobility training, new ways to do familiar, everyday tasks. The Department of Rehabilitation was my first stop. I was assigned to Robert Nestler, a totally blind counselor. He started the process going, assuring me that I would receive full financial support, necessary retraining, special equipment, whatever I needed to resume my life and return to grad school. Then one day Nestler announced, "My sighted assistant tells me that you are significantly obese. We are not prepared to help you unless you lose fifty pounds and keep it off for six months. After all, we are in the business of assisting the blind to move toward employment and self-sufficiency. Why should we pour our funds into you when chances are you are not employable at your weight."

Ah, this was familiar—the hostility at my fat, and my feelings of mortification and humiliation. It has taken years for the anger to surface: toward the people who hate me for my fat; toward Nestler, who accepted my blindness yet refused me the support of the government programs because I was fat; toward the graduate dean in Massachusetts who told me he had never heard of a blind historian; toward the people who find me "too disabled" and those who treat me as not disabled enough because, although I use a white cane, I may not move, walk, or act like a legally blind person "should"; toward people who insist on helping me cross the street, even if it is in the wrong direction; toward those who ignore me, discount me, don't believe me because I'm fat or because I'm disabled. And anger at being unable to read, drive, at having to struggle with issues of accessibility around both fat and vision.

And you know, even back in that hospital in 1971, I knew the attention would shift away from my fat and onto my blindness, and it would be a relief, and that pity would be easier to take than hatred.

The appalling truth is that for me, walking the streets is less frightening than it was before I used this white cane.

Now: after nearly forty years, and at the age of sixty-five, I would kick butt. What made the difference: the second wave of feminism, the fat liberation movement, the disability rights movement. Hallelujah!

Sound Off

After I closed the bed and breakfast in 2003, I searched for something to do that I would be good at, and which would be of some service to folks. The San Francisco Community Boards, a volunteer mediation service that helps people with disputes of all kinds, offered a ten-week class in their method of mediation. Ah-ha! I registered and spoke with the director about my visual disability and what accommodations I might need in order to successfully complete training. No problem. I had been advocating in this way for years around my blindness.

And then, at the first class, a new barrier struck me in the gut. The room was good sized, situated on a busy street, and had overhead fans whirring. I struggled to hear the teacher and the questions from fellow classmates, and no way could I understand what others were saying when we broke up into small groups. What gives?

In a panic, I found the San Francisco Hearing Center, called, and asked to speak with someone. I was anything but sanguine at the discovery of my hearing loss. I'd already had one sensory loss. How was it possible to have another one, at the age of fifty-seven? I was too young for hearing loss. There just had to be some mistake! It wasn't fair. Dual sensory loss, as I came to understand it, was unacceptable. And the label "deaf/blind" just couldn't be me.

At the hearing center I was connected with Laura Clark, a hearing loss counselor, and made an appointment to see her before the next mediation class. She said I needed to get an audiogram, which would show the results of a hearing test. Meanwhile, she loaned me an assistive hearing device to use in the class and said I would have to talk to the instructors about accommodating this new disability. Oh *no*! She offered to be an advocate for me if I chose.

With an extremely self-conscious apology, I once again spoke with the Community Boards' director about this new and unexpected development. I felt like I was a pack of trouble. She was very willing to accommodate as much as possible, making sure the small groups I ended up in were in a separate room alone. She spoke with the instructors about wearing a microphone, which sent their voice to headphones via a receiver I wore. This device was part of what I learned was called an FM system, and included various microphones for different situations. Eventually, I purchased one of these contraptions for myself.

I managed to finish the program and was eager to do the work. I even researched certificate programs at local universities for further training. Then I encountered another brick wall. Many of the clients had accents, and I could no longer understand people with accents or who spoke quickly or had high-pitched voices. There was no way I could keep interrupting the mediation sessions to ask them to repeat, speak more slowly or more clearly. The clients were anxious and up-tight as it was. Another door was shutting.

I acquired hearing aids at Laura's urging and with her support. She advised those called "behind the ear," which were big and visible but easiest for blind folks to deal with. They certainly improved matters a lot, but they do not bring back "normal" hearing. Any extraneous noise like traffic, nearby conversations, accents, fast talkers, etc. and so on leave me unable to understand what is being said to me. This means no eating in restaurants, no walking with a friend outside, no parties, no group activities. It is far more isolating than blindness, as far as I am concerned. There is nothing like being in a room with lots of folks socializing and feeling so utterly lonely and helpless. And avoiding such environments can give others the message that I am a loner, unfriendly, or stuck-up.

When my partner Suzanne and I got together in 2000, she knew that my being legally blind was part of the package. While it was at times frustrating for her that her lover had such a limitation, she was supportive of me. But with the hearing loss, there came huge and painful interactions between us. I was constantly asking her to repeat what she said, to speak slowly, to face me when she spoke. Our social life was severely curtailed. She was at times angry, impatient, and fed up. I don't blame her. It was very hard for me, too. She thought the hearing aids would take care of everything, and had a hard time believing that the technology was not advanced enough to simulate normal hearing. When I came home from a day out in the world after straining to hear and cope with sirens and overwhelming noise, I would take off the aids as I would my shoes, to relax. This meant Suzanne and I could not communicate with each other.

We had a couples' session with Laura Clark, and as a result, Suzanne has a more accurate idea of the limitations of the aids, and I keep one aid on even at home. It's rarely easy and so often fraught with painful emotions.

All I know is that I am way too over-accessorized, what with two hearing aids and a red-tipped white cane. How gauche! Nothing subtle about me.

ACTION

Soon after I returned to Amherst in 1972, and began to work with a counselor from the Massachusetts Commission for the Blind, I was astonished to learn of a doctrine taught to blind people, especially those who had gone through schools for the blind, like the Perkins School. That is to say, that the blind need to be grateful for any nod from sighted people and passively accept their charity. In other words, we should not make a fuss, and definitely not express any anger or indignation nor be pushy. Our attitude and demeanor will affect how *all* blind people will be treated, present and future. Needless to say, with my background, this did not sit too well with me. My people rock the boat!

In Amherst, I found very little understanding of disabilities at either my university or in the town. People asked what was my white cane for—playing pool, skiing? Once, when I was crossing the street, a car did not stop for me and sideswiped my cane, which went flying and struck the car. The driver charged out, yelling, "Why don't you look where you're going? You hit my car!"[40]

I asked my counselor if there was a support group in the area for blind students. He said no. There were five colleges in the vicinity, including Smith, Hampshire, Mt. Holyoke, Amherst, and U. Mass, and I bet that I was not the only blind student attending them. So I lobbied him and insisted one was needed — and with the commission providing transportation to and from each meeting for the students, of course. To give them credit, a group was organized. It helped a lot to be able to talk with others in a similar situation, facing all too familiar obstacles. And for me, I got much good guidance from those who had been blind or low-vision for a longer time and who had figured out alternate ways of getting things done. I took an action to organize this group, coming from my personal need for help and support. This motivation would drive me to other such activism in the years to come.

But it wasn't until the women's lib movement of the 1970s and '80s that I found my voice, feminist analysis, and was writing for and acting in performances with Fat Lip Readers Theater; found my anger in fat women's support groups; and came out as a lesbian, even marching down Market Street in San Francisco with my first lover while jauntily tapping my white "blind" cane. I eagerly joined a succession of women's support groups to raise our consciousness, learn assertiveness, unlearn racism and classism, and grieve with other women who had broken up with lovers or lost loved ones. There were study groups,

---

[40] I'm still not over my amazement that drivers do not know they are legally required to stop for a person using a white cane. Sadly, thousands of blind and visually impaired people are injured or killed every year because of drivers' ignorance.

coming-out groups, writing groups, and a myriad of others. If a group I needed didn't exist, I organized one. But, funny thing, it did not occur to me to find a disabled women's support group or start one. You know, it just wasn't an issue. Or so I insisted.

Why did it take me so long to figure out I had thoughts I needed to express, and feelings I needed to spill? It is called *resistance, avoidance, denial.* I didn't need to address my blindness. No big deal. Right!

Then friends urged, pestered, and nagged me to join a new support group for disabled lesbians at Operation Concern on Market Street. This was a clinic for GLBT counseling and the training of intern therapists. The group was to be facilitated by Ricki Boden, head of women's services, and Jill Lessing, who was building up her hours toward her licensing. Both were disabled too.

Reluctant, was I? Oh yes, but it turned out to be another one of those transformational experiences I've been so lucky to find in my life. The group lasted for many years, until Ricki retired, and even after that as we met for a while on our own. In that group, for the first time, I told the story of becoming blind and began to deal with the feelings over failing to get my masters and teach, of what it was really like being in the world as a blind woman. In that group, I met dear friends for life, like Dina and Melinda, and those now gone, like Silvia and June and Jean. There were Autumn and Adrienne and Ilene, and so many others over the years. Weekly, in that room, we faced our diminished capacities and grieved our losses. In that group, I found my anger at what had happened to me and felt safe enough to express it. We sobbed and railed and laughed together. There were lessons that have served me ever since. And eventually, once again, as a result of a women's support group, I was ready to take action by using my personal experiences to advocate and teach others, to become an activist in the disability rights movement.[41]

I'm proud of the work Fat Lip Readers Theater did on behalf of disability rights, as part of our mission to work against oppression and for greater accessibility. All our self-produced shows and workshops were wheelchair accessible, scent free, sign language interpreted, and provided special seating for deaf, blind, and supersized people. Outside producers were required to agree in writing to our list of such requirements before we would perform in their venues. In addition, my fellow Lippers were supportive and accommodating of me, offering ideas and understanding that enabled me to perform with my disabilities. They, of course, were able to refer to their scripts, which we all held, and read from them. I needed to memorize, as well as clip a little book light to the edge of the binder, so that I could refer to a key word now and then, to help remind me of words or blocking and choreography. When we performed on formal stages, I was afraid I would get too close to the edge and fall off—a terrifying prospect! They made sure I didn't. As a group we figured out how I could move around the stage in solos and group pieces, to be in the right place at the right time, smoothly and seemingly without effort as far as the audience could tell. I would come on stage with my white cane so as to be visible as a disabled fat woman, and then fold it under my chair and out of the way for the rest of the show.

I remember one panicky performance on stage in Santa Cruz, which was almost a disaster for me. The stage lighting was splotchy and we were constantly moving in and out of bright lights and spots of semi

---

[41] The disability rights movement began in 1970, to secure equal rights and opportunities in accessibility, accommodation, education, and employment, resulting in the passage of the Americans with Disabilities Act in 1990.

darkness. It was my worst nightmare. What vision I had (and depended on) could not quickly accommodate to changes in light. At times I didn't know where I was, let alone remember my lines. It was awful, and I felt like I had done a terrible job and let down my fellow cast members. They hugged and reassured me.

After I confronted my hearing loss, around 2002, I knew I needed a support group for the newly deafened and asked my counselor, Laura Clark, at the San Francisco Hearing Center to organize one. The group is still going on weekly under the auspices of the San Francisco Hearing and Speech Center and continues to be enormously helpful to folks with hearing loss.

I have been asked to present my story to a number of classes at San Francisco State University, on the psychosocial aspects of vision and hearing loss, to students interested in Special Ed and counseling programs. This is always enormously satisfying. After all, how often do we all get the chance to tell our life stories to eager and rapt listeners?

I was co-chair, along with Miriam Abdullah, an African American long-time activist, of "2010, A Year Celebrating the Activism of Bay Area Lesbians with Disabilities." I was recruited for this volunteer job by the directors of FABLED, ASP (Fabulous Activist Bay Area Lesbians with Disabilities, A Storytelling Project) and I am very glad I didn't know beforehand the full extent of what I was agreeing to do. It was a year of planning activities, including a major exhibit at the main branch of the San Francisco Public Library, on Larkin Street, along with concurrent events, fundraisers, writing proposals, media announcements, sample proclamations for city and state officials to sign, meetings and more meetings, and hundreds of other tasks. While I am proud of my part in this undertaking, I was ever so glad when the year was over.

My activism on behalf of disabled folks came from my experience as well as my personal needs as a partially blind and deaf woman. First, I had to deal with my issues in a supportive environment; only then could I move to take action, hopefully with others, to call for collective as well as individual accommodation, accessibility, and respect. The personal led, once again, to the political, as I'd learned in the women's liberation movement. This work was at times joyful and fulfilling and at times frustrating and hair pulling. But that's the nature of activism on behalf of a righteous cause.

What's next? My partner and I now live at The Redwoods, a senior community in Mill Valley, California. There are people here with vision loss—many from macular degeneration, and others with hearing loss— plenty of hearing aids around here. There is a monthly support group for low vision but not yet for residents with hearing loss, let alone people with dual sensory loss. Ah, another opportunity to help myself and organize something useful for others. Just you wait!

Bock's Bed and Breakfast mug offered to guests. c 1990

Feast or Famine

Tables

Written at the Old Lesbian Memoir Writing Group

I'm looking at a large rectangular table, covered with butcher paper and surrounded by twelve old lesbians, writing our memories and willing to take risks with each other as we reveal our secrets.

I'm remembering other tables:

1. Sitting in my high chair in our kitchen on Collingwood Street. There is a photo of me holding up my spoon and looking directly into the camera with a very unhappy expression. I'm scowling and my little brows are knitted tight and my forehead wrinkled. There might as well have been a pint-size black cloud over my head. I am about one year old. Years later, someone told me that my parents would put my plate or bowl on the little attached table and then take it away before I was finished. They were worried I was eating too much and needed to lose weight, at a year old! Perhaps it was my mommy who had served me my food

and my daddy who had removed it. I imagine I felt I had been a bad girl but not knowing what I had done wrong.

2. Sitting at the oval red Formica kitchen table on Willard Street, where Mom and Dad and I ate our dinners, and where every mouthful I took was watched, measured, judged by Dad and worried over by Mom. Where my table manners were criticized and where, in my anxiety, I would often knock into my milk glass, spilling it all over the table, resulting in disgust and anger from Dad about how sloppy and clumsy I was, and Mom trying to buffer between us as usual. I often left the table in tears, stomach clenched and faintly nauseous.

3. In the formal dining room of that house, there was another table for company meals. The maple dining room table, extended to its full capacity, could seat as many as eighteen. It was covered with one of what Mom called her colorful "peasant" India-print cloths, with candles and dishes and bountiful food. Animated, jovial people sat eating, talking politics, interrupting each other with excitement and impatience to make their point. There was laughter, and sometimes frustration, like when my mom couldn't convince my father to agree with her on a particular point, and would explode, "Oh Albert, be quiet!" My dad thoroughly enjoyed himself, playing devil's advocate and making comments designed to set off others at the table, stirring up the mix with an outrageous statement and a twinkle in his eye.

And there was me, mama's good little helper. I was quiet, glad that my dad's attention was not on me, listening to the discussion and what were mostly good-natured arguments. Anyway, what could I contribute that these bright, experienced adults had not already said or thought of, even if I could get a word in edgewise? Rather, I was complimented for being such a gem, busily seeing to the guests—passing platters, serving, clearing the table.

These gatherings with relatives and old family friends were among the few times I had permission not to diet. But sitting around that table was like being on display and I ate like a bird. I waited. My turn would come.

At meal's end, I insisted that I, alone, would clear the table and tidy the kitchen. I preferred no help, thank you, it would be much more efficient to do it all by myself. And I closed the kitchen door behind me.

Now my holiday feast began, nibbling to my heart's content as I cleared platters and put leftovers away.

I haven't had to do this secret eating in years but it seems to me, as I look back, that those tidbits and tastes enjoyed all by myself, away from the stares and the judgments, were particularly delectable.

Now, as I look around this table, in the community room at 190 Coleridge in San Francisco, and at all of us old lesbian feminist activists in our sixties, seventies, and eighties who have come together in 2009 to write our stories and risk the telling of them to this circle, I am so grateful for this most special table of all. Here we find the bounty and encouragement to fully partake of its delicious abundance, relishing every mouthful. Absolutely no "dieting" here!

AT ONE OF OUR memoir writing sessions, we were asked to write about broccoli, cabbage or cauliflower. My mom and her sister, my aunt Peg, each made a wonderful cabbage dish for special occasions. Mom made corned beef and cabbage, soaking and rinsing the corned beef over and over to rid it of some of the salt and then cooking it until the meat was as tender as butter and the cabbage full of the flavor of the meat and the vegetables and the broth. I never knew it was considered an Irish national dish. I just assumed it was one of my mom's peasant "Jewish" recipes!

And then there was cabbage borscht. Every year or so, our little family—Mom, Dad and me, along with a few lucky hangers-on—would be invited to a borscht feast at Aunt Peg's apartment across the street. These were special occasions, long anticipated and fully relished. Into the large pot my aunt put inexpensive beef chunks, along with tomatoes and tomato paste and water, to cook slowly, tenderizing and merging flavors with the cabbage. Eventually she would add the sugar and lemon juice to give it its signature sweet-and-sour essence. When we arrived we would be greeted to the most divine smells of cabbage borscht that had been simmering for hours on her old stove. The aroma of this peasant dish reminded us of our Russian Jewish stock, and the delectable repast soon filled our stomachs to the brim. We donned bibs to eat it, and the flavors were scrumptious. Along with the borscht were heaps of black pumpernickel bread we spread with cold sweet butter or dunked directly into the thick broth.

Those of us around her table were in heaven and always in good humor. Unlike other times when things could get tense, on these occasions there was no skimping on portion size, no dieting, no watching what and how I ate. I could eat my fill without comment from Dad. At the end of the meal—and this was part of the tradition—there were groans, a few belches, and the unzipping of pants and unbuckling of belts—sure signs of utter satisfaction.

As far as I was concerned, cabbage in slaw or stuffed with ground meat and covered with tomato sauce and baked in the oven or hidden in a casserole was to be avoided at all costs, but borscht—now, that was a different kettle of fish!

Then there was *zharkoye*, a very special Jewish way of cooking meat and vegetables, and it was my favorite thing my mom cooked. She'd lay a thick layer of chopped onion in the bottom of the large, dark blue, speckled roasting pan, then a layer of vegetables: peeled and chunked potatoes and carrots. And then in went the meat—she used this method with beef: cheap cuts of steak, stew meat, tongue, the cheapest, toughest meats were fine, even ox tails. She covered the roaster with its lid and cooked at a low temperature, maybe 300 degrees for three hours, I think. She never added liquid, to everyone's amazement. It came out browned and moist and falling-apart tender and with wonderful, natural gravy.

She called this a peasant form of cooking, and this was said with pride. It was shtetl cooking. It was poor folk's cooking. The aroma as it cooked was unforgettable.

I no longer eat red meat, but still that glorious taste is on my tongue memory.

Thanksgiving Highs and Lows

The ideal

Big table filled with friends and family
    Wonderful food

Lots of talk and everyone at once.

Feeling part of a community, connection secure, included, cherished

High: Childhood Memories

Our dining room table stretched out to the max, the "efficient" Susan in the middle (there will be none of that sexist "lazy Susan" business) reachable only by a few within arm's stretch. The food was bountiful and invitingly aromatic. The mood was ebullient from folks joyful to be with one another. The conversation lively and spiced with fast repartee and hilarious witticisms. This was our family of friends.

Low: Amherst

Amherst was so pretty in the late autumn. The brilliant leaves were mostly gracing the ground, in various stages of brittle decay and fun to walk amongst, and the sun was a slanty winter orb, the chill in the air beckoning the coming of the cold.

It seemed, to this twenty-three-year-old grad student experiencing her first New England fall season, that what she saw and smelled and felt led her to an anticipation of something wondrous—her first winter.

She lived two blocks from campus in a small apartment, which had been jerry-rigged from the attic of an original carriage house at the rear of a property on Sunset Avenue. Downstairs from her lived Miss Irene and Dr. Charlotte, two old women—one a former public health nurse, the other a retired osteopath. They were life partners and owned the house.

She knew nobody in Amherst and as a shy and self-conscious new grad student in the predominantly male history department of the University of Massachusetts, she had not made friends and so received no invitations for Thanksgiving. When Miss Irene and Dr. Charlotte invited her downstairs for the holiday dinner she gave her regrets since she, of course, had other plans with friends and colleagues. She considered their invitation a "charity" offer and would have felt pathetic and embarrassed if she had accepted.

So she prepared for Thanksgiving by buying some ready-made turkey sandwiches and other portable eatables and drinkables easy to consume. About the time she thought appropriate, she opened and closed the front door loudly. She had already arranged the food on the twin bed under the eaves, along with a number of good books to read.

She didn't get off that bed for hours, careful not to drink too much.

Eventually she tiptoed to the front door, careful to avoid any squeaky floorboards, vigorously opened and closed the door, and walked with purposeful firm steps through the living room, making a beeline for the bathroom.

High: with Sally

These were the years Sally and I organized Thanksgiving together at my house on Willard Street. Lots of people, lots of food, lots of laughter, lots of singing. Lots of hilarity, like the time when Tony was taking the turkey out of the oven and it slid off the platter onto the floor, and the year we all rewrote the "Twelve Days of Christmas" to "The Twelve Gifts My Lover Gave to Me," including five latex gloves and three ben-wa balls! Silvia's "days" were the funniest and most lewd.

Lows:

The years I went out to dinner with one or two friends, wanting to be part of a big family group. Always counting how many there were sitting together at other tables, envious, embarrassed. No family—no brothers or sisters with spouses and fretful kids, no grandparents, no boring uncles or obnoxious cousins, no automatic family for obligatory holiday meals. No group of close friends with whom to share the holiday, as had my parents.

Neither Very High nor Very Low:

Suzanne and I have been together as partners since 2000, and, as such, took for granted we would spend holidays together. She did not have the "baggage" I did. No yearning for family or a large group of boisterous friends with whom to sup and laugh. She was estranged from her family, had no fond memories of childhood feasts, and anyway preferred to be with just a few people at a time, in general. She did not understand but acknowledged my annual grief and anxiety as Thanksgiving approached and no invitations were forthcoming.

As time has passed, however, my yearly angst has lessened and I am increasingly content, or perhaps resigned, to our intimate celebrations. Sometimes we dine out at a lovely special restaurant and at times we prepare the traditional fare at home. We actually prefer the latter so that we have the pleasure of leftovers for days.

Last year we moved to The Redwoods in Mill Valley. This is a progressive senior community with a dining room. We cook our own food, but last November, as the day approached, we decided to join the crowd in the dining room. We sat at a table for two but were surrounded by other tables filled with fellow residents and their families eating and chatting away. I did not feel too embarrassed or self-conscious and enjoyed the meal and the lovely wine. We had even bought a turkey breast and all the trimmings, which we consumed the following days with "relish."

The ideal remains, but perhaps I am finally old enough to know that the number of people with whom I spend the holiday is not a reflection of my likeability, nor does it reinforce my old, very old, loneliness. I know I have wonderful friends and I am loved. At least this is true most of the time.

Holiday Chezerei ("Junk Food" in Yiddish)
Written for Fat Lip Readers Theater

I was raised in a secular Jewish household. The memory of my most favorite holiday family meal is vivid. Dad and I would go off together to our favorite Jewish deli and bakery on McAllister Street, and later on Noriega, and bring back this feast. We inhaled it with pleasure, each of the three of us happy in our annual ritual celebration.

Chezerei: Bagels, either water or egg only—*not*, God-forbid,
cinnamon or blueberry
Poppyseed rolls

> Lox
>
> Smoked codfish
>
> Cottage cheese and sour cream
>
> Pastrami
>
> Chicago-style salami
>
> Philadelphia Cream Cheese
>
> Cheese-filled pastries
>
> Time: Brunch
>
> Date: Every Dec. 25th, after presents.
>
> (Assimilated? *Nah!*)

We loved ice cream in my family. Mother's favorite was Rocky Road; my dad's was Maple Nut. I wasn't allowed any flavor of ice cream. All I was allowed was ice milk. Ice milk was not ice cream, was not low-fat ice cream, was not, I believe, even *non*-fat ice cream. It came in a frozen brick and, because I could rarely even have that, I could easily eat the whole carton at once. Sometimes I would sneak their cartons, skimming off the top, and if by mistake I went too far into the carton and knew they would notice, I would use my allowance money to rush out and buy a duplicate carton, eating down to the level where they had left it and finishing the original one. It was delicious and scary and humiliating.

About fifteen years ago I decided to have a "make your own sundae" birthday party. I had a table full of ice cream flavors (*not* ice milk), plus syrups, bananas, toppings, sprinkles, nuts—the works. Friends loved it, and loved the permission to enjoy it all. They made some of the most creative and colorful concoctions. What fun!

I made a big poster proclaiming "Do It Yourself Sundays." It was only days later that a friend told me I had misspelled "sundae." Correct spelling has never been my forte and I remain an unrepentant "creative" speller to this day. Needless to say, however, when I learned of my very public display of faux spelling, I had egg on my face.

The memoir-writing prompt at group one week was to "Teach me something." Smoothies came to mind.

Smoothies

It is my nightly treat and so yummy. Choose various fresh fruits you like: I frequently use cantaloupes or honeydew melon, blueberries, strawberries in season, pineapple or grapes and bananas. Use a large plastic container and start cutting up and dumping in the fruit, except for the banana. Mix well and place in fridge. Later, take some of the mixture and put into a blender and add a fresh banana. Add a little water to get things going and turn on at first or second speed. This will chop and mix the fruit roughly. In a minute or two, when all is churning around in there, change speeds to high blend. Put mixture in fridge for at least four hours to thicken. I generally let it be overnight. When ready for your smoothie, take out of fridge and blend a second. Enjoy!

This much-anticipated evening ritual started during my Weight Watcher years in Berkeley. Fruit was "legal" and it came as close as possible to ice cream.

Why give this treat up just because I got wise and stopped the dieting-binging roller coaster? After all, good is good!

And speaking of Weight Watchers: We were Karen—a hippie mom, and Sheryl, and Harriet—a UC doctoral candidate in experimental psychology, and Tom and Dick—a gay couple, and Julie, and me, and perhaps one or two others I've forgotten. We met at the weekly Weight Watchers meeting held in Berkeley at the Motor Inn on University. I was twenty-one, having just graduated from the University of Oregon, and living in my first apartment, on Euclid, a block from campus. I worked as a clerk typist at the UC Inventory Department. What else, after all, can you do with a BA in English?

This was 1968. We started going out together for coffee after the meetings. We enjoyed being in each other's company. We gathered for fabulous, raucous, and delicious parties—mostly at Karen's house in the Berkeley flats. We ate elaborate "legal" concoctions like mock chocolate cake and faux mashed potatoes (smashed cauliflower.) We drank wine and beer and smoked pot. (I confessed at one of these parties that I had never smoked anything and did not know how to inhale. They taught me on a cigarette so that I could—and did—try pot with them all. Fortunately smoking never did get its hooks into me.)

We all went together to see Jean Nidetch, the founder of Weight Watchers, at the Masonic Auditorium. She was our guru. We applauded heartily when any of us lost weight and commiserated when we did not or were stuck on a plateau.

We became buddies and saw each other frequently as a group as well as in twos and threes. Harriet invited me over to her and her husband Art's apartment for dinner and to fix me up with a fellow grad student, male. She thought we might hit it off. It was awkward and we did not.

This was a gang to laugh with, risk with, relax with, eat our fill with, and get support from. It was what I had always wanted, envied others for, and treasured.

In 1970, I went away to Massachusetts for grad school, losing touch eventually with most of them. Karen adored my parents and kept up with them and me for a few years. I exchanged annual cards with her and with Harriet. Sheryl and I remained close friends over many years, until she killed herself after she became extremely ill. She and I had been feminist activists, sharing our excitement and commitment to that movement from the early 1970s.

This group could never be duplicated again for one important reason. I stopped dieting in 1975. My new gang then became feminist fat women struggling with patriarchy and the indoctrination of women to loathe their bodies, of any size. The laughter was there and the tears and the food and the closeness. There was also anger and our shared drive to change how women felt about themselves and the system that perpetuated their self-hatred and discrimination.

Now, my "gang" days seem to be over. I have dear friends with whom I play and enjoy life but no girl gang to take on the world. I miss that.

Dairy-a-No-No

Written at the Old Lesbian Memoir Writing Group

You can have your chocolate boutiques and your coffee galleries, although those fragrances do entice.

I can easily walk past the zesty hamburger joint or even the cholesterol-enhancing odors of Kentucky Fried Chicken.

I do love the smell of fresh mown grass and eucalyptus trees expressing their pungency.

But if I knew I was to be dead in a day, I would make a beeline to Say Cheese or even the cheese department of some upscale grocery like Molly Stone's. I would arrange for myself to be locked in after closing hours to indulge, to savor, to gorge, and to hell with the digestive and LDL consequences.

First taste: smoked Gouda on rye, like I found in the street cheese market in Amsterdam—several blocks of nothing but stalls offering this nation's best, including a goat cheese from what I can only assume were the happiest goats on earth!

What then? A bit of Havarti on a chewy grainy cracker. In our Oregon days, my dear friend, Joanne, introduced me to this delectable comestible, both sharing a Finnish heritage.

I'd follow with a smelly Camembert or creamy Brie—what the hell, both—with a fresh baguette.

Next, sample some fondue—heretofore untried due to the diabolical early discovery of lactose intolerance.[42]

After several sips of a nice, dry imported water with a twist of lemon to cleanse the palette: some Stilton from a ceramic pot like the one I purchased in the food court at Harrods of London just before dashing to catch my plane home to San Francisco. One proud Brit told me that their cheese was "tip-top" due to the superiority of the English "grawss." Hang the extra baggage charge, I'll take a dozen!

---

[42] I intended to throw caution out the window and have, for my 70th birthday party, a "cheese blowout" with all my friends. On the tables, heavily laden with rounds and wedges with crackers and toast points, I planned to have decorative bowls filled with Lactaid!

Then time for a fruit course: a cold crisp Pippin apple with slices of cheddar—not the orange-color-added, mass-produced stuff, but a natural white cheddar from the Sonoma Cheese Factory on the plaza.

And now for nostalgia: a grilled cheese sandwich—possibly a Monterey jack dotted with caraway seeds, and using a long-handled, metal-clamped sandwich press just like the one my mom held over the gas flame on our O'Keefe and Merritt stove burner and flipping it over at just the right time, producing a crispy buttery melted wonder.

What then?

I'd go on a sniffing spree from one hunk and wheel to another, and when a bouquet caught my fancy I'd have a nibble or two or three.

Then off to the section marked "Cheeses Imported from the Lower East Side of New York," where I will find here a lovely aromatic and fresh mozzarella from the little mozzarella factory Sally took me to as we toured the culinary delights of her old neighborhood, introducing me to the unpretentious shop and the family who had been there plying their craft for generations. They smoked the cheese in a trashcan on the sidewalk, making it impossible to pass by with indifference. No pizza has ever been adorned with mozzarella like this.

As my night of ecstasy and indulgence ends in the dawning day, I will take leave of my cheese heaven, and return queasily but happily to the hospice, ready at last.

10

Ageing Matters

LET'S START WITH the body, right off the bat. The following pieces were written between 1989 and 2013 for Fat Lip Readers Theater, Mother-Tongue Feminist Theater Collective, and the Old Lesbian Memoir Writing group, as indicated. I've arranged them chronologically to show my thinking as I aged from forty-four to sixty-eight years.

Business Letter

(Fat Lip Readers Theater, January 1989)
To: My Complexion
From: The Body Company, Ltd.
Re: A Progress Report

Dear Madam;

In reviewing your current position vis-à-vis the total picture, I must make the following points:
1. We concur that you...are indeed aging, and while there are signs of wear and tear, your model, #1945, has by no means

outlasted its usefulness. We recommend reevaluation in twenty to thirty years.

2. Your hue remains the peaches and cream option originally selected for you. As I have told you for years, you will not be provided with an olive tint. Please do not request this again.

3. Your concerns regarding the elasticity of your outer layer are unfounded. It will expand and contract as needed, no matter how much is below the surface and how many chins appear. This is a special feature of this model.

4. Your model does come with an occasional pimple for variety and general facial interest. We are quite proud of this design feature.

5. I'm afraid we cannot promise you any significant degree of wrinkles soon. Our Research and Development Department informs me that in your body model, a generous supply of estrogen will not provide the wrinkle quotient you requested. You will, however, discover a few character lines as time develops. We hope this will suffice, even though you will not have the beautifully wrinkled and therefore extremely interesting face of your friend Miriam. She has an earlier model.

In conclusion, we are gratified that you are generally pleased and hope that you will adjust to those minor disappointments you have encountered with your model.

Yours very truly,
The Body Company, Ltd.

Aging Schmaging

(Written for MotherTongue Feminist Theater Collective, April 2000)

All right, I've been doing this aging business for almost fifty-five
years, and I've got a few things to get off my chest.

Forgetting a word? Please! Absolutely brilliant thoughts travel at
an irretrievable speed in and out of my brain.

I hate the first time some young twit selling movie tickets asked me
if I wanted "senior" or "regular."

And I hate it that I was fool enough to say regular.

Another thing, whose body is this? Spots, skin tags, creeping grey,
complaining joints, and so much stiffness I should be a mummy.

And what about those young ones with their so-cool piercings and
tattoos who look at me and can't see me for the rebel I am?

To all these insults, affronts, and plagues, I say "Feh" and "Feh"
again. And if you think I am going to take them lying down...

Oy vey, maybe now and then.

Rosie and Me

(Written for MotherTongue Feminist Theater Collective, April 2000)

How did it happen? I don't get it.

Just a minute ago we were in our mid-forties, full of energy,
endurance, a couple of grey hairs, a few midlife crises, but
nothing major.

Blink and it is years later

Me: hard of hearing in one ear — "whadjasay?"

You: an "overactive bladder," as the TV commercial puts it
Me: selective body parts painfully complaining
You: kidney disease that could kill you in a flash
Me: ecstasy is an afternoon nap
You: have to pause and sit every ten minutes on our walks
Both of us more salt than pepper
You: Seventy-seven
Me: Fifty-four

On the other hand, we are still gorgeous, frisky,
Enjoy a good meal and love to cuddle up together,
And if we're lucky, there's much more to come.
Rosie, my girl, my little Scottie dog.

I'm Waiting

(Written for MotherTongue Feminist Theater Collective, April 2000)

I've been told by a number of women past menopause how great they feel—renewed vigor, increased vitality, free from old limitations and concerns, a time of balance and discovery.

I'm *waaaaaaaiiiiiii*—ting!

At Sixty-Five

(Written in the Old Lesbian Memoir Writing Group, 2010)

Sixty-five and:
Smiling and thriving

Stumbling and fumbling

Ticking and clicking

Tripping and slipping

Dancing and prancing

Walking and balking

Falling and bawling

Thinking and sinking

Happy and sappy

Sad and mad

Working and shirking

Right on target and missing by a mile

Cruising and bruising

On top with a mop

Down under with a flop

Striving and thriving

Bumbling and tumbling

Ready and steady

Hiding and biding

In the pink and in the drink

Confused and bemused

Fearful and tearful

Knowing and crowing

Puzzled and muzzled

Proud and loud

Despairing and caring

Moody and broody

In pain and in vain

Controlling and strolling

Slouchy and grouchy
Decisive all knowing
    and wondering what to do
Filling in the holes
    and covering the cracks
Worrying and scurrying
Plannin' and planning
Settin' my limits
    and edging cross the lines
Bumpin' and stumpin'
Glowin' and growin'

At Sixty-five!

And then there are the hands. I am most certainly no Dorian Grey, with my portrait in the attic growing gnarled and wizened with age while my corporeal being downstairs remains youthful and vigorous. Oh yes, the hands.

I wrote about my hands in two exercises for the Old Lesbian Memoir Writing Group. Exercise 1: *Choose a body part; describe it in detail, and then write about your feelings about it.* Exercise 2: *Choose one sentence from what you've written and expand upon it.*

1) I don't recognize them; although they are still strong, grasp well, can twist off lids (with the help of a tap or two), they can cup Suzanne's face and participate in a bear hug—no problem.

But whose hands are they? Their skin is dry and loose on the back, the veins are prominent and spidering across the surface, the fingernails are brittle, cracking and breaking easily—an emery board must always be nearby. There is a silver ring on the middle finger of each hand and the fingers swell frequently, making it impossible to remove the rings.

For most of my life, I refused to wear any ring, ashamed of my fat, nail-bitten fingers. Eventually, it was the loving encouragement of two women who got me to swallow hard and try it out, one ring at a time.

I retain one fingernail on each hand for biting and often the skin around them is red and painful, when I've gone too far.

I can't see the actual color of my hands. I suppose they are beige. Perhaps they are spotted. The skin is so thin and easy to injure.

I don't know if my hands are very wrinkled, or if they look like those of my parents when they reached sixty-seven. I wish I did.

I'm happy that my knuckles are not swollen with arthritis and they are not painful. There is a very nice acupuncture spot on the back between thumb and index finger to help alleviate pain in the rest of my body.

All in all, I'm pleased with their usefulness and have few complaints. It's just that, whose hands are these, anyway?

2) Rings

I refused to wear rings for fifty years—my hands were fat, my nails bitten past the quick. My hands were to be hidden, not embellished and drawing attention.

The ring now on the middle finger of my right hand is a plain silver band. Knowing my "hang-up," a lover of mine one day took me to a ring stand on Market Street near the Embarcadero. There, the stall owner had coins—pennies and dimes to quarters. He measured my finger, chose a quarter with 1945 on it, my birth year, and somehow, with a nifty machine, transformed it into a ring—my birthday ring.

On my left middle finger I have a silver band with lovely braided patterns. Suzanne and I each acquired one for our tenth anniversary, in 2010, when we knew "it would last a while." But what finger to put it on? *Not* the "ring finger on the left hand"— the rebel in me would not be so conventional. We were not married—I didn't believe in marriage, faux or otherwise. And yet, not on my pinky or thumb—those wouldn't do.

That left two fingers—a ring on the index might get in the way. Somehow, wearing it on my middle finger is just right— meaningful, displaying the central strong importance of the relationship it signifies, but not marriage. Ah, there are principles, and then there are feelings!

And then there are the aging arms to consider, as I did in a piece written at the Old Lesbian Memoir Writing Group in 2013.

Grandma Berta's Arms

I remember my grandmother's arms. I was young and visited her weekly with my mom at the Jewish old folks' home on Mission and Silver Avenue in San Francisco. I didn't like going there because the smells were strange and, as we walked down the halls or in the gardens, old people would murmur comments and want to touch me.

My grandma's arms were a fascination. They were thin and spotted; the skin hung loose off her bones and there were so many lines and wrinkles. The skin felt like leather to touch, not like the plump soft arms of my mom's, which felt so nice when they went around me.

Now, at the age of sixty-eight, I look at my arms in amazement and with some curiosity, as if they did not belong to me. I feel the leathery skin as it loosely moves and wonder at all the spots on my forearms—some brown and some purple—that arrive dark and variously shaped and fade in time, only to return anew.

How did this happen?

This next piece was written for MotherTongue Feminist Theater Collective by my dear friend Susan Miller, who has left us. I offer the following to the younger ones, specifically the one who recently said she planned to "age gracefully" (as if she has a choice). I like the way my friend Dina puts it. She intends to simply "age."

To Those Who Babble Pollyanna Nonsense about the "Golden Years"

My hair is thinning
My sight is dimming
My hearing's failing

I'm always ailing.
You call this "golden"?

My teeth are going
My gait is slowing
My toes are curling
My head is whirling.
You call this "golden"?

My nose ain't smelling
My ankles are swelling
My knees are creaking
My bladder's leaking.
Hey, get real!

My hair color is extinct
My pubic area jinxed
I'm finally outta the kitchen
But still perpetually bitchin'.
On the other hand

My acts are daring
My anger is flaring
It's justice I'm seeking
For the truths I'm speaking.

Enough about the aging body! Let's move to ageism. That is to say, discrimination against old people, assumptions about us, and being made "invisible." We are not seen as intelligent or astute people worthy of attention, especially when we need some accommodation in order to be part of the conversation. In the following exercise for MotherTongue Feminist Theater Collective, I had fun coming up with smart-aleck retorts to stupid comments and questions, and some of which I used later.

Ageism Comebacks

A twenty- or thirty-something saying: "Oh I just can't think of it, I'm having a senior moment."

Comeback: "No, you're having a junior moment."

A person of any age saying: "Oh you're kidding, you don't look sixty-five."

Comeback: "Oh, I look seventy-five?"

A person: "You sure look good for _____."

Comeback: "Are you saying I am maturing well?"

Persons in their eighties, nineties or 100 saying: "You're only sixty-nine! You're such a baby."

Comeback: "I'm aging as fast as I can!"

I wrote the following piece about my aunt's aging for Fat Lip Readers Theater in January 1993.

Never Too Old: Aunt Peg

She's eighty-three, my favorite aunt—an activist, organizer, writer all her life for causes of peace and justice. Short and heavy like the other females in her family, she struggled always with self-hatred about her body size. Dieted, gained, dieted, gained, supportive of me yet skeptical about fat liberation politics—one movement from which she remained aloof.

And then her worst fears realized—a stroke leaving her partially paralyzed and speechless but with her mind intact. Enraged, despairing, disinterested in eating, in living, she lost weight, got little for the first time in her life.

We managed to get her into the Jewish old folks home—a victory—with an exemplary reputation for excellent comprehensive care, a lovely facility, activities, and stimulation. She began to eat, signs of life.

A year later she is given an ultimatum by the staff: if she outgrows her wheelchair, they will not find a larger one. Furthermore, unless she diets and loses weight they will refuse to get her out of bed at all.

So a threat—plain and simple: either stop eating or be punished by confinement and imprisonment.

She's eighty-three. It never ends.

I have had the very good fortune of following along in the footsteps of older feminist activists who founded a number of groups to address their issues as old women, as well as ageism in the women's community and in the wider population. I stood by, impressed, as they founded

Women Over 40, which morphed into Options for Women Over 40. I listened to their anger about how they were treated as middle-aged and old women, and watched as they organized newsletters and magazines like *Broomstick* to provide a forum for their voices. I did not relate to their experiences yet but tried to be a good ally.

And then it happened! With time, I too joined their ranks and took it personally. They founded OLOC—Old Lesbians Organizing for Change, and I joined up, learning from these older teachers. These women who had, for the most part, been activists all their lives for myriad causes and now, on behalf of old women, were fiery, angry, eloquent, articulate, and creative.

My friend Tita, on the national board of OLOC, organized WOW here in San Francisco. This stood for Wild Old Women, and for the past several years, they gather weekly at the Bank of America on Mission Street to picket and protest as part of the Occupy Movement. Tita, sadly, has left us, but this demonstration has continued. Women with their walkers and, at times, their oxygen supply, along with folding chairs and signs, come together to chant and sing their songs with vigor and purpose.

In the summer of 2014, I attended my first OLOC national gathering, in Oakland. It was bliss to be in a hotel filled with gorgeous old lesbians attending workshops, entertained and enlightened by our generation of lesbian-feminist writer luminaries who had aged right along with us, like Dorothy Allison, Christos, Cherrie Moraga, Jewelle Gomez, Elana Dykewomon, and others. We danced up a storm, grieved over our lost ones at a memorial, and kibitzed constantly. I ran into women I hadn't seen in years and lo and behold we were grey or white headed, wrinkled to various degrees, with one or another mobility aid, and still as enthusiastic as ever about agitating for change. It was a total high, and was hard to leave and reenter the "other" world after four days immersed in this old lesbian nation. I am truly the benefactor of the women who came before me, establishing what they needed and, by so doing, offering such a rich community to younger women as we came of age.

The year 2013 was a momentous one for my partner, Suzanne, and me. I knew I was finally ready to sell my family home on Willard Street when I found myself cringing at yet another old house repair crisis and dreading the next unknown one, certain to come. I wanted to be rid of the burden and responsibility of caring for this wonderful 108-year-old house and its renter occupants. Also, I wanted us to be in a senior community with "services" to help us cope when either of us was infirm or in a health crisis. We needed built-in support, as I saw it. It was obvious when Suzanne had a stroke and then a hip replacement and I had a knee replaced that we had been stretched beyond our limits as caretakers.

So we started looking around for such a community, touring several in San Francisco, which was my first choice. Suzanne preferred a more rural or countrified setting closer to nature, but we were open to whatever. One facility we looked at in San Francisco was swiftly removed from the list after a tour. I didn't get a good feeling from walking the halls or looking at the common areas, and then I knew all was lost when we asked if they offered a bus for excursions. The director replied, "Oh yes. We take our residents shopping and to a casino in Marin County!" We thought she hadn't understood us so we clarified: "What about museums, concerts, parks etc.?" She just looked at us, mystified.

Then we found The Redwoods in Mill Valley, just over the Golden Gate Bridge. In September, Suzanne trail-blazed for us and moved into this senior community. I remained on Willard Street, preparing the house for sale and arranging for things to be donated, consigned, tossed, or taken with me. I went through an arduous and painful negotiation with my two tenant-friends regarding what they needed in order to move out with a two-month notice. It was a grueling, intense two months that was physically and emotionally exhausting. I moved and joined Suzanne on October 25, and the house went on the market two days later. As I left my home for the last time, riding in a car down the hill, I sobbed and knew I would not go back ever for another look.

Horrified at the prospect of a new owner tearing down my home and building a mega-mansion, I told my realtor that I would not sell to a developer, wanting a new owner to love and care for the house as had my parents for twenty-five years and I for thirty-three years. The new owner, a woman, is a dentist and, as I was told, had been looking for months; when she first walked in the house, she fell in love with its warm, redwood paneled walls, curving staircase, and hardwood mahogany inlaid floors. Oh, and the views of course! It was a fit for both of us.

Suzanne has thrived at The Redwoods, where she immediately plunged into writing groups, play reading and poetry reading groups, and even an elite poet's writing circle. In these she has become known and appreciated and made new friends. Because we are located on flat terrain next to a marsh and bird sanctuary, she enjoys walking our dog, Louise, three times a day in all this beauty. On the Willard Street steep hill, she had been isolated and reclusive and very unhappy.

The Redwoods is a unique community and turned out to be the right choice for us. There already were other lesbians here, and being out and ourselves as a couple was absolutely no issue. As a matter of fact, the nine other lesbian residents had a welcome party for us soon after we moved in. In addition, many of the folks living here are politically progressive, and many are long time activists. So politics also was not an issue. There is a very active chapter of Seniors for Peace and a weekly peace demonstration at our intersection, complete with chairs set up by the staff, ice water on hot days, song books, signs, and cars honking in solidarity!

And yet how would I find my niche here? I could not go to the coffee or wine socials due to the noise and my inability to hear in crowds. I could not read plays or poetry aloud as did Suzanne in her groups, due to my blindness. As a result I felt unknown and a bit isolated away from my San Francisco activities and friends. What to do?

And then an idea: What about organizing something for Red Diaper Babies here? I knew there was at least one other, because two doors down the corridor I met Mary, an RDB and my age. How lucky was that! So, organizing juices flowing once again, I decided to organize four gatherings. The first would be to share our individual legacies from parents or other older family members. The second was to discuss what we did with that legacy in our own lives. The third came about because those who were not Red Diaper Babies started asking to come and just listen in. So the third meeting was for RDBs and "fellow travelers," who also had led activist lives but without the advantage of our radical legacies. The fourth meeting would be a sing-along in the garden, with all the old wonderful Wobbly, labor, and movement songs. I booked the rooms, made a flyer, and hoped I would meet people and find connection here.

Boy, did I get known fast! One day I was walking along the hall in front of the dining room and a guy with his walker bellowed as we crossed paths, "How's the red babies today?" I boomed back, "Just great."

To my delight there were a dozen or so other RDBs who attended the events, and told some wonderful stories. There was not the instant familiarity I had expected, due to the fact that these folks were in their late seventies, eighties, and nineties—and even one man aged 102. They grew up in times different from mine and thus had very different experiences. I was fascinated, if a little disappointed, by the fact that there was not the instant identification I had expected.

One of the RDB residents was Ronnie Gilbert, a member of The Weavers[43] and, years later, a beloved feminist folk singer on her own. The last get-together I planned, the sing-along, was open to friends and family as well, and we attracted a nice crowd in the garden. Ronnie sang two songs from the Spanish Civil War, and I just cried with gratitude and wonder. I invited my friend Sally to come with her guitar, and she and I had worked on songbooks, which I had copied for one and all. We ended with "The Internationale," which was sung in English and French since two people there had learned it while living in France. It was beautiful. My dear friends Nadine and Pam also joined us and I think they were as moved and joyful as I was.

---

[43] A folk music group which included Pete Seeger and was extremely popular in the late 1940s, '50s, and '60s, and which was blacklisted during the McCarthy period for their left-wing politics.

Red Diaper Babies
(Pink, too)
UNITE!

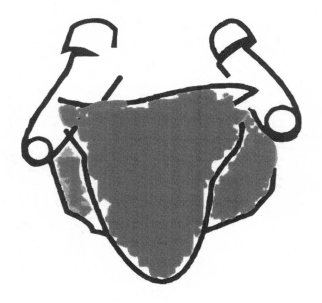

Or... Let's just get together to schmooze,
talk of the "good ol" and "bad ol" days,
and perhaps sing a tune or two.

Interested? Call Laura (13210)
I'll book the room and the time.

AVANTI!

In the fall of 2014, I again was thinking how I might become further active in this community, using the skills and experience I had to offer. What about a newcomers support group, which I could facilitate? Once again, it would be a way to be involved, doing service and feeling more connected.

Each new resident is assigned a buddy to help in orienting to living here, but many have problems with adjusting and feel overwhelmed for a while. With my background in and fervent commitment to the usefulness of support groups, this was a natural for me. I presented the idea to the social workers, who then discussed it with management. In early 2015, the group began, co-facilitated by me and another resident. Its purpose is multi-fold: to introduce new residents to each other and provide a roster so that they can call one another; to provide a forum to air issues and challenges they're facing as newcomers and get support and problem-solving ideas, if possible; and to assist in their integrating with the larger community. Also, as a result of this group, we've identified the need for new policies and programs. For example, one newcomer suggested a weekly "pop-up pub" every Sunday afternoon for folks to gather in the library with their libations for sipping and chatting in a relaxed setting.

Several months ago, one of "my" RDBs, Naomi, asked me if I, too, was disturbed about how white we are here at The Redwoods. After living in urban San Francisco my entire life, with its multiracial, multicultural richness, it quickly became obvious that living in Marin County, and Mill Valley in particular, felt foreign to me. Besides being so suburban, it is, with a few exceptions, very white. On the other hand, the staff working here at The Redwoods is primarily of color.

So Naomi and I decided to do a little research and then plan a diversity conversation and discussion group here. To this end, in March of 2015, we spoke with the chief operations officer, the marketing director, and the admissions director, who is the only African American on the management staff, to inform them of our intentions and to gather information. Soon thereafter we had our first residents' meeting, and the meetings and discussions still continue. We have had anywhere from ten to fifteen attend our meetings. Naomi and I arrange for the rooms, do the flyers, and facilitate the meetings. Several residents are now volunteering to take specific steps to reach out to local communities of color. I think the vast majority of residents support increased racial and ethnic diversity but are pessimistic about making it happen or just don't have the energy or physical ability to actively pursue it at this time in their lives.

How did I become a part of this community? By organizing, organizing, organizing, of course. From personal need to collective action toward social change. It worked for my grandparents, for my parents and other family members, and it works for me too!

Revolting
Written for the Old Lesbians Memoir Writing Group

If you think old women are revolting...
    We are!

But, lest you think my entire pleasure in life is rabble-rousing, here's a piece I wrote in the Old Lesbian Memoir Writing Group.

Bingeing on Books

What I Can't Live Without

I can't do without books to read—lots and lots of every genre, of all lengths, and of many weights, to please me with amazing writing, to amuse me with irony and satire, to distract me from the dailies, to inform me about lives and experiences foreign to me, to stimulate me to analyze what I did and didn't like in each, to bring me to anger and disgust and wonder and pleasure; to feed me, to remind me, to console me, to entertain me. I'm even filling in the holes in my Swiss cheese of books read, authors like Proust and Grass and Collette, and classics I had put aside for some future time in my life. This is it!

And there must be lots of books waiting in the queue, downloaded, all ready for the plucking; memoirs, novels, histories, biographies, tomes and a bit of fluff ready for whatever mood needs/requires attention with a good read.

I keep an index card for each author I read with the books listed below and each book rated from minus to blank to plus to checkmark to check plus to star.

Super organized, I am. Is this a surprise, by now? But can I remember days later what the book was about? Rarely! That's OK. My joy is in the present, reading, bingeing on books.

In the past, it has been to my frustration and sadness that joining a book club did not seem to work for me. The books chosen were rarely available on audio format or, if they were, it would take too long for me to receive them from the library service for the blind in time to participate in the discussion. Until now. At The Redwoods, where a number of residents have vision loss, the book club only chooses books that are readily available in formats we all can read. What a joy to discuss a book with others who are as passionate as I am about the written word.

Oh yes—there's also love, my partner, friends, my animals, luscious foods, and swimming. What's more, in November 2014, I started two huge projects dear to my heart. For eleven months I went into San Francisco once a week to process my papers, with the help of readers, at the San Francisco GLBT Historical Society. The pleasure of helping to preserve history is, once again, immense, and what made it even more gratifying was that I was preserving my own history as well as the history of the "the second wave" of the Women's Liberation Movement in the Bay Area.

Also in November of 2014, I began a second, even more daunting, project: writing my memoir, using as its skeleton all my writings from the Fat Lip Readers Theater, MotherTongue Feminist Theater Collective, the Old Lesbians Memoir Writing Group, and several other sources. I didn't know how to do it, and felt overwhelmed by the prospect. Flying by the seat of my pants, little step by little step, I spent months writing, organizing, thinking, planning, revising, and revising. I am astounded and proud, with my limitations as a blind person, to have figured out ways to create this book. Don't think I'm some "super-crip"—I could not have done it without the constant and crucial help of my sighted assistant, Peg Murphy.

With the completion of my archives and this memoir, I will have completed what was on my "bucket list." What then?

Perhaps I shall add new life goals to my bucket. Perhaps not.

It's time to move right along to the sexy topic of death and dying—the loss of dear ones, and eventually my own. I wrote the following list for my Old Lesbian Memoir Writing group.

Losses Connected with Getting Old

1. Eyesight
2. Hearing
3. Dear ones
4. Vigor
5. Fears
6. My reluctance to speak up
7. Temper
8. Inhibitions
9. Beloved dogs: Rosie, Bailey, and Louise
10. Words
11. Time
12. Ground
13. Flexibility
14. Spontaneity
15. Contact with beloved old communities
16. Demonstrating in the streets at moment's notice
17. Shyness
18. Going out with friends to noisy venues
19. Easily walking around Stow Lake, maybe twice.
20. The color of my hair
21. Trips to Sharp Park.

In the early 1980s, I discovered a beach community in Pacifica, just south of San Francisco. Sharp Park became my twice-annual retreat hideaway where, armed with scrumptious food and good reads to listen to, I stayed at a little hotel for three to four days at a time. I'd spend hours and hours walking the promenade and occasionally across the sand, to think, to write, to feel. Inevitably, I'd arrive stressed, grieving, anxious, and very needy. I would find solitude, occasional brief conversations with friendly strangers, and tears needing to come forth. At one particular spot, I pictured my dead dear ones. Sobbing and asking them for help, I could see their faces and hear their voices! Remarkably, at the close of these retreats, I would leave refreshed, renewed, calm, and acknowledging the bounty in my life. It seemed miraculous, each and every time, to this confirmed, non-spiritual atheist.

Now, living in Mill Valley, Sharp Park feels just too far from the security of home. Now, in my early seventies, the fears and the "what ifs," as well as being less sturdy and independent, find me more cautious and I have sorrowfully said goodbye to those wonderful interludes.

For decades, it seems, I have had to say goodbye to loved ones. There were sister-friends who died way too soon. And of course there were my dad, my mother, and Maggie; I was with each of them as they lived their last days and as they died. Each experience was so different.

Memory of a Smell
Written at the Old Lesbian Memoir Writing Group

The smell of my mother dying is one I don't want to remember. It is the smell of urine, catheter bag and tubing, of bedsores, of pain, of fear. It is the smell of the orange, which was used by the visiting nurse to teach me how to give injections of morphine to my mom. It is the smell of her decaying skin, her mouth. It is the smell of her dying on this ultra-hot day and her body lying in bed for the five hours it took for our family doctor to come and pronounce her dead. It was the smell of our grief, our relief, our disbelief.

Too painful to remember.

In 1977, my mother, Mini Karasick Bock, was so frail, not the vital and robust mother I had known, was dependent on her husband and her daughter for everything. She was forced to let others do all the intimate ablutions of her sick body, including treating the bedsores, doing catheter care, turning her, wiping her—I can only imagine what it took for her to allow us to help her. This was a woman who helped organize the San Francisco General Strike, who organized unions, who spoke at mass meetings, an independent, forceful and charismatic woman. And we never spoke of her dying. My dad was forever in "fight back" mode, her champion, unrelentingly in combat with the cancer, never giving up or giving in. My mom and I, following suit, spoke of good memories, her early life, our family vacations; in other words everything *but* her dying.

At the end of that year, I was trained to give her the massive injections of morphine, which hastened her death. She gave me life, I gave her death. Both were gifts of love.

And then there was Maggie. In March of 1996, at the age of seventy-five, my beloved friend Maggie died. The previous October we had danced together at my fiftieth birthday party.

Maggie had known me since I was three years old. I was aware of her from the time I was ten. She and her husband, Hollie, and daughter

Kate were family friends and, as a matter of fact, moved next door to us on Willard Street when I was twelve. I knew Maggie as my parents' dear friend, as Kate's mom, as a Texan with a soft drawl, as a leftie but different from others in my parent's crowd of fast-talking, excitable, and argumentative politicos. Maggie was soft-voiced and polite. One time at a dinner party with everyone talking at once, I heard a glass clink with a spoon. Suddenly, all talking ceased. No one could believe she had signaled for quiet. When she had it, she spoke her mind about whatever was in dispute, after which the heated gabbling resumed as usual!

It wasn't until I returned home from grad school, in 1973, that Maggie and I started being friends, peers, and contemporaries despite our twenty-five-year age difference.

When Mom and Dad died, in 1977 and 1979, she was there. And until she died, we checked in with each other every morning by intercom for a "planet call." Our lives were wonderfully intertwined. For several years, we went three times a week for early morning walks at Stow Lake—she power walking, me at my pace. We were different, but those differences added to the richness of our connection. She was "woo-woo," a psychotherapist always studying and becoming proficient in new, cutting-edge fields such as Transactional Analysis, sex therapies, and bioenergetic therapy. She was straight, thin, and able-bodied. She was direct and open in her communications with others and expressed her feelings easily.

I learned to trust her in spite of our differences. I learned to speak with an open heart and express my openness without fear with her. She was the first straight person I came out to as a lesbian, and she celebrated with me and helped me to find a lesbian therapist. We told each other when we were angry or sad. She was the first person who told me I was beautiful.

At my fiftieth birthday, in her weakened body, we came to my big birthday party together as dear ones, and as we danced together there was a sweetness and a pathos in our closeness.

In the days before her death, we shared some amazing times. With laughter and tears, we talked openly of the past and what was happening to her in the present. Once she pleaded with me to help her up from her hospital bed and dance with her one last time. She hardly weighed a thing by then, so I was able to easily get her upright and positioned her feet on top of mine. Humming a little tune and holding my arms around her, we managed a few dance steps.

Once, when she seemed so distressed, I reminded her of her study of the *Tibetan Book of the Dead* and how enlightened and tranquil she was by that reading. This Southern "lady" turned her head to me and retorted, "Fuck *that*"!

Another time we were holding hands when she said to me, "I don't want to die yet." I replied, "I don't want you to die yet either." And we cried together. There was no pretense, as there had been when my mother was dying. Both Maggie and I knew what was coming and talked and grieved openly with each other.

I gave the eulogy at her memorial in the form of a letter to her. My Maggie. Margaret Riley Northcott.

And then there are the future losses to fear, a painful subject I addressed in two pieces for the Old Lesbians Memoir Writing Group.

What-Ifs

1. I don't live to another birthday?
2. I remember horrible stuff from that time of few memories before I was ten.
3. My hearing decreases significantly and I can't listen to books any more.
4. I go back to bingeing on sweets.
5. I'm alive in my seventies or eighties, alone.
6. I end up in a nursing home, trapped.
7. I need a wheelchair and so can't go anywhere because no one can wheel and tap a blind cane at the same time.
8. There's no one to take care of me.
9. Suzanne dies first.
10. I die and am no more.

Good-Byes and Hellos

Goodbyes—people, things, self. Goodbye my Rosie, Suzanne's Amber, my Maggie, my Silvita. Goodbye my Joanne, my June, my two Susans, my mom, my dad. I can't live without any of you. And yet I do. I must.

Goodbye and good riddance—my fear, my self-hatred, the dieting, the bingeing, my silence, my loneliness. Goodbye and good riddance—"Shrub"[44] and Cheney and all of your noxious gang.

Hello—global cooling, fair fighting, conflict resolution, with plowshares and active listening, mediation, and acknowledging as the new weapons in our arsenal.

---

[44] Former President George W. Bush

Hello my darling, my dearies, my fur friends. Hello hugs and hugs and kisses!

Hello sentimentality!

My death is a concept I can barely conceive. However, I can think concretely about what I will miss and not miss. Again, the Old Lesbians Memoir Writing Group gave me the "opportunity" to confront these questions.

Won't Miss When I Die

1. Anxiety
2. Fears
3. Co-dependency
4. Poverty
5. Spiders
6. Snakes
7. Loneliness
8. Angry words
9. Worry
10. Setting goals
11. Taking steps
12. Rodents
13. The "what-ifs"
14. Meetings of any sort
15. Foreign films I wish I could see
16. Struggling to see and hear

17. Back pain
18. Constipation
19. Feeling stupid
20. Slurs about age
21. Slurs about size, race, gender
22. Feeling guilty when I'm not going to a demo
23. Feeling defensive
24. Clipping my toenails
25. Low-flow showers
26. Measuring and coming up short of my own standards
27. Al-Anon meetings

On the other hand...

Will Miss When I Die

1. Consciousness
2. Smells of eucalyptus and wet nature
3. Smells of my dog in the rain, or most anytime
4. Hugs and kisses and hand-holding
5. Laughing heartily and saying things that make others laugh in delight
6. The satisfaction of clear thinking and feeling the ease of expressing my opinions, even if contrary
7. Eating yummy foods like any noodle dish, crab Louis, tuna sandwiches, chocolate, monster cookies, Chinese food in general, lox and bagels, and my boiled chicken in particular

8. The sounds of foghorns
9. Sally's seder
10. Suzanne
11. Sharp Park retreats and the grandeur of the ocean even on foggy and rainy days

Bequests

Exercise: *Describe several possessions, how got, what mean, to whom will they go?*

There is a little rocking chair; it is glossy black and little Laurie sat upon it rocking to and fro. Mother said it was a child's version of a Boston rocker. Across the top panel were painted pretty flowers in vibrant colors.

For sixty-seven years this child's rocker sat empty in the upstairs living room at 1448 Willard Street in San Francisco—a room seldom used. I've lived in the in-law apartment downstairs, happily contained, and rarely venture into the upper regions of my family home. Yet I have been unwilling to part with it, waiting for whom, for what? I have no children, no grandchildren. My friends' children were grown. It sat, un-rocked, between two formal, tufted blue-velvet matching chairs for the adults who do come, occasionally, to visit.

Was it resistance to giving away evidence of my childhood, proof that I was cherished and delighted in and spoiled with love?

I have left a letter of instruction to be read upon my death, including particular bequests to special people. This includes my mom's china teacup collection, each cup and saucer unique, delicate and quaint. It was always hard to imagine why this working-class, strong, woman, rooted in a life of social justice activism, would seek and cherish these lovelies. She displayed herself as anything but fragile and quaint! She took them carefully from the china cabinet for dinner parties with friends, drinking their coffee as they vigorously and happily discussed and argued the politics of the day. Only recently did I discover the true story from her dear friend, Muriel, that Mom decided to have a tea cup collection and went out to find and purchase one intact. These cups will go to Kate, my sister-friend and daughter of our dear Northcotts, Maggie and Hollie, who lived next door. She has a fine artist's eye and appreciates lovely things and will display them in the glass-fronted corner hutch in the living room of her family home. She will bring them out with her friends and family to share their delicate beauty, telling stories of my mother, Mini, and will as well be reminded of and relish the loving history of our two families together.

And the little rocking chair? It still remains with me, in waiting.

A Dying Word

"Avanti"

It means onward, forward… For me it is into the nothingness, the absence of struggle,

This was a song we often sang in company with old friends, as I grew up in my crimson household. Our version of the old revolutionary anthem was sung with swelling ardor and comradely joy.

Avanti popolo
Bandiera rossa
Bandiera rossa.
Triumphera

Bandiera rossa
La triumphera
Bandiera rossa
La triumphera
Bandiera rossa
La triumphera
Viva la revolución
Y la libertad.

This song and others of its ilk were sung at every opportunity and occasion: Christmas, Chanukah, New Years, May Day, Labor Day, and any other time when comrades of a lifetime gathered to eat, schmooze, laugh, argue politics, and be in loving connection with each other. These were good times, even in the worst of times.

So "Avanti" solo or in solidarity, singing your songs, lifting your spirits, conscious of choices, choosing your paths toward the individual and the common good. Be righteous demanders of justice and proclaimers of truth. For me, struggle is over, fears of the present and the future have ended. I leave it all in your capable hands and hearts, with my love.

Laura and Suzanne at San Francisco Dyke March. c 2002

Laura and Suzanne, Columbia River Cruise. c 2005

LAURA BOCK
ILA 13210

Laura is a native San Franciscan, a 3rd generation social feminist. Although disabled, she's always been active in social justice.

She attended the University of Oregon for a B.A. in English and the University of Massachusetts working toward an M.A. in American cultural and intellectual history. While living in Berkeley, she worked as a substitute teacher in children's centers and as a senior clerk typist for the University of California. She ran her own business, a bed and breakfast in her family home for twenty-three years.

Laura has volunteered with the GLBT Historical Society on preserving and cataloging a collection from the San Francisco Women's Building and Women's Centers. Her personal papers are housed at the Historical Society.

Laura focuses on keeping her body moving with swimming and walking. She is a voracious reader. In 2009, she co-founded the San Francisco Old Lesbian Memoirs Writing Group and continues to share the facilitation of it. Her partner, Suzanne and their dog Louise, who is also a senior, reside happily at The Redwoods.

Laura at The Redwoods, 2013. A short bio and picture of all new residents is posted on a community bulletin board.

Epilogue—I've Got News

I GOT IT! I have one! My FBI file came! Okay, enough with the exclamation points. (Perhaps not!) Now I can hold my head up high among Red Diaper Baby circles (cells?), sing all the old songs with legitimate gusto, preen a little and spread my plumage here at The Redwoods where we live. Okay, end of hyperbole.

So what if it's not the FBI file of my dreams? It will do. I do, however, feel like writing back to them about all my subversive activism they left out. "As usual, you're a bunch of nincompoops and couldn't find a criminal on the Ten Most Wanted List if you tripped over him." But I will restrain myself. Perhaps.

They got at least two things wrong: they misspelled my name once or twice, and they claimed I was a member of the Progressive Labor Party. I never was. The PL, like the Trotskyites, were an anathema to my family!

You will find portions of the file(s) in the appendix section. The FBI redacted the names of their informants by "whitening" them out. I've removed the names of other radicals mentioned with "blackouts." It's up to them to publish their own affiliations. I have chosen to print these files as the FBI scanned them onto a CD-ROM for me. I have not prettied them up or straightened them out.

There may be general interest in what an FBI file looks like, as well as what they found subversive about me. Note the conversations their wiretaps picked up between my mom and Aunt Peg. I have left in the names of FBI agents for, as long as the FBI didn't bother to redact them, far be it from me to "protect" them from scrutiny of their misdeeds!

This file is really just the icing on the cake, the dot over the i, and the cross on the t. I'm a right proper subversive (improper?). I knew that already, but now I've been authenticated, verified, certified. I am my grandparent's progeny, the result of the ideals, beliefs, and radical activism of my parents. I have indeed followed in the family tradition, tweaking it and modifying it according to the times, my inclinations, and the influences from the movements of my day.

It's now up to you all. Since I have no future generation to pass these to, you, dear readers, are my surrogate children and grandchildren, nieces and nephews. I realize you did not volunteer for this job. Nonetheless, I trust you with these stories, to do with them as you choose. I was honored and proud to be the recipient of this subversive tradition and the bearer of my family's values.

In sum, how have I done so far in completing my life's bucket list?

1. Take a floatplane over the wilds of Alaska? (Not yet.)
2. Have sex for the first time. (Check—at thirty-six.)
3. Have feelings—turn the old rusted switch back on. (Check.)
4. Stop dieting and love my body. (Check.)
5. Love being on stage, acting my words, strutting my stuff. (Check.)

6. Do a striptease during the Fat Lip sex script, and do it in front of my ex and my therapist. (Check.)

7. Lose my shyness and become assertive. (Check.)

8. Stick my neck out with my opinions. (Check.)

9. Become a passionate activist (zealot?) on behalf of movements of my choosing and which relate to my life. (Check.)

10. Place my papers in an archive and process my own collection. (Check.)

11. Write my memoir. (Check.)

Not bad, so far! Now, who am I? Once again, that incredibly special and unique Old Lesbian Memoir Writing Group presented the opportunity to ponder who I am at the age of seventy-plus.

Self Portrait

She's big, oh she's big.
Boundless with substance
Bulging with confidence
Rippling with insight
Overflowing with opinions
Stuffed with knowledge
Jiggling with laughter
Fat with fervor
Brimming with life
Quivering with anticipation
Full of herself.
Oh yes, she's big.

Appendix I
Reflections on Me
Jewish Women Class

Laura J. Bock
March 3, 1981

HOW DIFFICULT it is to choose which aspects of my life to write about. Choice can be so liberating and burdensome at the same time. Before I succumb to waves of existential rhapsodizing, I better just begin.

I was born in San Francisco in 1945, when those around me were exulting at war's end, horrified by the excesses of the Holocaust and concerned at the flickers that would blaze into McCarthyism. The lifetime ideological commitment and political activism of my grandparents and my parents has been both a tremendous source of pride and, at the same time, an uncomfortable (if unspoken) pressure on me to excel in similar activities. This heritage in resistance to oppression and strong faith in a socialist future is one of the major themes of my life.

My paternal grandfather came from Vilna, Russia where, as a youth, he was an anarchist, active in the workers' movement of that city. I know far more of my mother's family. Her parents grew up with their families in a shtetl not too far from Kiev. As a girl in New York and Los Angeles my mother heard stories of shtetl life and related those she remembered on a tape we made before her death. I am reluctant to hear that tape, and her voice. For the purposes of this paper I can only depend on the wisps of my own recollections.

My mother's grandparents were Orthodox Jews. The man of the house was learned, and so protected by the women and the children who were responsible for the family's economic survival. In spite of the fact that these elders were afraid and critical of socialist ideology and activism, both my maternal grandmother and grandfather involved themselves from an early age while in the shtetl and later in Kiev where their activities and the harassment they encountered grew more intense. The workers' circles they helped organize discussed theory, wrote tracts, planned actions, etc.

Around the turn of the century, as the story goes, one of the Czar's police in Kiev, who felt friendly towards my grandparents, warned them that there was a warrant out for their arrest, and this time they would be separated and sent to the East. My grandparents fled in haste, knowing their usefulness to the movement in Russia was at an end. They made their way to London where they joined other family members and many immigrant Jews in Whitechapel.

I know nothing of what life was like for them at this time—working to earn money for passage to America. As a young woman I had little interest or felt the urgency in talking with my grandparents before they died.

They arrived in America about 1901, penniless, and were taken in by New York City relatives. They lived there almost ten years, working in the sweatshops of the needle trades, my grandfather tailoring, my grandmother in shirtwaist factories. My mother was born to them in

1905, and they still knew little English. My grandmother, in labor, was taken to a neighborhood hospital when her time came, with my grandfather being very protective and attentive. They could not understand what was being said to them, nor the puzzled looks of the staff. It turned out to be a hospital for unwed mothers! My grandmother wanted her first-born to have an American name and the staff pressured her to name the child quickly for the record. The more they pressed her, the more my grandmother kept her silence until one day when she heard over the hospital intercom, "Nurse Mini, Nurse Mini." And so my mother was named!

About 1909, the family moved to Los Angeles and settled into the large Jewish community there. Meanwhile my father's family had immigrated to St. Louis and from there to L.A.'s Boyle Heights, where eventually they bought a small, poor farm. My paternal grandfather worked as a tailor while his wife and children struggled to keep the farm going. Neither my mother's nor father's families prospered. They lived lives of struggle and poverty and worked toward their dreams of a socialist future. In New York, St. Louis, and L.A. these people continued their political involvements, in radical Jewish workers' leagues and some of them in the Communist party when it was formed.

My father saw his father participating in anarchist circles of the Jewish left wing, and my mother grew up in a large extended family who shared political beliefs and expected their children to carry on the work. The children were taught Marxist theory at an early age and expected to recite at family gatherings, as well as excel at school and actively work for social change in children's groups. At the age of ten or eleven, my mother organized a socialist children's performing troupe and wrote musical shows, changing the words of familiar songs, to be performed at rallies and meetings. She and her sister joined the Young Workers League and eventually the Communist Party.

Both my mother and her sister grew up with a strong feminist element in their socialist training. Their mother instilled in them a fierce independence and an aversion to domination by a husband. As a matter of fact she accepted my father only years later when he bought a car for my mother. For my grandmother this symbolized his encouraging my mother's independence. Similarly, she refused to teach her daughters to sew, fearing they would be trapped as she was in the sweatshops.

In L.A., in the California agricultural fields, in the canneries, on the waterfront, and in San Francisco, my parents were totally involved throughout the twenties and thirties—union organizing, strikes, my mother's party work, my father's well publicized trial and imprisonment for six months. (Earl Warren was the district attorney prosecuting him.)

I was born when my parents were forty. They wanted a child and were ready to curtail their political activities, but the house remained a center for lively discussion and reminiscences of past actions. My mother put her energy into the PTA, leading my Brownie troop, a socialist mothers' club, and organizing parents around school nutrition programs. As a child is was difficult for me to overcome the awe of who and what my parents and their friends were. I was extremely shy, unassertive, fascinated with the exciting and volatile discussions around me, and reluctant to participate in them. Knowing what my parents had accomplished before they were even twenty left me feeling I could not measure up.

Those first ten years of my life were a scary time. When I was five, my mother developed breast cancer and went away to a hospital for a time. My father was frightened that he might have to raise me alone.

Then I kept hearing the word "McCarthyism" and my parents and their friends were very much affected. I would overhear stories about people being taken away—my uncle was jailed under the Smith Act—and I was warned not to talk about these things in school or to my friends. I carried this fear and those admonitions with me though college, telling only a few close friends "who I was." So hand in hand went my extreme pride in my political heritage and the fear that we would be discovered.

I began my political activism in earnest in college at the University of Oregon in 1963. I plunged into the civil rights movement and then the anti-war struggle. My parents were proud of my activities and at the same time scared. At one point they persuaded me not to go to Cuba. Instead I traveled to Chicago (summer of 1964) where I worked in a CORE Freedom House on the Southside—organizing a children's day-care program and assisting in tenant strikes. My sophomore year was a time for intense political activity, not for many classes.

This heritage of left wing political activism is a major theme in my life. I have some of my father's skepticism of leadership as well as my mother's faith in organizational structure. My father, committed to socialism, blamed socialist leaders for corrupting it. Mother hung her faith on the Soviet Union until Czechoslovakia. For the past ten years I have kept away from working with any particular organization where frequently much of the work goes in to perpetuating the organization. I plug in, on an ad hoc basis, active on specific issues, attending demonstrations. I have a strong feminist identity and have been most involved within the women's community.

Another major area of who I am has to do with my oppression and evolution as a fat woman. I have always been fat, or told I was. For most of my life I have felt ashamed and embarrassed for existing, reinforced over and over by my parents and the world around me. I was living in a hostile world and guilt was my constant companion. It has been in the last five years that I have begun to purge those vile images, with the instrumental help of a fat women's support group. I became aware of the politics of body size as it relates to sexism, racism, physicalism, and I began to acknowledge my rage. I have forgiven my parents for their part in my oppression. They were victims as well. I have rejected the stigma and I am active with other women in the fat political movement. It's been a long, agonizing personal struggle and the confines of this paper do not permit further exploration of this area now.

The third, and last, area of my life I've chosen to mention is my disability. In 1971, I was living in Massachusetts, attending graduate school, when I lost my sight for no apparent reason. Equally unforeseen was its partial return, leaving me "legally blind." This sudden loss of sight was overtly more traumatic for my parents than for me. I handled it as I had handled other terrors in my life—by numbing my mind and feelings. I denied the extent to which I was impaired, and the degree to which I had to adjust my life. The thought of being dependent was abhorrent, and so I over-compensated. I did not, for example, train my friends to identify themselves to me. I thought I would know who they were with a few spoken words. I rarely asked for help and kept my frustration to myself.

People are forever saying to me, "But you don't look blind!" The stereotypes behind statements like these are beginning to make me angry. While I have been a non-active supporter of the disability movement, I have not developed my consciousness as a disabled person as yet. It will come.

So this is some of who I am and how I got here. I am a "romantic Socialist." I am an ardent feminist. I am a disabled person. I am a fat woman who has freed herself from much of her internal oppression and is working on the rest of the world. I am fiercely independent. I have a strong commitment to social change. I worry a lot—part of my heritage, too. I like to play with friends. And I like to learn and share ideas with others.

Appendix II
FBI Files

996 (5-31-98)

U. S. Department of Justice

(MATERIAL MUST NOT BE REMOVED FROM OR ADDED TO THIS FILE)

100

442060

FEDERAL BUREAU

of

INVESTIGATION

| Declassification authority derived from FBI Automatic Declassification Guide, issued May 24, 2007 | Screened By: RCR 2-6-2015 NARA FOIA case RD 44809 DOCID: 70000768 |

USE CARE IN HANDLING THIS FILE

NW: 15160

Transfer-Call 421

SHAW-WALKER 18-3019

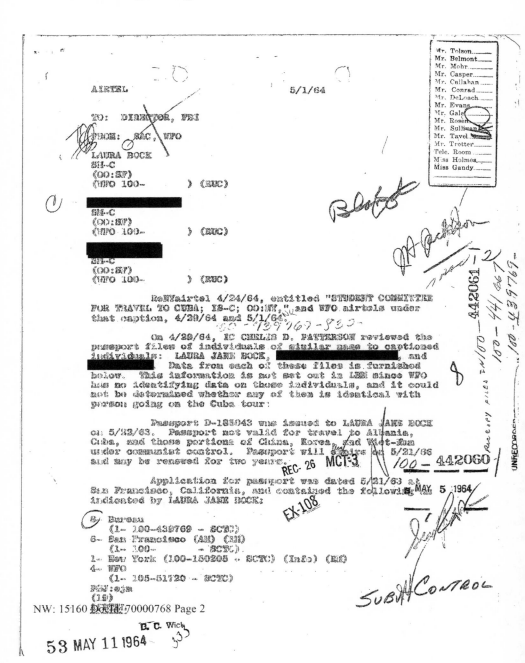

AIRTEL   5/1/64

TO: DIRECTOR, FBI

FROM: SAC, WFO

LAURA BOCK
SM-C
(OO:SF)
(WFO 100-   ) (RUC)

SM-C
(OO:SF)
(WFO 100-   ) (RUC)

SM-C
(OO:SF)
(WFO 100-   ) (RUC)

         ReWFOairtel 4/24/64, entitled "STUDENT COMMITTEE
FOR TRAVEL TO CUBA; IS-C; OO:NY," and WFO airtels under
that caption, 4/29/64 and 5/1/64.

         On 4/29/64, IC CHELIS D. PATTERSON reviewed the
passport files of individuals of similar name to captioned
individuals: LAURA JANE BOCK,   , and
                  Data from each of these files is furnished
below. This information is not set out in LHM since WFO
has no identifying data on those individuals, and it could
not be determined whether any of them is identical with
person going on the Cuba tour:

         Passport D-183043 was issued to LAURA JANE BOCK
on 5/22/63. Passport not valid for travel to Albania,
Cuba, and those portions of China, Korea, and Viet-Nam
under communist control. Passport will expire on 5/21/66
and may be renewed for two years.

         Application for passport was dated 5/21/63 at
San Francisco, California, and contained the following
indicated by LAURA JANE BOCK:

8- Bureau
   (1- 100-439769 - SCTC)
6- San Francisco (AM) (RM)
   (1- 100-   - SCTC)
1- New York (100-150205 - SCTC) (Info) (RM)
4- WFO
   (1- 105-51720 - SCTC)
RGN:sjm
(19)

53 MAY 11 1964

4-22 (Rev. 1-22-60)

Federal Bureau of Investigation
Records Branch

7/6 , 1964

☐ Name Searching Unit - Room 6527
☐ Service Unit - Room 6524
☐ Forward to File Review
☐ Attention _____
☑ Return to _Jackson P28RB_
        Supervisor   Room   Ext.

Type of References Requested:
☐ Regular Request (Analytical Search)
☐ All References (Subversive & Nonsubversive)
☑ Subversive References Only
☐ Nonsubversive References Only
☐ Main _____ References Only

Type of Search Requested:
☐ Restricted to Locality of _____
☑ Exact Name Only (On the Nose)
☐ Buildup   ☐ Variations

Laura Jane Bock
Subject _____
Birthdate & Place _____
Address _____

Localities _____
R # _____ Date _____ Searcher Initials _len_
Prod. _____

	FILE NUMBER	SERIAL
I mail	100 - 442060	
	100 - 439769 - 855	

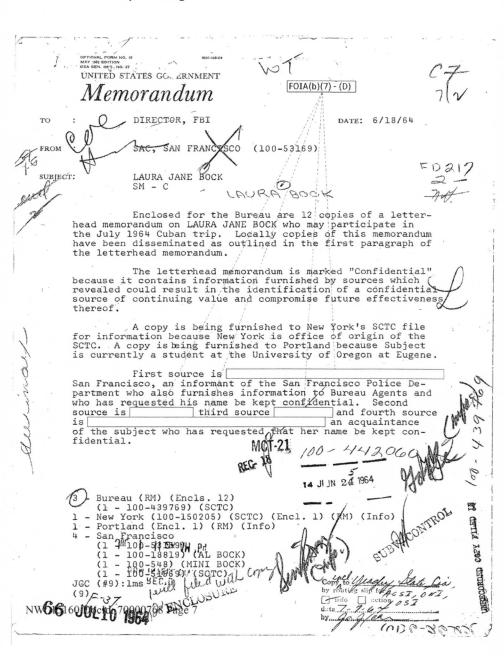

OPTIONAL FORM NO. 10
MAY 1962 EDITION
GSA GEN. REG. NO. 27

UNITED STATES GOVERNMENT

Memorandum

TO   :   DIRECTOR, FBI   DATE: 6/18/64

FROM :   SAC, SAN FRANCISCO (100-53169)

SUBJECT: LAURA JANE BOCK
          SM - C

        Enclosed for the Bureau are 12 copies of a letter-
head memorandum on LAURA JANE BOCK who may participate in
the July 1964 Cuban trip. Locally copies of this memorandum
have been disseminated as outlined in the first paragraph of
the letterhead memorandum.

        The letterhead memorandum is marked "Confidential"
because it contains information furnished by sources which
revealed could result in the identification of a confidential
source of continuing value and compromise future effectiveness
thereof.

        A copy is being furnished to New York's SCTC file
for information because New York is office of origin of the
SCTC. A copy is being furnished to Portland because Subject
is currently a student at the University of Oregon at Eugene.

        First source is
San Francisco, an informant of the San Francisco Police Department who also furnishes information to Bureau Agents and
who has requested his name be kept confidential. Second
source is   third source   and fourth source
is   an acquaintance
of the subject who has requested that her name be kept confidential.

(3) - Bureau (RM) (Encls. 12)
    (1 - 100-439769) (SCTC)
1 - New York (100-150205) (SCTC) (Encl. 1) (RM) (Info)
1 - Portland (Encl. 1) (RM) (Info)
4 - San Francisco
    (1 - 100-53169)
    (1 - 100-18819) (AL BOCK)
    (1 - 100-548) (MINI BOCK)
    (1 - 100-53169) (SCTC)
JGC (#9):lms
(9)

LAURA JANE BOCK   CONFIDENTIAL

        The following background information was furnished
by LAURA BOCK:

        She listed her date of birth as October 4, 1945, at
San Francisco, California, and listed her residence as 1448
Willard Street, San Francisco. Her father was listed as ALBERT
J. BOCK, born March 10, 1905, at Philadelphia, Pennsylvania, and
her mother as MINI KARASICK, born December 19, 1905, at New York
City on She listed her proposed itinerary as England, France, Italy,
Denmark, Switzerland and The Netherlands.

        Second source advised in March 1953, that LAURA JANE
BOCK'S father and mother, ALBERT BOCK and MINI BOCK, had been
Communist Party (CP) members from approximately 1927 to the 1950's.

        A third source in April 1951, advised that MINI BOCK,
who also used the name MINI CARSON, held numerous CP positions
such as CP Branch President, CP Educational Director, a member of
the California State CP Central Committee in 1934, and a delegate
to the CP State Convention in California in 1945.

        San Francisco office indices contain no information
identifiable with LAURA JANE BOCK.

        A fourth source advised that at the present time, LAURA
JANE BOCK is a freshman at the University of Oregon, Eugene,
Oregon. She is studying to be a teacher. Source advised that
during the summer months, LAURA BOCK resides with her parents
at 1448 Willard Street, San Francisco.

                        DESCRIPTION

        Name: LAURA JANE BOCK
        Born: 10/4/45, at San Francisco
        Height: 5'7"
        Hair: Brown
        Eyes: Hazel
        Occupation: Student at the University of
                           Oregon

                          - 2 -

                                        CONFIDENTIAL

OPTIONAL FORM NO. 10
MAY 1962 EDITION
GSA GEN. REG. NO. 27

UNITED STATES GOVERNMENT

Memorandum

TO   :   DIRECTOR, FBI (100-442060)   DATE: 7/20/65
                    1 - 100-443127

FROM   :   SAC, SAN FRANCISCO (100-53169)

SUBJECT: LAURA JANE BOCK
                SM - C
                OO: SAN FRANCISCO

ENCL

        Enclosed for the Bureau are 12 copies of a letterhead
memorandum on Subject who desired to attend the 9th World
Youth Festival at Algiers, Algeria, August, 1965. Local
dissemination has been given to the Department of State, Office
of Security and two copies to G-2, San Francisco.

        The letterhead memo is marked confidential because it
contains information furnished by sources which if revealed
could result in the identification of confidential sources of
continuing value and compromise future effectiveness thereof.

        First source is [   ]
San Francisco by request. The second source is [   ] The
third source is [   ]

no dissemination
warranted at this time
9th WYF postponed

2 - Bureau (Encls. 12)
3 - San Francisco
1 - 100-53848
JGC/bjd
(5)

12 - ENCLOSURE

ST-118

REC- 21   100-442060-3

18 JUL 22 1965

SUBV CONTROL

100-443127

ENCL COPY AND COPY OF ENCL FILED

228

Buy U.S. Savings Bonds Regularly on the Payroll Savings Plan

UNITED STATES DEPARTMENT OF JUSTICE

FEDERAL BUREAU OF INVESTIGATION

San Francisco, California

July 20, 1965

In Reply, Please Refer to File No.

C O N F I D E N T I A L

LAURA JANE BOCK

First source on July 9, 1965, advised that Laura Jane Bock, San Francisco, intended to attend the 9th World Youth Festival at Algiers, Algeria, during August, 1965.

Passport files, Washington, D. C., reflect that Passport Number D188043 was issued to Laura Jane Bock on May 22, 1963. The passport was not valid for travel to Albania, Cuba and those portions of China, Korea and Viet Nam under communist control. Passport will expire on May 21, 1966.

The following background information was furnished by Laura Bock:

She listed her date of birth as October 4, 1945, at San Francisco, California, and listed her residence as 1448 Willard Street, San Francisco. Her father was listed as Albert J. Bock, born March 10, 1905, at Philadelphia, Pennsylvania, and her mother as Mini Karasick, born December 19, 1905, at New York City. She listed her proposed itinerary as England, France, Italy, Denmark, Switzerland, and The Netherlands.

Second source advised in March 1953, that Laura Jane Bock's father and mother, Albert Bock and Mini Bock, had been Communist Party (CP) members from approximately 1927 to the 1950's

A third source in April, 1951, advised that Mini Bock, who also used the name Mini Carson, held numerous CP positions suc as CP Branch President, CP Educational Director, a member of the California State CP Central Committee in 1934, and a delegate to t CP State Convention in California in 1945.

C O N F I D E N T I A L

GROUP I
Excluded from automatic
downgrading and
declassification

COPIES DESTROYED

3330 DEC 14 1970

NW: 15 DocId: 70900768 Page

ENCLOSURE 100-442060-3

FD - 245   (REV. 4-13-60)

U. S. Department of Justice

(MATERIAL MUST NOT BE REMOVED FROM OR ADDED TO THIS FILE)

FEDERAL BUREAU

of

INVESTIGATION

Bureau File Number   *100-442060*

Declassification authority derived from
FBI Automatic Declassification Guide,
issued May 24, 2007

Screened By: RCR 2-10-2015
NARA FOIA case RD 44809
DOCID: 70000776

See also Nos.

NW: 15160 DocId: 70000776 Page 1

#9

FD-340 (REV. 8-17-62)

File No.

Date Received

From
(NAME OF CONTRIBUTOR)

(ADDRESS OF CONTRIBUTOR)

(CITY AND STATE)

By
(NAME OF SPECIAL AGENT)

To Be Returned   Yes ☐
                        No ☐

Description:

Laura Jane Bock
5/21/63

FD-36 (Rev. 12-13-56)

F B I

Date: 5/11/64

Transmit the following in _____
                                    (Type in plain text or code)

Via _____AIRTEL_____   AIR MAIL - REGISTERED
                                  (Priority or Method of Mailing)

TO: DIRECTOR, FBI (100-439769)

FROM: SAC, SAN FRANCISCO (100-51569)

RE: STUDENT COMMITTEE FOR TRAVEL TO CUBA
      IS - C

      OO - New York

          Re Washington Field airtel 5/1/64, re list of persons
participating in 7/1/64 trip and passport information on BOCK,
██████████

LAURA JANE BOCK (SF 100-53169)
          San Francisco indices contain no record on her.
However, she is the daughter of ALBERT JAYE BOCK (Bufile 100-8344),
who was a former SI subject and presently is on the RI-B index.
He operates an insurance company in San Francisco. He is the
brother-in-law of EUGENE DENNIS and was formerly a very active
CP member. LAURA BOCK's mother is MINNIE KARASICK BOCK who
formerly was a very active CP member. A LHM will be prepared
on LAURA BOCK.

3 - Bureau (AM-RM)
2 - New York (100-150205)(AM-RM)
2 - Washington Field (100-51720)(AM-RM)
5 - San Francisco (1 - 100-51569)(SCTC)
              (1 - 100-53169)(L. Bock)
              (1 - 100-53174)(████████)
              (1 - 100-49891)(████)
              (1 - 100-52341)(████████)
JGC/jr (#9)
(12)

Searched_____
Serialized_____
Indexed_____
Filed_____   100-53169-2

Approved: _____   Sent _____ M   Per _____
                 Special Agent in Charge

FBI

DATE: 6/24/64

TTransmit the Following in _____

Via   AIRTEL   _____

TO: DIRECTOR, FBI (100-439769)

FROM: SAC, NEW YORK (100-150205)

SUBJECT: STUDENT COMMITTEE FOR TRAVEL TO CUBA
         IS - C

         (OO: NEW YORK)

         ReBuairtel, 6/17/64.

         A review of the SCTC case file at NY shows that of the 46
people listed on BOAC reservations lists for flights on
6/27/64 and 7/1/64, the following have been identified:

```
3 - Bureau (RM)
3 - Boston (100-35192) (RM)
    (1 - 100-34291) (          NEP)
    (1 - 100-34493) (
7 - Los Angeles (100-64183) (RM)
    (1 - 100-65239)
    (1 - 100-61902)
    (1 - 100-64788)
   (1- 100-63949)
    (1 - 100-62228)
    (1 - 100-64667)
4 - San Francisco (100-65569) (RM)
    (1 - 100-53169) (LAURA BOCK)
    (1 - 100-49891)
    (1 - 100-53175)
4 - Seattle (100-          (RM)
    (1 - 100-24212)
    (1 - 100-27196)
    (1 - 100-
1 - New York (100-151519)
1 - New York (100-150859)              ROWSKY)
1 - New York
1 - New York (100-
1 - New York (100-
1 - New York
JWR:dtz
(28)
```

INDEXED

JUN 26 9 34 AM '64

FBI SAN FRANCISCO

100- 53169 -3

NY 100-150205

      LAURA JEAN BOCK. LAURA BOCK is the daughter of
ALBERT JAYE BOCK, Bufile 100-8344, former SI subject of SF.
Her mother is MINNIE KARASICK BOCK, who was formerly a very
active CP member.

      ████████████████████████ is a member of the
LA SWP and is a member of the Executive Board of the LA Branch
YSA, He received Passport Number ████████ on 4/9/64.

████████████████████████████████

      ████████████████ She is a member of the NY Local, SWP.

████████████████████████████

████████████████████████████

      It was reported on 4/27/64, that ████████ had intended
to make the trip to Cuba but was so disappointed with the
small number going from LA that he took his name off the list
of those making the trip.

      ████████████████ She is a member of the Seattle Branch
SWP. ████████

      ████████████████████████ is an SI subject of the
SFO who is active in the SWP and YSA.

- 2 -

FOIA(b)(7) - (D)

NY 100-150205

████████████████████████████ whose names also appeared
on the BOAC reservations list are presently in Cuba.
One ████████████ is also in Cuba but his true identity
is unknown at this time.

            For the information of receiving offices, the
Bureau has advised that arrangements should be made for
the immediate interview of the above individuals. It
is felt that the reservations on BOAC flights for 6/27/64
and 7/1/64 which have been cancelled by ████████████
may have been cancelled in order to divert attention from
this group and that arrangements could possible be made
on other airlines for them to travel to Cuba.

LEADS:

    BOSTON, LOS ANGELES, SAN FRANCISCO AND SEATTLE.

            Will conduct interviews of listed persons in their
respective territories as requested by the Bureau unless
some reason exists which would make an interview undesirable.
Each office is to attempt to determine from individuals
interviewed their knowledge of the SCTG to whom they submitted
applications, by whom they were interviewed and whether
or not they are still contemplating travel to Cuba in 1964.

            These interviews are to be given expeditious
handling and each office is requested to advise the Bureau
and NY of results of these interviews in form suitable for
dissemination.

                        - 5 -

UNITED STATES DEPARTMENT OF JUSTICE

FEDERAL BUREAU OF INVESTIGATION

San Francisco, California

June 18, 1964

In Reply, Please Refer to File No.

~~CONFIDENTIAL~~

LAURA JANE BOCK

      Copies of this memorandum have been disseminated locally to offices of the Army, Navy, Air Force Intelligence, Department of State (Security) and Immigration and Naturalization Service.

      On April 22, 1964, Mr. EDWARD O'NEILL, Ticket Manager, British Overseas Airways Corporation (BOAC), 530 Fifth Avenue, New York City, advised that ALBERT MAHER, New York City, made tentative reservations for 30 individuals to fly on BOAC Flight 4254 on July 1, 1964, from New York City to Port of Spain, Trinidad. Reservations were requested on July 2, 1964, from Port of Spain to Georgetown, British Guiana. Mr. O'NEILL advised that one of the names furnished to him by MAHER for reservation was LAURA BOCK.

      First source advised in 1964, that the Student Committee for Travel to Cuba (SCTC), formerly known as the Permanent Student Committee for Travel to Cuba (PSCTC), was sponsoring a trip to Cuba in July 1964, in order to test the United States Government ban on travel to Cuba. This source advised on May 29, 1964, that as yet it had not been determined by the SCTC exactly how many or who would participate from the San Francisco area in the July 1964 Cuban trip.

      A characterization of the Permanent Student Committee for Travel to Cuba is contained in in the appendix.

      Passport files, Washington, D. C., reflect that Passport Number D188043 was issued to LAURA JANE BOCK on May 22, 1963. The passport was not valid for travel to Albania, Cuba and those portions of China, Korea and Viet Nam under communist control. Passport will expire on May 21, 1966.

Serialized _u3_
Indexed
Filed   _u3_

~~CONFIDENTIAL~~
Group 1
Excluded from automatic downgrading and declassification

This document contains neither recommendations nor conclusions of the FBI. It is the property of the FBI and is loaned to your agency; it and its contents are not to be distributed outside your agency.

100-53169-4

LAURA JANE BOCK   ~~CONFIDENTIAL~~

PERMANENT STUDENT COMMITTEE FOR TRAVEL TO CUBA (PSCTC)

"The Columbia Owl," a weekly student newspaper of
Columbia University, New York City, December 13, 1962 issue,
page 1, contained an article entitled "Students to Visit Cuba
During Holidays." This article stated in part that the
Ad Hoc Student Committee for Travel to Cuba was formed October 14,
1962, by a group of students from New York City universities,
the University of Wisconsin, Oberlin College, and the University
of North Carolina, who stated that as students they would like
a chance to see and evaluate the situation in Cuba for themselves
and had received an offer of transportation and two weeks stay
in Cuba from the Federation of University Students in Havana
as guests of the Federation. The committee accepted the offer
and applied to the United States State Department for passport
validation which was refused; however, over 50 students planned
to defy the State Department ban and go to Cuba.

A source advised on December 6, 1962, that during
December, 1962, it was learned that the Ad Hoc Student Committee
for Travel to Cuba had recently been formed by the "Progressive
Labor" group.

"Progressive Labor," Volume 11, Number 1, issue of
January, 1963, page 11, in an article captioned "State Dept.
Pulls Strings to Keep U. S. Students from Cuba," states that
"For more information on the Cuban Trip contact the Ad Hoc
Committee for Travel to Cuba, 42 St. Marks Place, New York 3,
NY."

A second source advised on April 24, 1963, that a party
sponsored by the Permanent Student Committee for Travel to Cuba
was held on April 20, 1963, in New York City. At this party
it was announced that the Ad Hoc Student Committee for Travel
to Cuba is now known as Permanent Student Committee for Travel
to Cuba.

The same source further advised that at this party it
was announced that the committee had received a cable from the
Federation of University Students in Havana inviting the students
to spend the month of July, 1963, in Cuba, and a new trip was
planned whereby the students would leave New York City the last
weekend of June, 1963, for Canada and travel by plane from
Canada to Cuba.

APPENDIX

~~CONFIDENTIAL~~

- 3 -

LAURA JANE BOCK   ~~CONFIDENTIAL~~

PROGRESSIVE LABOR PARTY;
PROGRESSIVE LABOR MOVEMENT;
"PROGRESSIVE LABOR"

A source advised on July 2, 1962, that Progressive Labor
groups held a conference in New York City on July 1, 1962, where
███████████ acted as chairman. He read a statement at this conference setting forth their intention to form a new Marxist-
Leninist Party in the United States. ███████ stated that a more
formal organization was necessary, one which would provide a
framework for all who wanted to join in a united effort to build
an American vanguard. The functions of this new organization
are to consolidate all existing forces around Progressive Labor
and organize additional forces; expand and improve political
activities; win additional forces to an outlook of Marxism-
Leninism and increase the open advocacy of socialism; develop a
significant Marxist-Leninist program for the new party; and
organize a collective organization of leaders and members.

> "The Worker," an east coast communist
> newspaper, issue of January 7, 1962,
> page 10, column 3, reported the expulsion
> of ████████, former labor secretary
> of the New York State Communist Party,
> from the Communist Party, USA.

A second and third source advised in February, 1963,
that this new Marxist-Leninist Party had not yet been organized on
a formal basis but that Progressive Labor groups had been formed
in several localities in line with proposals of ██████████. The
sources advised as of February, 1963, that the leaders of this
group were referring to it as the Progressive Labor Movement.

The "Amsterdam News," a daily New York City newspaper,
dated July 27, 1963, page 22, set forth that the "Progressive
Labor Party is a new political formation based on Progressive
Labor Movement, a Socialist organization with groups in all parts
of the United States. The organization publishes a monthly
magazine called Progressive Labor."

The July-August, 1963, issue of "Progressive Labor" set
forth that it is published monthly by Progressive Labor Company,
G.P.O. Box 808, Brooklyn 1, New York.

APPENDIX

~~CONFIDENTIAL~~

- 4 -

OPTIONAL FORM NO. 10
5010-104

UNITED STATES GOVERNMENT

Memorandum   FOIA(b)(7) - (D)

TO   :   SAC, SAN FRANCISCO (100-53169)   DATE: 6/29/64

FROM   :   SA EDWARD J. O'FLYNN

SUBJECT: LAURIE BOCK
             SM - C

              [_____] on 6/4/64, reported that on that date
MINNIE BOCK, Subject's mother, contacted PEGGY DENNIS at
the PW at which time she discussed LAURIE and related that
LAURIE wanted to go to Mississippi this summer, but MINNIE
stated she couldn't because she is too young and too sheltered
and wouldn't be prepared for a trip like that.

RECOMMENDATION: Route to SA CARLISLE for information
regarding fact that Subject still present in this area,
did not travel to cuba and desires to go to Mississippi.

EJO/msl
(2)

100 - 53169 - 6

{*Translation of Previous Two Illegible Pages*}

7/3/64

AIRTEL   AIR MAIL

TO: Director, FBI

FROM: SAC, SAN FRANCISCO {*Illegible code*}

RE: STUDENT COMMITTEE FOR TRAVEL TO CUBA

            {*Illegible code*}

            {*Illegible code*}

      {*Illegible*} New York Airtel, 6/24/64

      References Airtel requests the San Francisco Office to interview LAURA BOCK regarding her intentions of travelling to Cuba during 1964.

      Through [FBI REDACTION, long] San Francisco, California, an acquaintance of the Subject, it has been ascertained that LAURA BOCK, for the summer of 1964, has gone to the State of Kansas to work for CORE.

      [FBI REDACTION] advised that LAURA BOCK, who was a freshman at the University of Oregon, had talked to her and told her that she was not going to Cuba but instead was going to work in Kansas this summer.

      For the information of Kansas City, LAURA BOCK is the daughter of ALBERT BOCK, a former security Index Subject of the San Francisco Office. Subject's mother is Minnie Bock, who was formerly a very active CP member.

      An {*Illegible. abbreviation*} has previously been filed on LAURA BOCK.

3 – Director (FBI)

2 – New York {*3 Illegible codes*}

1 – Kansas City (Info) {*2 illegible codes*}

4 – San Francisco (1 – 100 -53149)

JHC/lr

(4)

FOIA(b)(7) - (D)

SAC, CHICAGO

8/19/64

SAC, SAN FRANCISCO 100-53169 P

LAURA BOCK
SM-C

[blank] San Francisco, a
neighborhood source concerning the BOCK family, advised that for the
remainder of the summer LAURA BOCK is working at the Freedom House,
Chicago.

[blank] advised that LAURA BOCK who had been a freshman at the
University of Oregon and who will probably return to the University of
Oregon for the fall term, had wanted to take the 1964 Cuba trip sponsored
by SCTC but then decided to go to the Midwest to work for the summer.
BOCK intended to go to Kansas for awhile and work for CORE, and presently
is in Chicago at the Freedom House.

LAURA BOCK is the daughter of ALBERT BOCK a former Security Index subject
of the SF Office. Subject's mother is MINNI BOCK who was formerly
a very active CP member.

2 Chicago RM (for information)
1 Kansas City RM (for information)
1 SF 100-53169

JGC
(4)

Postp

Searched _____
Serialized _____
Indexed _____
Filed _____

NW: 15160 DocId: 70000776 Page 26

100 - 53169 - 9

OPTIONAL FORM NO. 10
5010-104

UNITED STATES GOVERNMENT

Memorandum

FOIA(b)(7) - (D)

TO   :   SAC, SAN FRANCISCO (100-53169)   DATE: 10/6/64

FROM   :   SA EDWARD J. O'FLYNN

SUBJECT: LAURA BOCK
              SM - C

                                on 9/28/64 reported that on that date
MINNIE BOCK (Subject's mother) contacted the PW to leave
a message for PEGGY DENNIS (Subject's aunt) that LAURA
BOCK's new address is "McClain Hall, Hamilton College of
Oregon."

RECOMMENDATION:

             No action. For information.

EJO:rap
(1)

SEARCHED _____ INDEXED ____
SERIALIZED ____ FILED ____
        OCT 5 1964
FBI — SAN FRANCISCO

100-53169-10

SAC, PORTLAND   10/27/64

SAC, SAN FRANCISCO (100-53169) - C

LAURA JANE BOCK
SM - C

FOIA(b)(7) - (D)

Re San Francisco letter and LHM, 6/18/64.

For your information, [   ] advised on 9/28/64,
that Subject is again attending Oregon University, and is
residing at McClain Hall.

2 - Portland (RM)
1 - San Francisco

JGC/jr (#9)
(3)

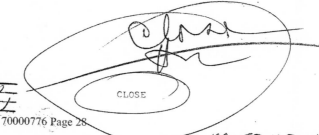

Searched
Serialized
Indexed
Filed

CLOSE

100-53169-11

NW: 15160 DocId: 70000776 Page 28

OPTIONAL FORM NO. 10
5010-104

UNITED STATES GOVERNMENT

Memorandum   FOIA(b)(7) - (D)

TO   :   SAC, SAN FRANCISCO (100-53169)   DATE: 11/6/64

FROM   :   SA EDWARD J. O'FLYNN

SUBJECT: LAURIE BOCH
            SM - C

              [   ] on 10/29/64 reported that on that date
MINNIE BOCH contacted her sister, PEGGY DENNIS, at the PW,
at which time MINNIE stated that she had a letter which
LAURIE wrote to AL BOCH in which LAURIE made a comment on
AL's little note on KHRUSHCHEV. PEGGY DENNIS stated that
LAURIE had two paragraphs on it in her letter. MINNIE commented
that LAURIE is boomeranging at AL and quotes from LAURIE's
letter as follows:

> "Now about Dad's comment about Mr. K. I
> was never so surprised in my life when I read
> it. I would never have expected a person, who,
> up to this date, had not expressed such ideas before,
> such ideas, and to the contrary had only but praise
> for the leader. According to this astounding new
> theory of his, Mr. K is a jolly Santa Claus man,
> fit for clowning, laughing, having fun, but nobody
> takes him seriously. As a matter of fact he was a
> detrimental force to the communist and collective
> leadership."

      LAURIE wrote that this is baloney and asked in
her letter if he were becoming one of those people who
always look down upon those who are party hacks and change
their ideas of policy as it is handed down without questioning,
without daring to disagree. LAURIE, in her letter, noted
that in her recollection he (AL BOCH) had never voiced such
ideas. Now all of a sudden he blacklisted a man he always loved
and that the Soviet leaders are trying to blacklist him (Mr. K)
in his own country. LAURIE stated that she doesn't agree
with him and is disappointed in him.

      PEGGY DENNIS replied that she thinks it is very
clear and it is true and that she, PEGGY, was very surprised

1 - 100-53169
2 - 100-32648
1 - 100-   (AL BOCH)
1 - 100-   (MINNIE BOCH)
EJO:rap
(4)

100-53169-

SEARCHED ___ INDEXED ___
SERIALIZED ___ FILED ___
NOV 6 1964
FBI - SAN FRANCISCO

NW 15160 DocId: 70000776 Page 29

SF 100-53169
EJO:rap

at AL's attitude. PEGGY stated that when she received the
news here at work, she, too, had many questions as to how
she would ever explain it and was sure that AL (BOCH) would
tear her to pieces, but the first day she talked with AL,
he was just the opposite. PEGGY stated that she is still
puzzled.

RECOMMENDATION:

For information regarding political interest
and allegiance of BOCH family in current political changes
in the Soviet Union. It may be noted that AL and MINNIE
BOCH's files reflect no political affiliations or activities
during the past ten years.

2

UNITED STATES GOVERNMENT

MEMORANDUM

FOIA(b)(7) - (D)

TO: DIRECTOR, FBI (100-443127)

                                              Date:7/2/65

FROM: SAC, NEW YORK (100-154578A)

SUBJECT: AMERICAN YOUTH FESTIVAL COMMITTEE aka
          IS - C
          (OO:NY)

          ReBulet dated 1/12/65 to all offices, entitled
"Ninth World Youth Festival, Algiers, Algeria, August, 1965;
The United States Festival Committee; IS-C."

          On June 17, 1965, [   ] who has furnished
reliable information in the past, furnished information
concerning payments made to the American Youth Festival
Committee (AYFC). The source no longer has custody of the
orginal information. The following payments were noted:

3 - Bureau (100-443127)(RM)
    (1 - 100-439754) (NINTH WORLD YOUTH FESTIVAL)
2 - Boston (100-   )
2 - Chicago (100-   )
2 - Denver (100-   )
10 - Los Angeles
     (2 - 100-   )
     (2 - 100-   )
     (2 - 100-   )
     (2 - 100-   )
     (2 - 100-   )
12 - San Francisco
     (2 - 100-   )
     (2 - 100-   )
     (2 - 100-   )   (LAURA BOCH)
     (2 - 100-   )
     (2 - 100-   )
     (2 - 100-   )
11- New York
    (1 - 100-   )
    (1 - 100-   )
    (1 - 100-   )
    (1 - 100-   )
    (1 - 100-   )
    (1 - 100-   )
    (1 - 100-   )
    (1 - 100-   )
(Copies Continued)
HPL:pmd
(42)
WTTN

SEARCHED____INDEXED____
SERIALIZED____FILED____
JUL 6   9 47 AM '65
FBI - SAN FRANCISCO

100 - 53169-13

NY 100-154578

Instrument	Amount	Bank	Maker	Remarks
				Marked "Tour"
				Marked "Tour"
Cashiers Bank check Date not legible	$290.00	Bank of America, U.S. Medical Center Branch, San Francisco, Calif.		Marked "3 tours for LAURA BOCH"

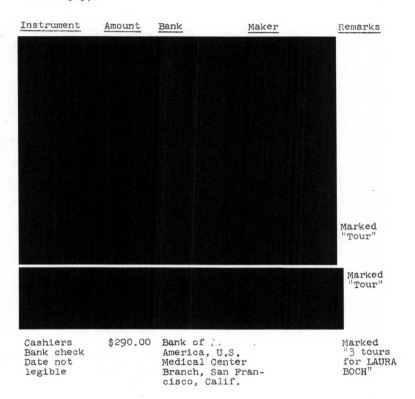

-5-

FOIA(b)(7) - (D)

NY 100-154578

It is noted that some of the checks above were
marked with a number, and it is believed that these are
the number of persons who have sent in money to attend
the Ninth World Youth Festival (NWYF). It is noted that
since the middle of April, 1965, the AYFC has added one
or more digits after the number, in an apparent effort
to put the numbers in a code. From a review of these
numbers, it would indicate that approximately 222 people
have sent in money to attend the festival.

The "National Guardian" 3/27/65, page 7, column 3,
contained an article which set out that the festival cost
$69.00 plus an optional $2.00 to help pay expenses of Asian
and African delegates. Eight dollars extra would be charged
for those desiring to go on trips before and after the
festival.

[   ] who has furnished reliable information
in the past, on 4/19/65, furnished information that a 10 day
tour to Moscow, Leningrad, Kiev, Brest, from August 8, to 18,
1965, plus air transportation would cost $228.00. This
source furnished information that a 14 day tour to Moscow,
Leningrad, Kiev, and Chop, August 8, to 22, 1965, plus air
transportation would cost $243.00.

A characterization of the AYFC is being submitted
for the individual copies.

Each office is requested to follow Bureau instructions
regarding individuals set out in this communication,
according to referenced Bureau letter.

-7-

NY- 100 -154578

1.   APPENDIX

AMERICAN YOUTH FESTIVAL COMMITTEE,
Also known as United States Festival
Committee, Committee For United States
Festival Participation

          A source on March 29, 1965, furnished a folder issued
by the American Youth Festival Committee (AYFC) which set out
"The American Youth Festival Committee, with representatives
from campuses and youth organizations throughout the nation,
is a non-partisan, non-political organization established as
a service to publicize and encourage participation in the
Algiers Festival, and to serve as the administrative body
processing all applications for the Festival."

          The folder set out that the 9th World Youth Festival
would take place in Algiers, Algeria, July 28th to August 7,
1965. The folder reported the AYFC has been recognized by the
International Preparatory Committee, the sponsoring body of
the Festival, as the sole United States Committee to administer
United States participation.

          The source advised on March 29, 1965, that the AYFC
is located at Room 1410, 104 Fifth Avenue, New York, New York,
having established that office on March 1, 1965.

          A second source advised on January 22, 1965, that
███████████████, National Youth Director of the Communist Party
(CP,USA) was contacting individuals concerning the Festival.

          On February 15, 1965, a third source reported ███████
███████, National Organizational Secretary, CP, USA, on February
13, 1965, stated that CP Youth would participate in the AYFC.

          A fourth source advised on March 30, 1965, that
the CP, USA, will lend support to the AYFC.

UNITED STATES GOVERNMENT

    MEMORANDUM   DATE: 7/9/65

TO   :   SAC (100-53169)

FROM :   SA DIRCK A. MERRILL

SUBJECT: Laura Bock
                sm -C

           Bureau letter to Albany dated 1/12/65,
captioned "NINTH WORLD YOUTH FESTIVAL, ALGIERS, ALGERIA,
AUGUST 1965; IS - C," advised that it desired investigation
to determine background and subversive activity concerning
any individual who makes any overture toward participation
in the Festival, whether it be actual intention to attend
or merely an inquiry concerning cost, additional information,
etc. Where information indicates intended participation
at the Festival by an individual, a letter should be directed
immediately to the Washington Field Office to secure data
contained in the passport records for inclusion in the LHM
which is to be prepared on each individual.

           Background information; subversive activity,
if any; and results of passport checks in cases involving
individuals, who have indicated intended participation, should
be furnished the Bureau under the specific case caption of
the individual by LHM with a copy designated for Bureau
file 100-443127 (United States Festival Committee), and a
copy for San Francisco file 100-53848 (Ninth World Youth
Festival). Twelve copies of the LHM should be furnished the
Bureau.

           Information contained in serial __13__
of this file reflects that investigation should be conducted
and a LHM submitted to the Bureau.

Also furnish 2 copies of LHM to G-2 locally

                                    100-53169-14

DAM:mhb
(70)

SEARCHED ___ INDEXED ___
SERIALIZED ___ FILED ___
JUL 0 1965
FBI — SAN FRANCISCO

LAURA JANE BOCK   C O N F I D E N T I A L

Description:

Name:	Laura Jane Bock
Born:	October 4, 1945, at San Francisco
Height:	5 feet, 7 inches
Hair:	Brown
Eyes:	Hazel
Occupation:	During 1964 was a student at the University of Oregon at Eugene, Oregon where she is studying to be a teacher

During the summer months, Laura Bock resides with her parents at 1448 Willard Street, San Francisco.

C O N F I D E N T I A L

FOIA(b)(7) - (D)

SAC, SF (100-53848)   6/3/65

SA EDWARD J. O'FLYNN

NINTH WORLD YOUTH FESTIVAL
IS - C

[   ] on 5/26/65 reported that on that date
MINNIE BOCK contacted PEGGY DENNIS at the PW, at which time
she noted that some of the ultra-leftist youth groups were
going to boycott the festival. DENNIS said that these are
disruptive tactics and these people will do anything to
create division. DENNIS told MINNIE that it is only fair
to point out to LAURIE (BOCK) that it is viewed as a Jewish
question and that if she wants to she could say that is
the way which AL (BOCK) views it. MINNIE stated that a large
group of Jews besides the Zionists feel this way about the
festival. MINNIE stated that she thinks it might be quite
a thing especially if the ultra-left really make something
of it. MINNIE stated it is pretty clear that LAURIE is
going to Alabama.

RECOMMENDATION:

        For information regarding possible boycott of youth
festival and information regarding LAURIE BOCK's proposed
attendance at Youth Festival and her plans to travel to
Alabama.

1 - 100-53848
    100-53169 (LAURA BOCK)
1 - 100-548 (MINNIE BOCK)
1 - 100-42399 (CP COUNTERINTELLIGENCE)
EJO:rap
(4)

SEARCHED_____INDEXED____
SERIALIZED_____FILED____
JUN J 1965
FBI—SAN FRANCISCO

100-53169 -17

Carlisle #9

OPTIONAL FORM NO. 10
9010-104

UNITED STATES GOVERNMENT   FOIA(b)(7) - (D)

Memorandum

TO   :   SAC, SAN FRANCISCO (100-53169)   DATE: 7/13/65

FROM   :   SA EDWARD J. O'FLYNN

SUBJECT: LAURA BOCK
            SM - C

            ███████████ on 6/21/65 reported that on that date MINNIE
BOCK contacted ███████████ at the "PW" and asked if he had
heard anything about the Youth Conference in Algeria and
whether it is called off. ████████ stated that he didn't hear
anything but understood that the Africa-Asia Conference for
June 29 had been cancelled because of the overthrow of the
Ben Bella Government. MINNIE stated she will call again as
LAURA doesn't have her ticket yet and was waiting to hear
about a charter plane and where it would leave from.

RECOMMENDATION:

            For information regarding Subject's intention to
attend the 9th World Youth Festival.

LHM Submitted

R/S - C
ARC
9/9

1 - 100-548 (MINNIE BOCK)
1 - 100-53848 (9th WORLD YOUTH FESTIVAL)
EJO/eja
(3)

SEARCHED _____ INDEXED
SERIALIZED _____ FILED
JUL 1 3 1965
FBI — SAN FRANCISCO

100-53169-18

Made in the USA
San Bernardino, CA
25 April 2017